Praise for *Luck Through Adversity*

"This book tells the story of Rudy Zeeman's escape from Nazi officers in Paris, and his harrowing trek over the Pyrenees Mountains with downed Allied flyers, to achieve freedom in England. His research and recall of times, names and places, combined with his unvarnished prose, shines a light on the courage shown by Dutch and French resisters in World War II. Rudy does not promote himself as a hero, but he was brave—and he was lucky!"

—Coleman O'Flaherty, Member of the Order of Australia, Professor Emeritus, University of Tasmania

"Rudy Zeeman is a unique and valuable witness to World War II. Like many other young people in the occupied countries of Europe, he went into hiding rather than submit to deportation for work in Germany. He escaped to England from The Netherlands through France with a grueling and dangerous crossing of the Pyrenees on foot through deep snow. He held many administrative positions in the Pacific in the final months of the war with Japan and in the postwar period. His is a fascinating and vivid account."

—Janet Holmes Carper, author of *The Weidners in Wartime*

"Zeeman's escape through Nazi-controlled territories makes for compelling reading. His colorful descriptions and encyclopedic mind put the reader at his side as he side-steps capture. He has to be one of World War II's most resourceful and elusive evaders."

—Kurt Ganter, The John Henry Weidner Foundation for Altruism

"This is a compelling story of escape from Nazi-occupied Europe in World War II. It was fascinating to compare with my father's own experiences, with many similarities as well as striking differences. Highlights of this tale were the hair-breadth escape from the Gestapo in Paris, and the grueling crossing of the Pyrenees in winter. These stories need to be told, and the experiences remembered for future generations."

—Ian Schagen, co-author of *A Wartime Journey Revisited*

"One gets a sense of Rudy's humour immediately in the first few paragraphs of his fascinating memoir, when he details his first meeting with Robert van Exter in Spring 1943. This was the first step in his extraordinary journey from Holland through Paris, across the Pyrenees to Spain. Hiding from German patrols, climbing up the snow-covered mountains, hiding in abandoned houses, it describes his arduous, physically demanding and adventurous escape to freedom."

—Jos Scharrer, author of *The Dutch Resistance Revealed*

LUCK THROUGH ADVERSITY

The Memoir of a Dutchman's Flight to Freedom
Through the Dutch-Paris Escape Line of World War II

By

PIETER RUDOLPH ZEEMAN

WEIDNER FOUNDATION BOOKS

Weidner Foundation Books is a part of the John Henry Weidner Foundation for
Altruism and serves to further the Foundation's mission of cultivating selfless and
courageous action in the spirit of John Weidner and the Dutch-Paris escape line. For
more information about the Weidner Foundation, visit www.weidnerfoundation.org.

Luck Through Adversity is the second publication by Weidner Foundation Books. See
also *The Weidners in Wartime: Letters of Daily Survival and Heroism Under Nazi Rule*,
selected, translated, and introduced by Janet Holmes Carper.

Cover painting by Pieter Rudolph Zeeman of his escape across the Pyrenees
Mountains. (The man in the white coat in the painting is Rudy.)

Cover design by Terrill Thomas and Ronald E. Osborn.

Map by Ronald E. Osborn based on notations by Pieter Rudolph Zeeman.

Set in Garamond type by Weidner Foundation Books.

Riverside, California
Printed in the United States

Library of Congress Control Number: 2020909943
ISBN: 978-1-7346999-1-3

For those who did not make it

Contents

Part III: Around the World in 1014 Days

Preface

If a young lady called Robyn Post, a granddaughter of my widowed sister-in-law, Hetty's, second marriage, and some friends had not exhorted me to write my wartime memoir, before I left for the Valhalla of my very distant ancestors, I would not have put pencil to paper nearly 60 years later.

This is a personal account of events during World War II in which I was involved. It all happened a long time ago, well before many who read this preface were born. Some in passing will only give a cursory glance at the cover. My prose will not set the literary world alight and others have had more exciting adventures during the 1939-1945 years. But I hope that those who urged me to write my wartime experiences, and those of later generations, may find it of some small interest to read about the wartime experiences of a young man who escaped from German Occupied Europe to join the forces of the Netherlands in England to fight the enemy.

The fallibility of human memory and the passage of time have, of course, blunted my memory of much. But some incidents are still, after more than half a century, fresh in my mind. I have a total recall of the Paris incident and near total recall of all events of the journey to freedom.

To paraphrase a passage of an issue of the Reveille, the magazine of the Australian War Veterans, when danger walks so close as it did on our journey to freedom our senses were more acute and the memories left are more detailed and indelible.

Keeping diaries and notes during those dangerous times in the Netherlands was quite unwise, and I do not possess them. However, I have, from the first days after crossing the Spanish frontier, made written notes in notebooks and on sheets of paper when recalling names, places and incidents still fresh in my mind. I also kept photos and newspaper and magazine cuttings which related to my wartime experiences, and I cross-checked dates and facts from books.

I wrote part of my story in its original form in 1945 on Red Cross paper at the US General Hospital in Hollandia and added to it later. I was never happy with those efforts but they were of use when writing this final edition.

A strong visual memory has been most helpful when describing the route and ways of travel. Maps, particularly the No 71 Carte Topographique of the St Gaudens to Andorra area of southern France and northern Spain, have been of great assistance in fairly accurately retracing the route followed through the Pyrenean Mountains. Pierre Treillet, one of our two guides could—when we met up again in 1994—confirm that my reconstruction of the route we had taken was fairly accurate. I was thus also able to put many more names, accurate heights and distances in my narrative.

When mentioning my old country, I often follow the general custom of calling it "Holland" but Holland is actually the western part of Nederland along the North Sea and north of the province of Zeeland. A person born or living in the provinces of Limburg or Groningen would object, if not be insulted, at being called a Hollander. They call themselves Limburger and Groninger.

To the British, the people of the Netherlands are Dutchmen; to Americans they are Hollanders since in parts of the USA, like Pennsylvania, German settlers are called Pennsylvania Dutch, while the Germans call us Niederlander or, more commonly, Hollander.

Part of my story is not much different in essence but only in detail from those whom the Dutch call *Engelandvaarders*, who made similar journeys to freedom from Nazi oppression. We had one thing in common—the confidence that we would not fail. The description *Engelandvaarder* will be used throughout my memoir when referring to the Dutch evaders and escapees who managed to reach England.

Just like those who go to war, some are convinced that they will survive and only others will be killed. *Engelandvaarders,* when they set off, believed that they would succeed in reaching England. Only those who did not make it were proven wrong. We also learnt, if we did not already know, that being without fear does not exist.

Should readers discover errors and, no doubt, omissions, then I, having, among other things, been in the import and export business, claim E & OE.

Launceston, 5 January 2004

Map of My Route to Freedom

My escape from life under Nazi occupation took me from Holland to Gibraltar by foot, rail, car, and sea—and then onward to England, sailing deep into the Atlantic and around the coast of Northern Ireland to avoid German U-Boats.

Part I:
Occupation and Resistance

1. The Gathering Storm: 1930-1939

My father was a great admirer of Winston Churchill and the likes of Duff Cooper and the diplomat Sir Robert Vansittart. He shared Churchill's anxieties about the military build-up in Nazi Germany—in contravention of the provisions of the Versailles Treaty—after Hitler came to power in January 1933. Because of his position at Holland's largest bank, my father was privy to information not readily available to the general public and often expressed his fears about developments in Germany after Hitler came to power.

He believed strongly that the world would have been a different place if in 1936 the most powerful army in Europe, the French, had interceded when Germany re-occupied the demilitarised Rhineland in March 1936. Poland would likely have joined the French since the Poles had no illusions about Hitler's intentions to reclaim German territory lost after the 1914-1918 World War.

For whatever considerations the French sat on their hands and allowed Hitler to tear up yet another provision of the Versailles Treaty. No doubt the anti-war sentiment then prevailing, with the slaughter on the Western Front in 1914-1918 still fresh in their minds, played a role, as did the Great Depression of 1929-1934, brought about by the Wall Street financial collapse of October 1929. Another factor that may have influenced Western European Governments, ever since the Russian Revolution of 1917, was the general and great fear in "The West" of Communism. Any other ideology was viewed as a lesser evil and some believed the Nazi dictatorship was a bulwark against the Soviet Union where mostly innocent men and women had been transported to the Siberian gulags and between 8 and 14 million perished. Who could have foreseen that the Nazi regime with its extermination camps would be as bad as Stalinism and its gulags?

Many years ago, I read and made a note of an article about the Rhineland affair. As I recall, Hitler's generals told him, that they could not risk re-occupation of the Rhineland "as we have only enough ammunition for a few hours. If the French march we are done for." Hitler answered that the French would not march, but if they did, "we would be finished".

Whether this anecdote is true or not, it is one of those crucial moments in history that makes one speculate: What if the French had marched across the German border?

The *Anschluss* with Austria in 1938 was followed by the Sudetenland crisis and the Munich Conference in 1938. The British Prime Minister's "peace in our time" pronouncement was thereupon put to ridicule when Hitler occupied the rest of Czechoslovakia well within a year. In May 1939, in a forlorn gesture of goodwill, the English national soccer team was ordered to give the Nazi salute on the pitch in Berlin, a vignette of those troubled times which stay in the mind.

In spite of my father's exhortations, my great interest in history, and being aware of the Schlieffen Plan and its possible implications if a new European war would break out, I must admit that in 1938, I did not fully appreciate the likely consequences for my fatherland. I was at the time of the Munich Conference only interested in a settlement that would make it possible for the postponed Donnington Grand Prix for Grand Prix motor-racing cars to be held in October and for me to attend. That was, for a car-mad young man who had asked for a subscription to a motoring magazine for his 9th birthday, the most important matter of the moment. I also wanted to meet the sports editors of two British motoring magazines who had published some of my artwork for illustrations.

It was therefore with great pleasure that I took the Hoek of Holland-Harwich ferry across the North Sea and the boat-train to London with my friends Jean Paul Perez and Lody Muskens. I wanted to stay at the home of Perez's parents in Beckenham in the south of Greater London. His sister Paulette drove us in her Hillman to the circuit near Derby where we watched the kind of exciting motor-racing compared to which the present 21st-century Formula One races are dull affairs. The great Italian racing driver Tazio Nuvolari would win the Grand Prix and my portrait of him would be published in the British motoring magazine, Speed. My original drawing is now displayed in the Nuvolari Hall of the Donnington Motorcar Collection Museum at the circuit near the city of Derby in central England. It was for me personally the most satisfactory result of the Munich Pact but most certainly not for the Czech nation.

My tea-planter older brother Tom, who came to Amsterdam on home leave at the end of 1938, did not believe that war had been averted by the Munich Conference of Chamberlain, Daladier, Mussolini and Hitler. He must have feared that the Netherlands would not remain neutral and, not wanting to be stranded in Holland, he cut short his home leave. In April 1939, with his newly-wed wife Hetty Potjer, he boarded the boat-train for Marseille where they embarked on the MV 'Dempo' of the Rotterdam Lloyd Line to return to the Indies and his tea plantation near Pematang Siantar in North East Sumatra. Tragically the Pacific War would catch up with them.

In March of 1939 I had to report to the Army's Medical Service for a physical examination and there, at one moment, four young men born in 1919 and all named Zeeman, stood naked next to each other awaiting their turn. They were the sons of a well-known eye specialist, a foundation garment factory owner, a butcher and myself. In 1986, 47 years later, Bill Zeeman and I would meet again on the other side of the Earth, on the island of Tasmania, named after its discoverer, the Dutch Navigator Abel Tasman. Bill, as his father before him in North Amsterdam, had built up a successful butchery in the town of Westbury where he lived with his wife and 13 children. His eldest lawyer son would become a Supreme Court Judge in Hobart some years later.

The day after having been declared fit for Military Service I went back to the school benches but at the end of the summer break on the 28th of August the Dutch Government called a general mobilisation and I boarded the train for Alkmaar, a town northwest of Amsterdam, to report to the commanding officer of the 2nd Battery *Luchtdoel Artillerie* (Anti-Aircraft Artillery) in that well-known cheese-market town, where my good friend Jan Doornik would serve with the 1st Battery AA.

The troops of the 2nd Battery AA were housed in a requisitioned primary school which was fitted with toilets tailored to receive children to age 12. The resulting blockages can be imagined without describing the unpleasant details of the frequently returning overflow problems. We slept on straw mattresses plonked on the bare classroom floors, partitioned by the suitcases we had carried when leaving home. It was a quantum change from the rather privileged life I had become used to.

I still remember with amusement the selection of cooks for our unit. On the first day, after a pathetic mustering ceremony of us raw recruits, the sergeant major called for trained cooks to step forward. Nobody moved. He then ordered butchers and carpenters by trade to declare themselves. Four 19 and 20-year-olds stepped forward and were promptly assigned to be our cooks. No need to elucidate on their cooking expertise but only to mention that the local cafeterias, restaurants and the ubiquitous so-called brown cafés, which are still hugely popular in the Low Countries, did a roaring trade.

The Dutch are truly democratic and self-reliant but they have scant regard for authority. Military rules and discipline were not taken too easily by many, if not most, of the young men of the Netherlands contrary to our fellow Saxons across the eastern border whom I consider the best soldiers in the world.

In the summer of 1939, my father had left for England where he had been temporarily posted to the office of the NHM Bank in London, the great financial centre, where he as a youngster had learned the ropes at Lloyd's Bank before joining the NHM Bank (now called ABN-AMRO). This time however he did not stay in digs as in 1901-03, but at the renowned Savoy Hotel.

On that 3rd of September in 1939, when England and France declared war on Nazi Germany, he was in London. We still have a photo of him which appeared in a British magazine carrying a gas mask slung from his shoulder and entering an air-raid shelter.

The prevailing belief that Holland, as in 1914-1918, would remain neutral made most conscripts consider military training a bloody nuisance. The average Dutchman does not care for military discipline. He takes a dim view of the unquestioning obedience demanded of the military. Weapons training and drilling of these young conscripts must have been, at times, highly frustrating for the officers and NCOs.

The feigned ignorance and deliberate stupidities at drill made me recall the antics of the mentally backward (challenged is now the appropriate word) Austro-Hungarian soldier Schweik of that most humorous of books, *The Good Soldier Schweik*.

There was a larrikin who on route marches, to the distraction of the drill sergeants, would boo at cows, neigh at horses, quack at ducks and whistle at girls. There was also a comedian who, when marching through the streets and singing songs like "who has put sugar in the pea soup", would, in step, make 'escaping wind' noises to the amusement of the good burghers of Alkmaar. I, who consider food to be one of the great delights of life, have always remembered the solid black army bread, probably as served at the Battle of Waterloo, which was so indigestible that it made three of us, my delicate self included, pass out on a rifle exercise. To the envy of our 'mates', our army doctor prescribed white bread for us chaps with less robust constitutions.

When Holland mobilised I was 19 years old and in year 12 of the Lyceum. My application for study-leave was granted after only two and a half months of the Army trying to make a soldier out of me.

To lay stress on the strict neutrality proclaimed by the Dutch Government, defensive positions on the North Sea coast had to be maintained. However, since the probability of an invasion by the British and French troops was non-existent, the under-sourced Army had logically assigned their oldest equipment to the seacoast defences facing Britain. As a consequence, an artillery regiment in the province of Zeeland was outfitted with guns dating back to 1861. It does illustrate Dutch unpreparedness. Even those units like the AA batteries in Alkmaar were short on the excellent new Bofors AA guns, while my section had only one rifle for every ten men.

It was therefore no surprise that in May of 1940, while the Dutch Marines and some Army units fought with great bravery, other units consisting of badly-trained and under-armed reservists and conscripts, when faced by the powerful German Army, quickly retreated or hoisted a white flag.

We Dutch had learned at high school about the 'Schlieffen Plan' which called for a German Army advance through Belgium and Holland, and which the German General Staff of 1914 had not adhered to. After World War I, the French had constructed a strong defence line of fortresses called the 'Maginot Line' named for the then French Minister of Defence. It ran from the Swiss Border across Northern France and, quite incomprehensibly, ended way short of the North Sea coast. It just passed the border of Luxembourg, leaving most of the border with Belgium unprotected. The French Military did not believe that an attack by tanks and motorised forces through the heavily wooded Ardennes was feasible.

The short-sightedness of the planners of the 'Maginot Line' is truly breathtaking for it could not but induce the Germans to attack through Belgium or Switzerland and outflank this defence line if another war broke out.

The invasion of Denmark and Norway in April of 1939 should not have left the peoples of The Low Countries in any doubt that they would be next to fall victim to Hitler's quest for dominance of Europe if not the world. However, the majority of the Dutch people nevertheless remained naïve enough to believe that, as in 1914-1918, the Netherlands would remain neutral while some hoped against hope and kept their fears to themselves, as did my father who had returned from London at Christmas of 1939.

That April of 1940, the surname of the Fascist Party leader of Norway, Vikund Quisling, would become synonymous with traitor.

2. The German Invasion of the Netherlands

Very early on the morning of the 10th of May, 1940 I was disturbed in my sleep by the then still unfamiliar pop-pop sound of bursting anti-aircraft shells and the distant but constant drone of aeroplane engines interspersed with the dull, deeper sound of exploding bombs in the general direction of Amsterdam's Schiphol Airport.

From the large windows of our second-floor apartment at 96 de Lairessestraat in Amsterdam Zuid (South) I could see Junkers and other types of German military aircraft flying over and the smoke bursts of exploding 'ack-ack' shells. Quickly changing from pajamas into clothes, and shouting to my family that Schiphol was being bombed by German war planes, I ran down the stairs to the cellar, collected my bicycle and pedaled furiously through still nearly deserted streets on a perfect spring day towards and through the village of Amstelveen. When within about 300 yards of Schiphol Airport, I got off my "Raleigh" and, leaving the bicycle path, crawled up the embankment of one of the many canals near the airfield. The canals are many feet below sea level on land called "polders", reclaimed a few centuries ago. Peering over the top of the rise of the embankment I could see aeroplanes with the German Iron Cross marking swooping across and dropping bombs on Schiphol. I witnessed a series of explosions on or near the buildings and at the perimeter of the airfield. I noted a Junkers JU-52 transport plane which had crash-landed, a few aircraft wrecks burned beyond recognition and small fires burning all over the place. I watched the bombardment for nearly an hour before returning home.

On that night, from the 9th to the 10th of May, the people of the Netherlands had been literally and figuratively awoken by the start of an unprovoked and undeclared war. The country was shaken literally by the over-flying aeroplanes, the roar of guns, the sound of marching troops and the blowing up of bridges in the eastern provinces by Dutch demolition squads, and figuratively by the realisation that the country would not remain neutral as in 1914 to 1918.

The expectation that the Germans would be held at the Grebbe Defence Line, which runs through the centre of the country from the IJsselmeer (the former Zuiderzee) to the great barrier of the mighty river complex fed by the waters of the Rhine and Meuse, seemed not unlikely at first. The Dutch Air Force had been annihilated on the first day but reports on the radio and in the newspapers that the German parachutists had been killed or captured to a man cheered us up.

Mr. Michielsen Snr., my father's friend, phoned us from The Hague and confirmed the apparently successful elimination of the German paratroopers who landed near Rotterdam and Valkenburg Airfields, whose task had been to capture the Royal Family and the Government ministers. He could also proudly tell us that his younger son Ady, a Reserve Sub-Lieutenant of the Field Artillery, had personally captured two *Fallschirmjäger* (Paratroopers).

At the Huis ten Bosch Palace, Prince Bernhard had joined a detachment of the Dutch Army guarding the palace. Firing a machine gun at a low-flying German aircraft, he hit the plane's petrol tank causing it to crash on the open space of the Malieveld in The Hague.

On that first day of the war, a JU-52 Junkers transport plane had been shot down and in the wreck the body of General von Sponeck (and the kidnap plan for the Dutch Royal Family and Government) were found. For his glorious ceremonial entrance into The Hague, the *Herr Generaal* had packed his parade uniform in a suitcase.

It had been the intention of the Germans to capture The Hague by a large airborne assault on the first days but it would be one of the very few failures of their military campaign in Western Europe in May and June of 1940.

For the rest of that day and the next four days we watched the goings on in the air, listened to the news bulletins on the radio and avidly read the newspapers.

After the bombardment of Schiphol, very little happened in Amsterdam. Apart from a nervous mood, we noted little of the war in contrast to Rotterdam and The Hague where daily life was profoundly affected by the German attacks.

We had a few air-raid warnings when German aircraft flew over the city. The *Burgerwacht* (Home Guard), dressed in World War I French uniforms and helmets, patrolled the streets, occasionally checking the identities of persons considered suspicious.

From the morning of the 10th of May I had tried to rejoin my unit in Alkmaar but, like most conscripts and reservists on leave, had not succeeded in the general confusion prevailing. I was told to await instructions which never came. When the situation became desperate and defeat became inevitable, the Dutch Royal Family left for England on the 12th of May. Prince Bernhard first escorted his wife, the future Queen Juliana, and their three children in an armoured car to IJmuiden and by the RN Destroyer 'Codrington' to Britain. A day later, after having returned to Holland, the Prince boarded a British destroyer in IJmuiden in the company of Her Majesty Queen Wilhelmina.

Nowhere in Holland during those four hectic days of war were there so many goings on as at the Port of IJmuiden on the North Sea from where the Noordzee Kanaal (canal) runs to the docks of Amsterdam. At Scheveningen and Hoek of Holland, many tried and a few succeeded in escaping to England aboard fishing boats. Ships carried the Dutch Government ministers and some bureaucrats to safety across the North Sea while most of Holland's reserves of gold and stocks were safely transported to England.

The Dutch passenger ship 'Texelstroom' managed to leave IJmuiden with more than 500 and perhaps as many as 1500 captured German Airmen and Paratroopers aboard, a feat that caused the German Reichs-Marshall, Hermann Goering, to explode in anger.

After the capitulation on the 15th of May, more than 90 per cent of the Dutch Merchant Navy was operating outside Occupied territory and would give valuable assistance to the Allied war effort, while the war ships of the RNN, which had survived the German onslaught, took refuge in the British Isles.

At first the news of the Royal Family and the Government having fled to England to continue the War from our British Ally's island was received with great consternation by the population. It aroused irrational thoughts and emotions in many who would soon regret that they had vilified the Government and in particular Queen Wilhelmina.

3. Blitzkrieg: May and June 1940

The Second World War had started at 00.45 hours on the 3rd of September of 1939 when German Panzers rolled into Poland. A sad and sombre Neville Chamberlain, Prime Minister of Great Britain, announced in Parliament, and by radio to the British nation and the world, that his country and France were now at war with Germany. The Netherlands on that day had declared its strict neutrality but the Dutch Government had been aware of the German attack plan. That plan had been recovered in Belgium from a downed German war plane in late 1939, while very reliable information had also been received from Dutch Military Intelligence (GS-III) and particularly from the Dutch Military Attaché in Berlin, Major Sas, who had been kept informed by a friend in the *Abwehr* (German Military Intelligence) about Hitler's intention to invade the Low Countries.

The Dutch General Staff, having learned of the Germans' intention to invade the Netherlands at dawn on May the 10th, had already dispersed the Navy's ships over many ports and the Army had been put on alert.

General P. W. Best, Commander of the Air Force, had ordered all 125 operational aircraft to be combat-ready for take-off by 03.00 a.m., but had not expected the *Luftwaffe* to over-fly the country from east to west to make it appear that they were going to attack Britain and then to reverse course once they were over the North Sea. Dutch Air Force planes, consisting of 183 aircraft, of which only the 23 Fokker G-One Fighters could effectively oppose the 959 German planes, were therefore caught on the ground while waiting for orders to take off. More than half the Dutch Air Force was consequently destroyed when Hitler's *Luftwaffe* pounced without having declared war. The remainder took to the sky and fought valiantly, against the odds, to the last plane. The Air Force and the anti-aircraft batteries downed 350 German planes during those four hectic days of war.

The rapidity of the Dutch collapse gave the Allies the false impression that the Dutch had not fought very hard for their country. However, after the War, *gründliche* (detailed) German war documentation reported unexpectedly strong defence at the Grebbe-Line. They also reported heavy losses suffered by the *Wehrmacht's* 207th Infantry Division and the two supporting SS Panzer Regiments. Aside from the stand at the Grebbe-Line, the *Wehrmacht's* 18th Army had also not yet broken the defence elsewhere in the "Fortress Holland". The Dutch Marines put up a tremendous fight at the bridges over the Maas River at Rotterdam and the 2000 or so *fallschirmjäger* dropped near The Hague had all been hunted down and killed or captured without meeting any success in their task of capturing the Royal Family and the Government. Also, on the Afsluitdijk (the dam across the former Zuiderzee) at Kornwerderzand and at the Moerdijk bridges, where parachutists had been dropped in the early morning of the 10th, the *Wehrmacht* met stiff resistance.

About the best weapons in the Netherlands Armoury proved to be the AA-guns which were equipped with a superior Dutch firing system, which accounted for most of the 350 downed *Luftwaffe* aircraft. These setbacks had ruined the German timetable which called for German troops to enter Amsterdam within 48 hours of the outbreak of hostilities. Only the terror bombing of the City of Rotterdam by 90 Heinkel HE-III Bombers on the 14th, followed by the German ultimatum to surrender on pain of the destruction of the Cities of Utrecht, Amsterdam and The Hague, forced General H. G. Winkelman to capitulate. The official document of surrender was signed at the small village of Rijsoord near Ridderkerk. Rotterdam, by the way, was not an 'open' city but defended by the Dutch Marines, Army and Navy.

In afterthought, it would have served no purpose to have the heart of the economic and government centres bombed to rubble in an effort to gain time since it very soon became apparent that the British and French were not capable of rendering any effective assistance being themselves soon engaged in a hopeless fight against a better armed and tactically superior German Army and Air Force.

The Dutch Forces in the south western province of Zeeland put up a strong defence for a few more days, ably assisted by two French Divisions and a British Sabotage Unit. It is not well known that when the German advance was halted in Zeeland, the Germans, as in Rotterdam, bombed the heart out of the regional capital Middelburg and destroyed or seriously damaged historical buildings dating from the Middle Ages.

As in Norway and Denmark, a 5th Column had assisted the German troops. There were 50,000 German nationals living and working in the Netherlands, among whom were many female domestics who had found work in our country after World War I, while some NSB members (Dutch fascists) must also have provided the *Abwehr* (German Intelligence) with information of importance to their war plans as well as actively assisting the *Wehrmacht* during their invasion. German troops disguised in Dutch uniforms had reportedly been employed on the first day of the attack.

As desperate as the situation appeared, to my family who were descendants of Royal Netherlands Navy and RN East Indies Army officers, the capitulation of our country did not mean that Holland had lost the War; it was only the beginning of the fight to ultimately beat Hitler.

The news from the warfront was only of German successes. Calais fell on the 24th of May. Belgium capitulated four days later and King Leopold II chose to remain in his now German-occupied country. By the 4th of June, over 300,000 British, French, Belgian and Dutch soldiers had been evacuated at Dunkirk, thanks to a masterly defensive retreat by the British, and as we would only learn years later, aided by one of the less-than-brilliant decisions made by the Führer Adolf Hitler himself.

The Fall of France on the 16th of June stunned everyone. However we still did not realise how desperate Britain's plight had become at the time of Dunkirk, nor a few months later, when the Battle of Britain had been a near-run thing.

4. German Occupation and First Acts of Resistance

On Adolf Hitler's orders, SS Troops from the *Leibstandarte Adolf Hitler* were to enter and parade through the City of Amsterdam, the capital of the Netherlands. On that fateful 15th day of May 1940 I stood in a silent crowd lining the Apollolaan, only a hundred yards away from my high school, Het Amsterdamsche Lyceum, watching the motorised German SS Troops pass by. No Dutchman or Belgian, Dane, Norwegian, Pole, Frenchman or Czech alive in 1938 will ever forget the day he or she witnessed the humiliation of watching the German troops enter their village, town or city in triumph.

Remembering the drunken orgies followed by assaults and rape committed by soldiers throughout history, and in particular the assault and rape perpetrated by drunken German soldiers in Belgium in 1914-1918, that morning of the 15th of May the wine stocks of churches as well as alcoholic drinks in many private homes like ours, on our Government's advice, were poured down the sink. This act of caution was soon regretted by all, including my father, who promptly had his whisky and sherry stocks restored when the German military behaved impeccably. Assisting my father, at his request, in the folly of disposing of the contents of bottles with precious liquids from Scotland, Portugal and France, has remained with me all my life.

The Kingdom of the Netherlands had been created by the European powers after the fall of Napoleon in 1815 to ensure that France would have a large state on its northern border. The Dutch had not been at war since Waterloo, except for some minor skirmishes when the Catholic Belgians seceded from the mainly Protestant north.

Since Napoleon, Holland had not suffered incursions of a conquering army or experienced occupation by a foreign army. Thus the Dutch were stunned and it took a while for the population to awake to the reality of being a conquered people and under the heel of a ruthless totalitarian regime.

The Jews who had fled from Central Europe and who knew what they could expect under Nazi Occupation tried to buy passages on ships, small or large, to reach safety.

IJmuiden, the port at the North Sea entrance of the Noordzee Kanaal was the prime destination for the crowded motorcars and trucks. Few succeeded and some of those who failed to depart on fishing vessels of various sizes were reported to have committed suicide. Three well-known Dutchmen also preferred suicide to living under German rule. We would come to know about the *Sicherheitsdienst* (SD) and *Ordungspolizei* in their green uniforms (and therefore called *Grüne Polizei*), the SS, Gestapo *(Geheime Staatspolizei)* and the *Abwehr (*Military Intelligence*)*.

After some confusion regarding the disbandment or internment of the 200,000 or so Dutch Military, the German Commander, General Von Valkenhausen decided, for military and economic considerations, as well as reportedly on Hitler's instructions because the Dutch were considered Aryans and part of Germania, to let all Dutch military personnel not yet made POWs by the 15th of May to go free, including those on leave who had not been able to rejoin their units. After the first 50 per cent or so had been disbanded and sent home as 'prisoners of war on extended leave', a new order was issued on 22nd of May that all those thus released were to report back to their units. Nearly all the men who had been sent home on 'grand leave' ignored the 22nd of May order.

On the 20th of June the German Occupiers issued a new call-back of POWs but now excluded conscripts and reservists. Professional soldiers who refused to sign a declaration of loyalty by giving their word of honour not to engage in any activities against the German Reich were sent to POW camps in Germany on the 14th of July. Among ten of the regulars who refused to sign was the KNIL (Royal Netherlands East Indies Army) Lieutenant Luyting who would successfully escape on the 5th of January 1942, from the infamous 13th-century Colditz Castle near Leipzig. He was in the company of Airey Neave, who at MI9 in the UK had the codename 'Saturday' and after the War would write several books about the War. One of the books was named after his pseudonym, *Saturday at MI9*. In May of 1942 all demobbed professional officers, who had earlier been released on signing the declaration of loyalty, were transported to Stanislau Camp in Poland.

After that sombre day of the 15th May, life, to the surprise of most, returned to the normalcy experienced before the 10th of May, except for the black-outs which understandably stayed in force. One rapidly got used to seeing German uniforms in the streets, cinemas, trains, shops, cafés and restaurants. The Dutch settled down in some disgust to tolerating the presence of the enemy and the galling sight of the NSB (Dutch Nazis) now flaunting their black uniforms. Schools resumed classes and university students attended lectures. My friends and I stored our hockey sticks at the end of the competition season and resumed sailing on the Dutch lakes. Quite a few members of my Amsterdam Hockey and Bandy Club, like my lifetime friend Philip Altes, played cricket which like golf was, at that time, quite foreign to nearly all Germans and indeed most Dutchmen. Meanwhile the Nazis rapidly extended and tightened their grip on life and a curfew was imposed from midnight to 4 a.m.

The German Military, as ordered by Berlin, behaved very correctly to create a favourable impression with the populace, for it had been Hitler's intention to incorporate the Netherlands into a post-war Greater German Reich. It was therefore the Netherlands, as distinct from Belgium and France, where the German military governed. It had a Nazi regime under *Reichskommissar* Arthur Seyss Inquart and Hans Albin Rauter, who was Heinrich Himmler's personal lieutenant, and who along with his Gestapo henchmen ruled with an iron hand. The Austrian Nazi Seyss Inquart had one stiff leg and, also because of his name, was promptly called *Zes-en-een Kwart* (six-and-a-quarter) by the population. Street urchins, to our amusement, would imitate his walk.

The importation of goods ceased on the day of the German invasion, while the Nazis soon carted away the prized large stocks of coffee, tea, rice and fats. Food and clothing were rationed, while imported cigarettes, tea and coffee, amongst other things, were soon only available on the black market at ever-increasing prices until the black-market stocks ran out. The quality of bread and soap declined slowly and, by 1943, was quite terrible. After the severe winter of 1941-42 the supply of all vegetables and other foodstuffs reduced further and we got used to surrogates like chicory coffee. Bread, milk, potatoes and meat rations were gradually reduced and the black market, as time went by, became more and more important to stave off under-nourishment, at least for those who could afford it. The poor, especially towards the last year of the war, suffered terribly from malnutrition.

The black marketeers took very high risks. The penalties imposed by the *Ordungspolizei* were extremely severe. All daily necessities gradually became scarcer and the quality and quantity available in the shops for purchase on our ration coupons declined. The terrible quality and appearance of grey-coloured soap and revolting greyish sodden bread still stick in the mind. Food, which my parents could luckily afford to buy on the black market, became more and more scarce and expensive. By the later summer of '43, I would bicycle to farms well outside of Amsterdam to buy food. I shall never forget the horrible taste and smell of sheep fat, which we mixed with potatoes to make up for the lack of fats. Later in life I could, as a consequence, not stand the taste and smell of mutton.

Money inexorably lost its value and goods, particularly gold, silver and, by the middle of 1943, precious stones, were demanded in payment by the black marketeers as well as by at least 11 farmers. My mother was forced to part with some of her jewelry. Food had become more important than possessions.

While the standard of living had declined sharply and the daily calorie intake was barely adequate, there was however no famine until the terrible *Honger-winter* ("hunger winter") of 1944-45, when people literally died in the streets from starvation.

In September of 1942 the Occupier ordered all silver, copper, nickel and bronze coins to be handed in. Non-compliance would incur a punishment of six months' jail or a 1000 guilder fine. However only 10 per cent of the coinage in circulation was handed in and the rest disappeared. It was realised that compliance meant assisting the German war effort. Zinc coins now came into circulation and paper money replaced silver coins.

Your country is important and becomes more so when you fight a war. It did not take long for the first stirrings of resistance to the enemy to manifest itself. The first open act of dissent came on the 29th of June 1940, on Prince Bernhard's birthday. A whispering campaign and handwritten exhortations on orange paper had been passed around asking citizens to show loyalty to the Royal Family in defiance of the Occupiers. We were urged to lay flowers at royal palaces and monuments of royals as well as to wear Prince Bernhard's favourite flower, a white carnation. That morning of the 29th, unusually large numbers of white carnations were offered for sale at Holland's ubiquitous flower stalls and sold out in no time.

On *Anjer Dag* (Carnation Day), as it became known, flowers were laid at the entrance of Soestdijk Palace, the home of Princess Juliana and Prince Bernhard, where they were hastily removed on German orders. However, many royal monuments were soon covered with flowers and untold numbers of the population displayed a white carnation on their person. The German authorities and the NSB, the Dutch fascists, were not only taken by surprise but could not effectively act against individuals wearing a flower in their button hole, stuck into a hat-band or pinned on a blouse, nor could they clear away all the floral tributes on the monuments.

Some people wearing a white carnation were accosted by members of the NSB but I did not learn of anybody being arrested. That day my friends and I also stuck a white carnation in the buttonholes of our sports coats (dress in those days was much more formal and hats were invariably worn when dressed in a suit) or pinned on the girls' dresses or cardigans. Thus festooned, we bicycled to the famous flower town of Aalsmeer on the Westeinder Lake where our sailing boats were tied up. There is a photo taken on that day of my friend Fred Braat and me, complete with white carnations. The photo was sent to Prince Bernhard on one of his birthdays. By sheer coincidence the Nazi Minister of Propaganda, Joseph Goebbels, visited The Hague on that *Anjer Dag* and he could not but have heard the singing of the Dutch National Anthem by a crowd of demonstrating Dutch Royalists not very far from the small palace on the Voorhout belonging to Princess Juliana, where he held a meeting.

The next act of passive resistance came on the 31st of August, Queen Wilhelmina's birthday, when the front lawn of the Palace was inundated with orange marigold petals, orange being the colour synonymous with the Royal House of Orange.

The first three evaders bound for England pushed their small boat off the Noordwijk beach in early July and they, and all those that succeeded in reaching England, were soon called *Engelandvaarders*. Radio Oranje in London announced on the 9th of July that "the *Bebek* had arrived" and the meaning was soon passed on by word of mouth and received with smiles and great satisfaction by one and all. From Mr.

Michielsen we learned to our delight that one of the three men was his son Ady (the nickname by which Karel Jr. was known in his youth) and the others, Kees van Endenburg and Freddie van Nunez.

There is little doubt that the broadcasts from London by the BBC, and from July by Radio Oranje, kept up our spirits and hopes in the dark days of May, during the Dunkirk evacuation and after the capitulation of France in June. Only the Dutch collaborators must have been elated to listen to or read the German war bulletins of 1940 and 1941, triumphantly announcing their victories by starting with the announcement: *"Das Oberkommando der Wehrmacht gibt bekannt."*

It is said that one believes what one wants to believe and this was never more true than in those dark days and years when, in spite of the continuous defeats suffered by the Allies, many like my family never doubted that the Allies would in the end be triumphant. The successful evacuation of some 330,000 troops from Dunkirk was viewed by us as a battle won, while it was of course only a withdrawal at the cost of all of the heavy and most of the light weapons after a crushing defeat. In fact, on the 2nd of June in 1940, Great Britain came nearest to losing the war and France, victorious in 1914-1918, was conquered in just six weeks. France's surrender had stunned us but our spirits lifted after Churchill's defiant speech in the British Parliament. It was just as well that we had no inkling that England was practically defenceless and only the Royal Navy stood between the victorious *Wehrmacht* and the shores of the British Isles. Ever since the Fall of France, marching German troops sang *"Wir fahren gegen Engeland"* and from the activities in the ports of Holland, Belgium and France, it was clear that preparations were in progress for a German attack on the British Isles.

From the battles of May and June of 1940 it was also clear however that air supremacy was crucial to a victorious military campaign and we therefore rejoiced when the Battle of Britain was won by the RAF. Thereafter there was no need for the Nazis to announce that Hitler had called off "Operation Sea Lion", since the perennial autumn storms in Western Europe would have made it a great folly to attempt a crossing of the Channel and North Sea in October or November. German troops also ceased singing *"Wir fahren gegen Engeland"* and we knew that while the Allies had not won the war, they had not lost the war either.

The successful evacuation at Dunkirk, the victory in the Battle of Britain and, particularly, British sea power had and would continue to deny Hitler the full fruits of the astonishing land victories. This had an immense psychological impact on the enslaved peoples of Europe—as did the news reported in, if I remember correctly, one of the illegal newspapers, that a resistance group calling itself De Geuzen (after a similar band of patriots in the 17th century in the fight against the Spanish Overlords) had succeeded in scuttling a U-boat in Rotterdam Harbour that Autumn of 1940. It was, however, realised that it was almost beyond belief that Britain would be able to defeat Germany on its own, and that the enslavement of Western Europe by the Nazis and the East by the terrible Stalinist regime in the Soviet Union would be inevitable if the USA did not join the Allies in the fight against the Nazis. Thankfully we were not aware in 1940 and 1941 of the strong anti-war feelings in the USA and the general wish of the American people not to get involved in yet another European war.

5. Nazi Persecution of the Jews

Nowhere in Europe would the persecution of Jews be as cunning and systematic as in the Netherlands. Perhaps with the exception of Eastern European Jewish refugees, hardly anybody else could foresee the terrible consequences of the compulsory registration of the Jews followed by their deportation to the Westerbork and Vucht internment camps in the province of Brabant. Some months later it would lead to forcible 'relocation' to 'the East', which meant, as the world would later learn, deportation to extermination camps in Germany and Poland.

In January of 1941 all Jews were required to report for registration and in May of 1942 an order was issued for them to wear the Star of David on a yellow background on their person at all times. The first deportations commenced in July, against which on the 26th of July, both the Catholic and Protestant Churches issued strong protests which were, of course, ignored by the Nazis. It was the beginning of the great tragedy that was to follow when 105,000 out of 140,000 Dutch Jews perished in concentration camps. The bullies amongst the NSB, the Dutch fascists, would now let no opportunity pass to denigrate the wearers of a Star of David. This and other provocations by the fascists did nothing to endear the Black Shirts and their leader Anton Adriaan Mussert to 98.5 per cent of the Dutch population. In 1917 when Mussert was 23-years-of age, he had married his mother's younger sister, Marie Witlam. The fact that he had married his auntie who was 18 years older had caused great merriment for which Mussert would constantly be held up to ridicule.

Some 25,000 Dutch Jews who were suspicious of the Nazi's true intentions and did not wish to be 'resettled' in Eastern Europe went into hiding.

Brave people from all walks of life were prepared to help Jews as well as evaders and escapees, disregarding the very real risk of arrest and fearsome reprisals taken by the Nazi Occupier's security police, the *Sicherheitsdienst*, for aiding the enemies of Hitler's 1000-year Reich. When betrayed by collaborators or discovered by the Gestapo, they, as well as about 8000 Jews and others in hiding, lost their lives in front of firing squads, by hanging or in concentration camps.

The first big round-up of Jews took place on 22nd and 23rd of February 1941. The second *razzia* (raid) commenced on the 11th of June and continued until 1943 when representatives of the *Herrenvolk* proclaimed Amsterdam to be free of Jews. There were however, still those in hiding like the tragic Anne Frank whose diaries would subsequently make her a famous victim of Nazism.

After receiving a warning from Guus Camaert, a Dutch Police Lieutenant, through his wife Milly that a *razzia* was expected that evening, I hid in the apartment (on the Minervaplein in Amsterdam South) of my brother's mother-in-law, Mrs. Pauw, and witnessed the arrest of a Jewish family on the same floor of the building. I still remember the sound of loud, harsh German commands and, when furtively looking out of a window, the dejected posture of the Jewish family of four and their frightened faces when they were herded into a SS truck.

The first protest against the systematic anti-Jewish measures of the Occupiers was made by the six large Protestant-Christian Church Associations through a petition to the *Reichskommisar,* Seyss Inquart. It was read from all the churches and prompted a protest from the students at the University in Delft. At Leiden University on the 26th of November 1940, the day on which the renowned Jewish law professor, E. M. Meyers, was forbidden to lecture any longer, Professor Cleveringa made a speech. It was a most courageous act by a highly principled academic which made a deep impression on us all. That same day, thousands of Leiden University students went on strike and thousands of copies of Prof. Cleveringa's text were disseminated all over the country. The next day the Occupier closed Leiden University and arrested Prof. Cleveringa. It was re-opened some time later, but Delft University students went on a protest strike in November and their university remained closed until after the war.

On the 25th of February 1941, the first of the three big strikes against the Nazi Occupiers started in Amsterdam; this was later named the "February Strike", in protest against the persecution and deportation of Jews. The strike took the Germans totally by surprise. Never before in Germany or any of the other occupied territories had there been a mass protest against the Nazis. People in the German-occupied territories simply did not strike! Rauter's SS and SD henchmen acted forcefully. Strikers were arrested and executed. By the 26th the strike was broken. A statue of a wharf labourer now stands on the JD Meyerplein in Amsterdam in honour of the Amsterdam wharfies who started the strike and were executed.

It was, however, clear to our Nazi Occupiers that to Dutchmen in general, who practised a policy of non-discrimination, it was an affront to denigrate the Jews and forbid them to use parks, cinemas, concert-halls and public transport. They would soon learn that, except for the 30,000 NSB members and collaborators, the Dutch did not want to become a part of the Greater German 1000-year Reich of Adolf Hitler.

Virtually nobody in Holland knew about the Nazi extermination camps although we did know about concentration camps for anti-Nazi Germans and Resistance members and we had feared for the well-being, but not for the lives, of the Jews in Holland. However, the brutal manner of 'collecting' Jews and their dispatch in delivery wagons to Eastern Europe had not passed our notice. Resettling the Jews of Western Europe in Poland and the Ukraine, where a large Jewish population was known to exist, seemed harsh but it was beyond our comprehension that the Nazis intended to exterminate a race by shooting and gassing people. Hitler's "Final Solution" for the Jews in German-occupied Europe, and executed with ineffable brutality by the SS, was and is simply beyond the understanding of a civilised mind.

6. Illegal Newsletters and the BBC's Radio Oranje

Quite soon it became evident that the Nazi German civil administration was imposing a dictatorship far worse than a military regime like those in Belgium and France. They were clever enough to retain virtually all civil servants and most of the high placed bureaucrats as well as the police to execute their orders and only placed NSB members in key positions. Dutch fascists were also placed in key positions but they were not given any real governing power. The Dutch people would receive a continuous stream of *Verordungen* (orders) in the newspapers and as announcements in large print on bulletin boards found on the streets and in government buildings. Among these were the 'wanted' posters for criminals, often with their photos, which the population from the very first correctly interpreted were not criminals at all but members of the Resistance, secret agents and POW escapees.

Although it took some months before organised resistance came into being, the first illegal publication had already appeared on the 15th of May 1940, that is, within 24-hours of the capitulation. It was called the *"Geuzenbericht"*, initiated by Bernard IJzerdraat of the City of Schiedam. (The name *'Geuzen'* was symbolic for the acts of resistance against the Spanish overlords of the Low Countries by a group of insurgents who called themselves the *Geuzen*: this occurred at the start of the war of liberation from Spanish rule in the 16th century.) IJzerdraat was subsequently betrayed, arrested and shot by the SD.

Yzerdraad's execution was very soon followed by *"De Niewsbrief"* (newsletter) edited by Frans Goedhart, a communist in his youth, who would become an avowed socialist and who I would meet briefly in Spain in 1944. The *"Niewsbrief's"* first run was only 150 copies.

These illegal newsletters were at first written in longhand or typed and stencilled. Not until a year later, in August 1941, would the first printed underground paper *"Het Parool"* (The Parole) be handed around. After the war, *"Het Parool"* would become one of Holland's daily newspapers.

Other major underground newsletters which my family and friends would receive regularly were *"Trouw"* (Loyal) and *"Vrij Nederland"* (Free Netherlands). The Communists printed the *"De Waarheid"* (The Truth) which continued publication after the War. There were many clandestinely printed newsletters which appeared only a few times, which was not surprising considering the risk of arrest or betrayal as a result of production and distribution. Many an intrepid newsletter contributor was arrested during those years of Occupation. Amongst them was the law student Han Gelder who, when the SD raided the office of the illegal newspaper *"Ons Volk"*, shot himself in the head to prevent disclosing names of his fellow Resistance members under torture.

Another true hero was Kees Verloop, a member of an escape line, who, when arrested by the Gestapo, jumped out of a high-storied window to his death.

The underground press would grow from these small beginnings of a print of only 150 copies to have a monthly printing of some 150,000 copies. They were read and passed on until worn out—at the risk of severe penalties imposed by the Germans for having even one in your possession.

In January 1941 the Archbishop of Utrecht, Jan de Jong, forbade Catholics to be members of the NSB *(Nationaal Socialistische Bond)* or the WA (Stormtroopers of the NSB) and the SS, which did not endear him to the Nazis and NSB but made him admired and most popular with everybody else.

In January 1941 the Archbishop of Utrecht, Jan de Jong, forbade Catholics to be members of the NSB *(National Socialistische Bond)* or the WA (Stormtroopers of the NSB) and the SS, which did not endear him to the Nazis and NSB but made him admired and most popular with everybody else.

In that same month of January of 1941, a radio tax was introduced. It was abundantly clear that the purpose was to register the addresses of radio owners and to confiscate them at a later date. My father, like so many others, ignored the order and henceforth covered our radio (which was situated in the remotest part of the apartment) with a cloth to keep it away from prying eyes. It was risky but then one had to take risks during the Occupation.

In spite of the severe penalties imposed, the Dutch showed a reluctance to listen to the rigidly-controlled radio stations *Hilversum 1* and *2* and preferred instead to bolt windows and doors and tune into the BBC and Radio Oranje from London. The *Höherer Polizeiführer der SS* Rauter's solution was simple. On the 18th of May 1943 he confiscated radio sets by the hundreds. The SS swooped down on houses and blocks of flats and the haul was reportedly 800,000 sets. Having a radio became illegal throughout the Netherlands.

None-the-less, every evening we listened to Radio Oranje, which started broadcasting in July of 1940, and to the comforting sound of Big Ben announcing the BBC News. A feature on Radio Oranje was the broadcasting of old Dutch songs of which the words had been changed to express defiance, anti-Nazi and pro-House of Orange feelings. If, during the next few days, someone whistled these tunes, passers-by would know they had listened to Radio Oranje and acknowledged the whistler with a wink or a smile. To do this in the presence of uniformed Germans was particularly pleasing.

The (figuratively speaking) sober Dutchman considered German Military music bombastic and the goose-step comical, while Hitler's toothbrush moustache reminded them of Charlie Chaplin and the Nazi salute and Heil Hitler greeting were held up to ridicule. Acronyms, usually coarse words, of SS, NSB, OKW, etc. were painted on walls and fences. German propaganda posters were defaced or over-painted with anti-Nazi or pro-Allied slogans. It helped to lift the gloom, if only temporarily, of the humiliation of foreign domination.

Humour is a marvellous medicine for the mind. Jokes, humorous remarks and using satire as a tool of dissent helped the people to endure the trials of shortages as well as the presence of German uniforms and the depressing war news.

Felicitous remarks at which the Amsterdarnmer is particular adept could put smiles on worried faces and many a tram driver and tram conductor has caused me and fellow passengers to chuckle, grin or smile.

I recall that once, standing near the front in a No 16 tram, a German *Feldwebel* asked the driver for directions to the district's *Ortskommandantur.* He was advised to get off at the next stop on the Stadhouderskade and then to walk along the canal. My fellow passengers and I had to contain ourselves, until the *Feldwebel* had alighted and the doors had closed, for we knew that the street along the canal ran in an easterly direction (towards Germany!) and that he would have a very long walk since the bureau of the local military commander was in a totally different part of town.

Of the many jokes told early in the Occupation I recall to this day a Jewish one of Mosie having been arrested by the Gestapo. He was taken to the Gestapo HQ in the Euterpestraat in Amsterdam-Zuid, where a sadistic Gestapo officer beat Mosie black and blue with blows of his fists and a truncheon. At the moment a mighty wallop caused Mosie's nose to spurt blood, the telephone rang. Annoyed at being interrupted, the Gestapo brute lifts the receiver and, after listening for a few seconds, barks, *"Sie wissen doch dass ich kein Hollandisch spreche?"* (You know that I do not speak Dutch?). At the same time the Nazi signals to Mosie to take the receiver and orders him to ask the bloody fellow what he wants. Mosie wipes the blood from his nose, puts the telephone receiver to his ear and says: *"Hello, you are speaking now with Mosie from the Gestapo".*

After the capitulation of the Dutch Forces on the night of the 14th of May, petrol supplies quickly ran out and all traffic, apart from the motor vehicles requisitioned and painted field-grey by the Germans, disappeared from the roads. Soon however a few motorcars, taxis and buses appeared, running on gas generated by wood or coal burners attached to the back of vehicles and stored in large mattress-like inflatable containers carried on the roofs. Horses were also employed to draw motor vehicles. Bicycle taxis appeared briefly before being outlawed by the Occupier.

Then, in the Low Countries, ubiquitous bicycles became even more indispensable. New bicycles were unobtainable as the production of bicycles was now sent directly to Germany. Stocks of new tyres soon ran out and by 1942 the ingeniously-constructed wooden tyre had appeared. Many simply drove on the bare wheel rims. Theft of one's bike became an even greater worry.

Trains and trams had to accommodate an enormous increase in the number of passengers and postal services reverted to horse-drawn mail vans while postmen on bicycles and on foot continued as before to deliver the mail. In December of 1940, gas and electricity were rationed but we could cope.

On the 20th of July, 1942, our dear *Generaal Komisssar* announced that they needed 100,000 bicycles for the *Wehrmacht*. Those who owned men's push-bikes were ordered to turn them in. Non-compliance would be severely punished. Virtually the whole population ignored the *Verordnung*. They simply did not use their bicycles for a while. Two weeks later we were informed that the order was rescinded because our type of bicycle was not suitable for the *Wehrmacht*. This excuse caused much mirth and engendered jokes about the type of bicycle suitable for the *Wehrmacht* in the mud and snow of the Eastern Front. Those who, for fear of repercussions, had handed in their prized bicycles never saw them again, but it gave rise to another spate of jokes thought up by Amsterdammers, known for their marvellous sense of humor.

7. 1941: Operation Barbarossa and Pearl Harbour

The astounding news that Hitler's deputy, Rudolf Hess, had bailed out from a Messerschmidt 110 over Eaglesham Moor in Scotland was received with glee. Hopes were raised of disagreements and tensions amongst the Nazi hierarchy, but these were however soon dashed.

I still remember clearly how we rejoiced when Hitler tore up yet another treaty and unleashed "Operation Barbarossa" on the Soviets in June 1941.

Ever since the 1917 Revolution in Russia there was great fear in Europe among the conservatives and liberals of the threat of communism which was considered a greater danger to the democracies than fascism. The Soviet Union's invasion of Finland in November 1939 strengthened our fear of the ruthless Stalinists. Everybody but the communists admired the heroic Finnish people who fought the Soviets to a standstill and were dejected when they were forced to give in to Stalin's demands.

This sentiment was so strong that when Hitler invaded Soviet Russia many in Holland, like us, were pro-German on the Eastern Front while remaining strongly anti-Nazi and praying for an Allied Victory. We hoped, nay believed, that the Soviets, like the Tsarist Russians in 1812 against Napoleon, would employ the same tactics and draw Hitler's armies into the vastness of Soviet Russia where they and the Red Army, aided by Partizans, would fight each other to a standstill. When (and not if) America, like in 1917, came into the war the Nazis would be defeated and the communist threat also eliminated. It, of course, did not pan out that way.

When the German war machine annihilated several Soviet Armies and made hundreds of thousands prisoner, many despaired as did our highly respected and admired former Conservative Prime Minister Colijn who openly expressed his disbelief that Germany could still lose the War.

It would be the "Russian Father Winter" that came to the rescue of the Red Army and halted Hitler's hordes in sight of the spires of Moscow. Then the Japanese attack on Pearl Harbour on the 7th of December 1941 allowed President Franklin Roosevelt to declare war on Japan. Adolf Hitler, the *Führer* of the German 1000-year Reich had, on the 3rd of October, announced that Germany had already won the war against the Bolsheviks; now, in a rush of blood, he declared war on the USA. That the great dictator Benito Mussolini, in support of his Axis partners, followed suit went largely unnoticed.

Our euphoria at this turn of events, and particularly that the USA had, as in 1917, joined the Allies, was however dampened by our fears for my brother Tom, his wife Hetty and their one-year-old baby girl Patricia, as the Netherlands East Indies was now at war with Imperial Japan.

The news of the Japanese landings on the Malay Peninsula, the sinking of the 'Repulse' and 'Prince of Wales' battleships followed by the fall of Singapore and the landings on the coast of the province of Deli, were very worrying. On the north east coast of North Sumatra, Tom and his family lived on a tea plantation and this was particularly worrying to my mother. We were now cut off from news about them which we, in spite of the German Occupation, had received through Hetty's sister in New York.

Newspapers reported the Japanese rampaging through Sumatra and Java. Then came the news on Radio Oranje that all Europeans—men, women and children—were interned in camps. This was most distressing. We, who knew about life in the tropics, worried about Hetty and her small baby living in cramped quarters and deprived of proper medical care and proper nutrition. Recalling the treatment of Chinese POWs by the Japanese Imperial Army we feared for the treatment Tom would receive.

8. Identity Cards and 300,000 Go into Hiding

In April 1941 personal identity cards were introduced which carried a passport photo, signature and fingerprint. These had to be carried on one's person at all times. It was so perfectly designed that neither the Resistance nor the SOE in England ever succeeded in producing a copy which could pass close scrutiny by the Germans. The Resistance, however, managed to 'acquire' blank forms with the help of professional safecrackers and anti-German employees of the Government department involved.

As early as July of 1940 the first contingent for the *Arbeidseinsatz* (labour in Germany) departed for Germany. They consisted at first of volunteers, attracted by the seemingly generous wages and conditions offered. Soon a larger number of unemployed men, who had been threatened with withdrawal of unemployment benefits unless they signed-up, were forced to leave for Germany. Thirty-percent returned within a few months because of the employment and housing conditions and went into hiding.

In 1942, all able-bodied 18 to 35-year-olds were declared liable for compulsory labour in Germany and ordered to register at the labour exchanges. My friends and I ignored the order.

My cousin Wim Portengen was one of the unlucky ones and had to work 10-12 hours a day for six days a week in Germany. He slept in barracks which were infested with lice and fleas and was subjected to the frequent air-raids by the RAF at night and USAF by day; to top it off he was also required to help clear the rubble after air-raids.

However, not all were as unfortunate as Wim. My Tasmanian friend, the French-Australian Pierre Lecomte, was similarly forced to work in Germany, where he was housed with a German family and was treated with kindness, while his employers were understanding and helpful. Pierre, like hundreds of thousands of others, was caught up in the chaos at the War's end. His experiences from the end of April 1945 during and after the Russian onslaught on Berlin, and his telling of his amazing adventures when travelling from Russian-occupied Germany to the British/American lines, would make fascinating reading, if he chose to put it in writing.

By the spring of 1943 the shortage of manpower in German industries became so serious that in May all men between 18 and 40 years of age, unless exempted by the authorities, were ordered to register at the labour exchange for the *Arbeidseinsatz*. Non-compliance with this *Verordnung* meant arrest and deportation to a forced labour camp.

A day earlier, on the 29th of April, the *Wehrmacht's* General Christiansen had, no doubt for the same reasons, issued an order for approximately 240,000 former POWs to report for immediate captivity. On Friday, the 30th of April 1943, in a broadcast on Radio Oranje, the Dutch Government-in-Exile in London urged us not to report and, if necessary, to go into hiding. Thus only 11,000 ended up in a POW camp.

In early May 1943 the churches protested vehemently against what they described as deportation to Germany and openly advised us not to comply with the order.

These simultaneous call-ups by the Germans caused spontaneous strikes to break out all over the Netherlands, at first in Hengelo and in the eastern province of Twente. The next day, strikes were reported all over the country. The April-May strike did not however end up in a general strike when the railways and population in the big cities in the West and the province of Zeeland did not put down "tools and pens". The German reaction was swift and ruthless. The SS and Gestapo Chief, Hanns Rauter, announced a police summary justice *Verordnung* to the effect that groups of more than 5 persons would be shot on sight and a curfew from 20.00 hours to 06.00 hours imposed. This resulted in many arrests and indiscriminate shooting of factory personnel and innocents by the *Ordnungspolizei* and the *Waffen* SS. In one village the SS perpetrated the wholesale slaughter of villagers—men, women and children.

The arrested strikers, after a short hearing in court, were immediately executed. The death sentences were reported on the front pages of the German-controlled newspapers and on billboards. The newspaper

"Prom" that day reported that the *Grüne Polizei* and SS would act with even more intimidating brutality.

I belonged to those fortunate young men who could hide in an ancestral home—we also had a storeroom on the 4th floor attic of the apartment building—or stay with close relatives as well as occasionally with friends or at a sports clubhouse. My parents were also financially able to look after my welfare, but other families required financial assistance. Only after the end of WWII, would I learn about a marvelous clandestine operation which came into being towards the end of 1942.

The *Landelijke Organisatie* (LO) was instituted for the sole purpose of rendering centrally-organised assistance for *Onderduikers* ("under-divers" or evaders) going into hiding. Members of the LO would gather regularly to exchange information regarding all matters connected with helping evaders find a hiding place, paying for expenses incurred by those offering shelter, and acquiring forged identity and distribution cards and food coupons. At one time 14,000 people, spread out over 100 districts, worked for the LO. The Resistance provided the LO with 'liberated' blank forms of identity cards and ration coupons, while some public servants also rendered assistance in this regard, as well as issuing certificates for exemption from labour in Germany.

To meet the expenses incurred by the LO on behalf of evaders another clandestine organisation, the *Nationaal Steunfonds* (NSF), under the inspiring leadership of Mr. Walraven van Hal, had been empowered by the Netherlands Government-in Exile in London to effect payments to the LO and also to provide guarantees for any loans provided by third parties.

Mrs. G. L. M. Smit, who was responsible for the payout in Amsterdam, told, in the *"Contactblad Stichting 1940-1945"*, how towards the end of World War II she carried two small suitcases, each containing 400,000 guilders in banknotes, on the luggage rack of her bicycle from the De Ruyterkade to her home in the Rijnstraat for distribution to 12,000 families.

Those who have read Nancy Wake's wartime story will know that young women were the preferred couriers in Occupied Europe. Girls had the best chance of passing scrutiny and could use their womanly wiles to flirt themselves past ogling soldiers and the sternest of *Wehrmacht* or *Polizei* checkpoint inspectors.

The *Engelandvaarder* Miss Jos Gemmeke was awarded the MWO, the highest decoration for bravery, for bicycling through the warfront in Brabant and bluffing her way through German checkpoints to personally deliver microfilms hidden in the shoulder pads of her overcoat and under the mirror of her powder compact, to Prince Bernhard at his HQ in Belgium.

After May of 1943, the total number of *Onderduikers* increased to over 300,000. Many evaders now also disappeared into the marshes of the Biesbosch and joined the eel fishermen and rush cutters who, in primitive circumstances, made a meagre living. Here they would hide in sheds, straw huts, and small boats invisible to the German Occupiers. It was in these marshes, resembling a true wilderness and situated in the delta created by the confluence of the mighty Rhine/Waal and Meuse/Maas Rivers called the Biesbosch, that Allied soldiers after the Arnhem Battle found refuge. Among all those evaders in hiding were also German deserters, an occasional escaped Russian POW and downed Allied airmen. Most of the latter would however soon be passed on to the escape lines to be spirited back to England.

One cannot but greatly admire the readiness of farmers, peasants and ordinary people in all the occupied territories of Europe who rendered assistance to escapees and evaders with shelter, food, clothing and sometimes even money, all this in spite of the danger they ran in doing so.

Apart from the physical and financial problems facing those who had gone into hiding, there was also the emotional strain of living cooped-up and, at all times, the fear of being detected, arrested and transported to a forced labour camp, or executed.

According to the Dutch historian, Dr. L. de Jong, in no Western European country did so many go into hiding as in the Netherlands, although our densely populated country was not an easy place in which to hide, unlike countries like France or Yugoslavia where one could retire to the forests and mountains, and from where the *Maquisards* and *Partizans* could strike at will against the Nazi Occupiers.

The SD searched attics which they logically assumed were used to hide family members. But the attics were often so ingenuously constructed that evaders, more often than not, were never detected. Attics could also often offer a chance of escape over the roofs of adjoining buildings. My good friend and a participant in the *Ondergrondse,* John

Reys, was one of those who escaped from the Huis van Bewaring (jail) in Amsterdam over the roofs of adjoining buildings. He forced the window of an attic and ran down the stairs of the house. Upon reaching the street he looked left and right and noticed uniformed men already blocking the side street corners at the bridges running across the *gracht* (canal). John quickly crossed the street, passed the large trees planted alongside the canal and slid over the quayside into the water. The worst part was, he told us, having to disappear under the stinking dirty water for short periods when the chasing *polizei* were passing nearby. With the help of strangers, including a boat-owner, he succeeded in reaching his home town of Nijmegen on the day before the Arnhem assault by the Allies. Talk about timing!

After the War, Dutch Government documents stated that of the 8 million inhabitants, 420,000 either signed up for the *Arbeidseinsatz* or were deported to forced labour camps in Germany, as well as 20,000 military and 6,500 students. All told, 120,000 Dutch Jews were arrested and most died in extermination camps. Over 300,000 went into hiding by August 1944; some of these evaders enlarged the ranks of the BS (Interior Forces/Resistance) to 25,000 after D-Day. By the time the Allied Armies reached Arnhem the active Resistance according to official figures reached 45,000 men and women.

9. Intelligence, Sabotage, and Reprisals

After Dunkirk and the capitulation of France, it was generally accepted by those staunchly believing in an ultimate Allied victory that it would take many years to defeat the efficient German war machine. This strengthened the determination of many young men to join a resistance group or to try to get to England to join the forces and actively participate in the fight against Nazi Germany.

My father, well aware of this desire, had however, quite early after the capitulation, made it clear to me that he considered it essential for me to obtain that "bit of paper", as he called the high school diploma. "Without it you will probably end up selling shoelaces on a street corner." I had therefore to promise him that, whatever I intended to undertake, I was first to get my leaving certificate. The 1939 mobilisation, plus my father's frequent transfers during my primary school years—when we moved from Holland to Kobe in Japan, then to Shanghai, Soerabaja, The Hague, Jakarta and finally Amsterdam in the space of eight years—and my failing the first form at the Batavia Lyceum would delay my matriculating by four years. Returning to the school benches after my spell in the Army I had not found it possible to catch up sufficiently on lost tuition to enable me to sit for my final exams and I repeated Year 12 at the Amsterdamsche Lyceum.

In June '41, I welcomed the awarding of my diploma with great relief for I was, in some subjects, a mediocre student. It had been a hard slog. It has always been a great mystery to me how my teachers could have advised my parents to send me, after year nine, not to study Commerce/Economics but to a Mathematics Division to prepare me for University. The only real talent I possessed, apart from a small talent in art, was in Commerce, the proof of which was soon demonstrated by my ability to trade in progressively scarcer consumer goods and provide for my parents' smoking habit with a regular supply of, albeit deteriorating quality, cigarettes. As the War progressed, the supply of quality tobacco products like "Capstain" and "Camel" cigarettes and "Sobrani" pipe tobacco ran low even at the exorbitant black-market prices. On the ration card we could only acquire terrible cigarettes sold under the brand name "SOPLA", which in popular language soon became the acronym for *Stinkt Ontzettend Probeer Liever Anderen* which translates into *"It stinks terribly please try others"*.

In the autumn of 1940, sabotage by 'illegals' induced the military *Kommandant General* Christiansen to issue a warning that henceforth such acts of sabotage would result in the taking of hostages or the setting on fire of homes in the area where the sabotage had taken place. Executions of saboteurs and, heinously, of innocent hostages were announced in the newspapers. A well-known hostage executed by the Nazis was Mr. Willem Ruys, after whom a Rotterdam Lloyd passenger liner was subsequently named. The MV 'Willem Ruys' would years later end up in Italian hands and, as the "Achile Lauro", become famous when hi-jacked by terrorists.

When the Germans invaded on the 10th of May 1940 our Government did not have an organisation in place which could provide important and necessary intelligence to the Allied HQ. It illustrated yet again the near total unpreparedness of the Netherlands. It would take years for an efficient intelligence network to be created.

The first secret agent sent to the Netherlands by the Dutch Government in London was the RN Navy Lt. Lodewijk van Hamel, who parachuted into the western province of Holland and immediately found helpers amongst his friends at Leiden University. Misadventure at a seaplane pick-up on Tjeuke Lake in the northern province of Friesland in November 1940 resulted in the arrest of van Hamel and the other occupants of the rowing boat by the Germans. (More about this later.)

Amongst those involved and who watched the drama unfold but got away, and were wanted by the Gestapo, was Erik Michielsen, who would hide for nearly two months in our Amsterdam home and share my bedroom where he would write part of his book, *Tegen de Vlagen van de Oostenwind*. Sheltering people wanted by the Germans was, of course, not without danger, but Erik's father, who had been the Managing Director of the Javaansche Bank in Batavia, was a very close friend of my father.

From the end of 1941 onwards, it became even more dangerous to shelter evaders, even if they were one's own children, when hiding secret agents or members of the Resistance. Whole families ended up in jail or in a concentration camp and the head of the family executed. Before the War, both Erik and Karel Jr, whom I had first befriended in 1929, would spend many weekends at our first home in Amsterdam, in the J. J. Viotta Straat 37 opposite the present Hilton Hotel, until their parents and sister settled in The Hague in the late thirties.

In the exceptionally severe winter of 1941-42, a summons was deposited in our letterbox ordering Mijnheer Pieter Rudolph Zeeman to report for guard duty at homes belonging to members of the NSB because of recent attacks by dissidents on homes of aforesaid citizens of the fascist ideology. I was to report at the Overtoom Police Station on a number of evenings. It became known that those selected for such assignments were prominent citizens like university lecturers, industrialists, bank directors, politicians and teachers, and were generally middle-aged.

Since my father and I had the same Christian names and no mention was made of age it therefore went without saying that I would present myself on the days Mr. Zeeman had to fulfil his duties of walking up and down the streets on packed snow and ice in front of the NSB members' homes. The owners of these fascist-owned or rented dwellings must have been red-faced with anger and green with envy when they noted their neighbours providing us 'guards' frequently with hot soup and even once with a cup of real tea, which by this time was a highly-priced luxury. Occasionally, we might even receive a cigar or cigarette.

By the time I returned with my companion to the Overtoom Police Station—a walk of about half an hour on shoes covered by old socks to prevent slipping on the icy streets—we were half frozen by the Siberian temperatures and the biting east wind. I can still picture the kindly sergeant in his Amsterdam Police uniform serving us 'ersatz' coffee, or just a cup of hot water, while we gathered around the potbelly stove to defrost.

I usually took the risk of sleeping in my own bed but would regularly stay with friends or family when tipped off by reliable sources or by rumours about impending raids. These rumours were or seemed more often than not without foundation but, of course, had to be taken seriously to avoid the hospitality of a Gestapo jail or at best the luxurious barracks of a forced labour camp in Germany and Poland!

I have always wondered whether two P. R. Zeemans living at the same address caused confusion both at the City's Registry Office and with the German authorities.

My father, then aged in his fifties, because of his position at the NHM Bank was obviously the PRZ required to do guard duty. It would explain why there was no house search at No 96 until after the order signed by the *Wehrmacht-Befehlhaber in den Niederlanden*, General Christiansen, on the 29th of April 1943, which required all Dutch servicemen 'on extended leave' to report immediately for captivity. Dutch military records would show clearly that a P. R. Zeeman of the 2nd AA Battery was born in 1919 and, in 1939, lived at No 96 De Lairessestraat in Amsterdam. When the knock on the door came in June 1943, I had already left (having been warned) for The Hague to stay with my parents' friends Mr. and Mrs. J. Bennink in Benoordenhout.

Having a surname starting with the last letter of the alphabet could, of course, also have played a part in not receiving an earlier visit from the police for failing to report for the *Arbeidseinsatz*. In any case, it did mean that I quite likely, and quite unnecessarily, often did not sleep in my own bed because of the confusion caused by my father and I having the same first names.

By coincidence my Uncle Jacob Portengen, who lived in The Hague, was staying overnight at No 96 and it was he who the German Sergeant found in the spare bed in my bedroom and caused the good *Feldwebel* to remark *"Er ist zu alt"* (He is too old). When asked, my family told him that I was an independent 23-year-old whom they had not seen for a long time and that they did not know where I was. After also looking under my sick 82-year-old grandmother Sophia's bed and apologising for having to inconvenience her, he departed and joined the other soldiers who searched other apartments in the building.

In the course of 1942, the *Moffen* (Dutch slang for Germans) commenced making random raids at offices and factories and conducted drives in cinemas, on sports fields or simply in the streets. Evaders now had to be more alert not to be caught in raids or at the increasingly-held identity card checks. During these SD raids, often assisted by the municipal police force or by the SS (military units), one or more house blocks were cordoned off and all the young men caught in the dragnet were carried off for whatever interrogation. When such a raid was in progress and you happened to walk or cycle in that direction, total strangers passing by would invariably manage to warn you by remarking softly, or loudly when you passed by on a bike: *"Ze zijn weer bezig daar" ("They are busy there again")*, or simply *"Identiteitskaart controle"*, and make a backward nod with the head. Once, I was nearly caught in a dragnet of SS soldiers in South Central Amsterdam who started surrounding a few street blocks. I was in a bicycle shop situated on the corner of one of the streets being cordoned off when the first arrests were made. The SS men had already blocked the main entrance of the corner shop before I noticed them but I somehow managed to leave unnoticed through a side door leading into the side street. I quickly unlocked and jumped on my bicycle, which I had placed against a lamp-post, whilst more SS men jumped out of their trucks and ran on the double into the cordoned off main street.

By 1942 we had to be constantly vigilant when moving about town on foot, in trains or trams, or on our bicycles and, if stopped for proof of carrying the compulsory identity card, not give the impression that you were afraid or apprehensive. You learned to scrutinize the faces and posture of people and it happened that a feeling of tension would descend on the occupants of a tram or train when certain types of men "who did not belong" or uniformed SS or SD men boarded the carriage.

In all of those years I avoided staying overnight in a hotel because hotels were required by the Authorities to inspect and register the identity cards of their guests. Only twice did I stay in "safe" hotels where the guests were not registered by the proprietor.

We did not let the fear of a knock on the door or being caught at identity card checks or SS drives for the *Arbeidseinsatz* completely rule our lives and we still had parties which, because of the night curfew, had to end before midnight.

It was however not the nerve-racking existence it may sound like and especially so from 1940 to early 1942. One seemed to develop some immunity against fear. A complete mastery of fear is, of course, quite a different thing.

10. Planning My Escape

In the summer of 1941, I celebrated gaining my diploma by mostly sailing on the Westeinder Lake south of Amsterdam with my friend Fred Braat and other friends on his sailing boat called '*Snark*'.

During that summer, while I did not neglect pursuing avenues of getting to England, I prepared myself for my future career which as a matter of course was to be in the Netherlands Indies and the Far East where the previous two generations had spent their working lives. I therefore first acquired a certificate in commercial English and then read *Indologie* (i.e., culture, language, trade, history and government of the Indies) at the Colonial Institute in Amsterdam. There I would meet young men of a similar disposition with whom the possibility of escaping to England was a common topic of discussion.

I realised all too well that making one's way to England would be a risky venture and, while I was prepared to take a calculated risk, it was against my nature to 'beard the lion in its den' and set off in a southerly direction by foot or bicycle trusting solely on my luck and ability to overcome all obstacles on the run. Some adventurous and brave chaps however did just that with a few Belgian and French francs in their pockets, a rucksack on their backs and a trust in their initiative, and good luck, to reach Switzerland or Spain. How many never made it is anybody's guess but a handful of *Engelandvaarders* actually did so and succeeded in reaching freedom. But being of a careful nature I did not trust myself to succeed in overcoming all obstacles on a huge wave of luck.

Very early in the German Occupation of Belgium and France very little was known about the (still chaotic) situation in those countries and less about whether evaders, escapees and refugees could expect a welcome mat or get a hostile reception from the neutral Swiss (many with German sympathies), the Vichy French or the fascist government of General Franco in Spain.

By the summer of 1941 we knew that trains were rigidly controlled and the stations' platforms and waiting rooms could be dangerous. Forged Belgian, but particularly French, identity cards were therefore the next most important item after a good pair of shoes to brave the mountains of the Jura or Pyrenees. An identity card was however not a foolproof protection when, under questioning, poor French or good French with a foreign accent could raise suspicions. A foreign or Jewish appearance was not helpful either and some of those with a good dash of genes from the native population of the Indies also could not pass as pure Saxons but, once in the South of France, a very few might well blend in with the local population. We were also well aware that the *SD/Gestapo* had the power of preventative arrest and could imprison anybody simply on a mere suspicion, the consequence of which could be most unpleasant. I should mention that for all practical purposes the dreaded Gestapo *(Geheime Staatspolizei)* and SD *(Sicherheitsdienst)* were indistinguishable, and the *Ordnungspolizei* nearly so.

Simple logic told us that it would be difficult to cross the Jura Mountains to Switzerland without a guide and the Pyrenees even more so. It is not surprising that very few who tried to trek across the daunting Pyrenees without a *passeur* made it to an inhabited part of Spanish soil.

Rudi Hemes (General Rt.) the present Chairman of our *Engelandvaarder's* Association, told the story of a school-mate who, soon after matriculating in 1940, made it to the Pyrenees on his own but was shot dead in the mountains by a German patrol. The Germans made sure that the newspapers carried stories about failed attempts by *Deutschfeindliche* to cross the North Sea or of their arrests in Belgium or France.

I was told a most amusing story of an intrepid character who, suitably and flamboyantly dressed as a bicycle racer, sprinted across the border on his racing bike past astonished German and Spanish border guards. On reflection, that was a prime example of clever and good planning.

The time of the year to try one's luck was, of course, a major consideration. Late spring and early autumn would logically be the preferred time to make the journey to Spain or Switzerland. The most favourable time for a sea crossing was mid-summer when the weather on the North Sea could be expected to be benign.

Cold and snow were a deterrent against crossing the mountains of the Jura and Pyrenees in winter, while leaving a trail in the snow increased the chances of being spotted and arrested by German or Vichy French ski patrols. Yet many of these considerations were very often put aside and escapes overland in winter were nevertheless made as well as hazardous sea voyages over the fickle North Sea throughout the year.

Most of those who took the risk to make their way to England did not, as young men in their late teens and early twenties tend not to do, let their minds dwell too long on the dangers and consequences of failure. If they had, they might never have attempted it. A few even reached England in a foldable canoe.

The direct route to England by sea was, of course, the shortest journey but by the end of the summer of 1940 the *Wehrmacht had* tightened its surveillance of the whole coastal area. Leaving from a beach in daylight, like the threesome on the *Bebek* in July, was now hardly possible. Nevertheless, several attempts were made at dusk and during the night, departing from dunes north of Scheveningen and further north from the Hondsbosche Seawall, east of the town of Bergen. From what has become known, most of these attempts failed with loss of life in the notoriously treacherous waves and unpredictable sudden storms of the North Sea. Those caught died by firing squad execution in the nearby Waalsdorper dunes or in a *Nacht und Nebel* concentration camp, usually after a sojourn in the Gestapo jail at Scheveningen. This jail came to be known as 'Oranje Hotel' because all of its occupants were evaders, escapees, secret agents and members of the Dutch Resistance. The name *"Nacht und Nebel"*—or "night and mist"—was used by the Nazis to indicate that nobody would leave these concentration camps alive.

In June '41 *Reichskommissar* Seyss Inquart, in *Verordnung* No 100, forbade water sports in the coastal zones of Holland and Zeeland, the IJsselmeer and the Wadden Islands, which are situated along the North Sea and form an arc to the north-west tip of the province of Friesland. Overnight stays in cabins of all pleasure boats on all waterways and lakes were considered criminal offences. It did not however deter us from overnighting in the *"Snark"* on the Westeinder Lake that summer of 1941. But in 1942 we considered it prudent not to test our luck and, before darkness set in, would bicycle back to 'ye olde Amsterdame'.

From October 1941 it was forbidden to be on the beaches or dunes along the North Sea after sunset and before sunrise. In the spring of 1942, to meet and prevent an Allied landing on the coast of Western Europe, the Germans started the construction of the 'Atlantic Wall' coastal defences, declaring it a 24-hours forbidden coastal zone for all except those with a *Sonderausweis* (legitimation paper). The population of whole coastal areas were evacuated and large swatches of buildings along the coast were demolished to afford coastal guns an unobstructed field of fire.

In May of 1942 more than 100,000 inhabitants of Scheveningen and The Hague had to vacate their homes in this coastal area and whole quarters of these adjoining towns were pulled down. The whole coastal area between Hoek of Holland and the naval base at Den Helder was proclaimed a forbidden zone and people living in the provinces of North and South Holland, Zeeland and Western Brabant were no longer allowed to remain.

Thereafter, most of those who still made it by the North Sea route succeeded through well-organised group attempts.

The so-called Swedish route, which involved signing on as crew on a coaster and making a getaway when moored in a Swedish port or by jumping into the sea when not too far from the Swedish coast and swimming ashore, did not appeal to me at all. Besides I feared that getting from Sweden to England would be most difficult. The land route to Switzerland, taken by Erik Michielsen, or the route to Spain appeared to me to offer the best chances of success.

However, by 1943 a new danger came into being when the Allies started to increasingly attack trains and railways, particularly in North West and Central Western France. In those years when vigilance against betrayal through collaborators and Gestapo spies was a *sine qua non*, it was far from easy to come into contact with a resistance group or escape line. It was for instance only years after the end of the War that I learned that a resistance group was operating from a house only 100 yards away in the very street where I lived. In fact, there were several other groups in close proximity.

When Erik Michielsen left our home in early 1941, it had been agreed that any contact between Erik and my family would be avoided to eliminate the risk of a visit to No 96 by the Gestapo who were still, at that time, keeping his home in the van Alkemadelaan and his family in The

Hague under surveillance. When, in February of 1942, I received a postcard from him from Berne, the capital of Switzerland, I deeply regretted having lost contact with Erik since, by the time I had matriculated in July of 1941, I knew that he was still active in the Leiden 'Underground'. Among my circle of friends, who had not yet gone underground or disappeared, nobody had contacts in the Resistance.

Towards the end of 1941, the Dutch Government in London, through Radio Oranje, issued warnings that those contemplating escaping to England should avoid going to Vichy-France, and that those who were already *en route* to Spain should divert to Switzerland. Some amongst my friends however believed the danger to be exaggerated and chose to disregard this warning even when, in early 1942, the arrests and executions of several young Dutchmen at Dyon and Besançon became known.

I had befriended several young men from the pleasant towns east of Amsterdam like Hilversum, Bussum and Utrecht with whom I also discussed and planned possible avenues of escape to England. The early plan concocted by these enthusiastic young men to reach Spain via Vichy-France was based on the knowledge of a reliable address in Brussels and of 'an address' in Paris, as well as a smuggler on the Netherlands-Belgian border who could guide us to the tram-stop at Turnhout in Belgium. The first twosome would send a postcard from Brussels and Paris, whereupon the second twosome would depart. The postcards were duly received and the second twosome departed. Nothing was ever heard again from either twosome. If arrested, they would, in accordance with German decree for having tried to escape with a view to joining enemy forces, have been executed or punished with a minimum of two years' jail for *Feindbegunstigung* (assisting the enemy).

We, who were to follow the first two twosomes, deduced from the two failed attempts of our friends, and from a Radio Oranje warning, that travelling through the Vichy France of Marshall Petain was no different from travelling through German-occupied France.

We also concluded from this experience that a 'safe' address could, at any time, through treachery, turn into a trap set by the Gestapo for the unwary escaper. What worked for a friend might become sure death for you. It made me even more circumspect.

After the *Wehrmacht* occupied Vichy-France in November 1942, as a consequence of the Allied landings in North Africa, we did not have to contend any more with the obstacles presented by the demarcation line. The SD and Gestapo would now be ensconced openly, and no longer covertly, in Vichy-France and would be well disposed to offer us the Gestapo's secure accommodation in their 'luxurious' cells or be ready to dispatch us to a concentration camp or, without further ado, to the heaven or hell of our religious belief or the oblivion of the unbeliever.

In the course of 1941-43, the arrests of *Deutschfeindliche,* 'illegals' and 'criminals', most with illegal identity documents were, on German orders, printed, often on the front pages of newspapers. We, of course, expected that, as in the Netherlands, identity card checks were regularly conducted by the Belgian and French police in the streets, trams and trains and often accompanied by the *Grüne Polizei,* especially at railway stations. The Gestapo chaps in mufti could also be watching and were NOT always dressed in long leather coats (as they are now often characterized in the British "Allo-Allo" and other movie spoofs).

I only learned after I had reached Spain that, when crossing into Switzerland, it was essential to get as far into the country as possible since the Swiss border police often handed escapees caught at or very near the border, to Vichy-French police or the Germans.

Although the German news reported someone being shot by patrols in the Pyrenees, it did not deter eager young men who do not tend to dwell too long on the possible consequences of failure or allow the dangers to weigh too heavily on their minds.

Erik Michielsen, who travelled with an established escape line, wrote in his book that he believed that to be successful, you needed 40 per cent planning, 40 per cent guts and 20 per cent luck. He later, after reaching England, revised this to at least 40 per cent luck and 60 per cent planning and controlling one's fear. Good planning of the escape route was vital and a failed plan would also make it more difficult for those who followed.

Many young men who wanted to escape to England or to join a resistance group must have, like me, been frustrated by their inability to make contact with an escape organisation or resistance faction through friends or their jobs.

One simply needed to have the good fortune of meeting a friend or acquaintance who could introduce you to an organised escape line, and when one from my circle of friends suddenly disappeared, like Eddy Jonker and De Gast, I could only assume that he had been one of those lucky ones.

When the opportunity presented itself, it was very seldom possible to have a friend included in a twosome or, as was often the case with the sea route, in a five or six-man escape party. I would myself be faced with that predicament in October of 1943 by not being able to include my best friend Jan Doornik. He, like a sizeable number of young men who never joined a resistance organisation or made contact with an escape line, had to find a safe hiding place on a large farm in the Province of Friesland.

When sports fields and particularly sports complexes became targets for identity card checks and raids to arrest evaders of the *Arbeitseinsatz* and POW call-ups, I decided to give up playing field hockey, which had been my passion ever since I started classes at the Amsterdam Lyceum in 1934. There, hockey was part of the compulsory sports program.

Fortunately, this decision was made easier by my taking up the ancient game of golf, to which I was introduced by my friends Jan and Jean Paul, and my Club membership (at a much-reduced student's fee) was arranged by the dentist father of my friend Jan Doornik in the summer of 1942.

The Amsterdam Golf Club (AGC), which was situated among meadows, although not far from a railway line, was also a safe place for us *onderduikers* (evaders) to pleasantly while the time away. When a telephone call informed us about nefarious goings-on of the police authorities or SS and warned us to avoid check points or areas being cordoned-off when house searches were expected, I would occasionally spend the night on one of the Club's many couches or large armchairs.

New golf clubs were of course unobtainable and my eight or so clubs consisted of a hickory-shafted mashie, mashie niblick, mid iron, spoon and putter complemented by a metal-shafted brassie and four iron. To carry this assortment I acquired a near prehistoric golf bag. The importation of new golf balls from Britain and the USA had of course also ceased with the invasion by Hitler's armies. The thin-skinned golf balls of those days were quickly damaged and their useful lifespan was way short of today's far superior golf balls. The members of the Amsterdam

Golf Club were however fortunate to have a special source of supply from the many ponds and cross-and side-ditches where, for years, golf balls had disappeared into the mud. Retrieving these became a boon for members and a steady source of income for the young lads and caddies from the village of Duivendrecht and nearby farms, who would dredge the ditches and, in the summer, also dive in the ponds. We would punch our initials into our golf balls and, when retrieved and handed-in, we paid the retrievers a standard fee; unmarked balls were offered for sale at the professionals' shop. A local rule allowed balls to be replaced on the greens with an undamaged and perfectly round one.

But for Hitler's war, I would perhaps never have taken up golf, a game that would strongly influence the course of my working and social life. It would also, totally unforeseen, provide me, finally, with a chance to leave German-occupied Holland and totally change the course my life would take.

Via the grapevine we kept hearing about *"De Illegaliteit"* (a newly coined word for illegals/Resistance). We heard about a resistance organisation called the OD *(Orde Dienst)*, created by ex-military men and others who were preparing themselves to assist the Allied Armies in the liberation by acquiring weapons. The OD would however have to wait many years before they could fulfill the task they had set themselves, but during that time they would occupy themselves by entertaining the Occupier with other activities.

It would be only well after the end of the War that I read in a news magazine about the resistance group called CS-6 which engaged in espionage and other activities near our home in the de Lairessestraat. There were also others working from a house in nearby Corelli Straat and Koninginnenweg.

I must have frequently passed by these houses and also, unknowingly, had amongst these Resistance members a personal (and a year or so older) friend of mine, Tony van Renterghem. Tony was the son of our dental surgeon, a long-time friend of my father. At the turn of the 19th to 20th century our fathers had played first division soccer (at that time still an amateur sport and not yet widely popular in the Low Countries) in the first team of Vitesse in Arnhem (now Premier Division professionals) and a club called Volharding (Perseverance). Tony's life was centered around cameras and I recall him, at the age of 16, making a movie in the dunes at

Zandvoort on the North Sea in which my sisters and I had minor acting parts! After the war, Tony ended up in Hollywood and retired, when in his seventies, to Noordwijk.

In the course of 1941 Tony had quietly disappeared from the scene and, since the Gestapo wanted to 'interview' him, started moving from attic to attic. We would not meet up again after the War although his father would resume applying the (old style!) dentist's drill to my molars in 1947. If we, per chance, had come across each other sometime in 1941-43, I could well have ended up in his resistance group out of frustration for not being able to find a way to get to England.

During the Occupation Tony became a commander in the Amsterdam Resistance and was also involved in taking photographs of the Occupation. One of those photographs was of the infamous strafing by German troops of the crowd celebrating the end of the War in Holland on the 7th of May 1945 on Dam Square in Amsterdam.

ID cards were indispensable for obtaining food and clothing coupons and Tony's *Ondergrondse* (underground/illegal) unit would also provide passport photos for forged identity cards. ID cards were of course an essential means of exercising control over the population. The 'liberation' of blank ID forms and food coupons by the Resistance was therefore of the utmost importance to those in hiding. Apart from the occasional raid, everyday policemen or policemen in SD uniforms (and you could never be sure whether they were pro-German) would sometimes conduct arbitrary spot checks.

11. The Tide Has Turned

In early 1943—after the British victories at El Alamein and the Russians at Stalingrad—a new mood had swept through the German-occupied countries. These battles had proven that the seemingly invincible *Wehrmacht* was beatable.

My family's unshakeable belief in an ultimate Allied victory, in the face of extreme adversity encountered in the first three years of WWII, now seemed to be vindicated. However, as Churchill proclaimed after the victory in North Africa: *"It is not the beginning of the end but the end of the beginning,"*

The OKW *(Oberkommando Wehrmacht)* would soon report glorious retreats or 'adjustments of the frontline' of the Eastern Front and while the BBC announced British and American victories in North Africa and reported the landing in Sicily, conditions in the occupied countries grew steadily worse.

In totalitarian regimes the police soon take over and it was no different in Holland, where by 1943 the most powerful individual was Hans Albin Rauter, the *'Hohere SS und Polizeiführer Nordwest'*. Rauter, also had the imposing title of *Generaalkommissar für der Sicherheitswesen (Public Safety)*. The Gestapo, SD and *Ordnungspolizei* became more ruthless under his direction. Captured resistance workers were now promptly, without trial, executed by firing squads. The names of executed persons appeared in ever-greater frequency in the newspapers and so did the announcements for 'criminals' wanted by the German authorities. I recall one announcement for the 'street-robbers' Dourlein and Ubbink, who were actually two outstanding *Engelandvaarders* and secret agents who had escaped from a Gestapo jail. The most inhumane reprisals were surely the executions of hostages: the killing of hostages is the vilest and most cowardly of acts.

We had not expected the war to end any day soon after Stalingrad or when the Allies triumphed in North Africa. We had understood that the disastrous Dieppe assault by the British and Canadians in 1942 had been made to probe the German defences and to test their landing craft and, thus, gain the necessary information and experience for the invasion on the western shores of Europe.

The euphoria after Mussolini was deposed and Italy capitulated on the 8th of September was short-lived when the *Wehrmacht* checked the Allied advance at Casino. The Anzio Landing, ended in a part-failure due to the Allied inability to break through the German encirclement. This made us fear that a successful invasion on Europe's western shores (which was expected to take place in 1944) might not result in an early victory for the Allies. Dieppe had also caused the *Wehrmacht* to further strengthen the 'Atlantik Wall' and not only around Calais.

We knew about the heavy water production in Norway and concluded that the air raids on Penemunde were aimed at the Nazi establishments working on the secret weapons which were to bring the *'Endsleg'* to Hitler's Third Reich. Was Germany soon to use these new secret weapons which could, if not bring them victory, prolong the War?

In the spring of 1943, SS and *Ordnungspolizei*—in addition to drives in streets and squares—started to raid offices, factories, cinemas and sports complexes by surrounding them and making arrests, instead of only checking identity cards at the exits.

As a consequence of Goebbels' announcement in February that Germany was henceforth waging "total war", Generaalkommissar Schmidt's *Arbeidseinsatz* order in early May of 1943 declared that anyone who had not reported would be outlawed. This order did not meet with the success Schmidt had expected, for Dutch civil servants liberally handed out Certificates of Exemption from Work in Germany to individuals or through their employers (who were required to furnish full backgrounds on all employees). Many more went into hiding. Those who were detected were sent to forced labour camps.

Meanwhile the bombing of railway lines and similar strategic targets by Allied aircraft, which had intensified since early that year, had not gone unnoticed by those wanting to make their way to Allied territory. It was a new danger when travelling by train in a southerly direction to Switzerland or the Iberian Peninsula.

Furthermore, if an Allied landing on the west coast of Europe would take place in 1944, we feared it would no longer be possible to get to Switzerland or Spain regardless of the outcome of the invasion and we were not, as explained earlier, optimistic about an early Allied victory.

Meanwhile, I and no doubt many like-minded young men—while coping with difficult and dangerous personal situations—remained in the frustrating position of wanting to get to England to take an effective part in the fight against *"de Moffen"*, but were unable to find a way to accomplish this.

September 1939: British magazine cutting showing my father (far left) going down the steps of an air raid shelter in London.

The clubhouse and 18th green of the Amsterdam Golf Club.

1935: Erik Michielsen in his Artillery Officer's uniform and me (age 16) in the garden of our house at No 37 JJ Viottastraat, Amsterdam.

1938: My brother Tom and his bride Hetty Potjer leaving the Municipal Registry in the town hall of the City of Haarlem, followed by my mother and father.

1940: Fred Braat (right) and me at the Westeinder Lake on "Anjer Dag" (Carnation Day), 29 June, showing the white carnations we wore in honour of Prince Bernhard's birthday.

The frozen-over canals near the St Nicholas Church in Amsterdam in the severe winter of 1941-1942.

January 1942: Eddy Jonker (left), myself and Just Klinkhamer (right).

October 1939: Jan
Doornik (left), Vlasta
Kôkes (center) and
myself at the Kôkes
residence.

October 1939:
Visiting Milly
Geelhuijzen, fiancé
of Guus Camaert.

Summer 1939. Many happy weekends were spent on the "Snark" and "Harlekijn" on Westeinder Lake at Aalsmeer, a 25-minute bicycle-ride south of Amsterdam. The Lake was a relatively safe refuge during the occupation when there were rumours about the Germans holding round-ups in parts of Amsterdam. When staying overnight we would sleep in a floating boatshed hidden in the reeds of a tiny island.

February 1942: I received a postcard from Switzerland signed "Geoffrey", Eric Michielson's pseudonym. Eric wrote that he was leaving for a short holiday with his younger brother. For us it was clear that he had escaped safely to Switzerland and would soon leave for England, since his brother Karel was one of the first three Dutchmen who had escaped from Holland to England in July 1940.

September 1939: My father with compulsory gas mask container in London.

Part II:
My Escape to England

12. A Fateful Meeting

In the spring of 1943, at the Amsterdam Golf Club, I first met Robert van Exter, an Economics student at the University of Amsterdam. I had completed 18 holes and was having a drink in the small, but lovely, clubhouse when Robert, who I later learned had just recently started playing, ran excitedly into the club's lounge and bar-room, followed by his girlfriend, shouting he had made a hole-in-one on the short 8th hole when practising.

It was with great sympathy that we told him that it would not stand as a hole-in-one, since he could not submit a completed scorecard duly signed by a golf partner and witness of the great feat.

After this, for a golfer, tragic news, Robert—one of the university students who had not, on the 6th of February 1943 signed the declaration of loyalty to the Germans—joined our small group of mainly *onderduikers* (those who had gone underground to evade the German authorities for various reasons). Nearly every day the *onderduikers* played golf in the relatively safe environment of the AGC's 18-hole golf course, situated just outside the boundaries of Amsterdam's outer suburbs near the village of Duivendrecht.

Golf was, in those days, still an exclusive sport played by few people in the country. Most Germans would not have known of its existence. In fact, I do not know of any of the ten or so golf courses in the Netherlands having ever been raided by the *Sicherheitsdienst* (better known as SD), Gestapo or *Ordnungspolizei*.

It was in the month of October that year, at a lunch in his mother's flat in the Beethoven Straat in Amsterdam-Zuid, that Robert, aware of my longstanding desire to try to get to England and join the fight against the Nazis, outlined a plan to reach England via Spain.

From the moment that Robert mentioned that his father lived in Paris, and the plan was to reach Spain, I was all ears for I had always considered it essential to have one or several 'safe house' addresses on the overland route.

Robert's father, his parents being divorced, lived in Paris where he was the Representative of the Engineering Office *De Nederlanse Havenwerken* (Dutch Harbour Construction Works). Ir. B van Exter was a graduate of Delft University and had previously, in his capacity as Overseas Director of van Hattem & Blankevoort been involved in harbour projects as far away as China.

One of Mr. van Exter's friends, and a member of the Dutch Resistance in Paris, was a young engineer, also a graduate from Delft University, called Albert Starink, who was to be our contact and who would organise falsified French identity cards. Albert could also arrange for *passeurs* to get us across the Pyrenean Mountains. Only after the war would we learn that Albert, apart from his own endeavours in assisting Dutchmen to escape to Switzerland or Spain, also worked with an escape organisation which became famous for their exploits during the War-the Dutch-Paris Escape Line, set-up and led by the Dutchman Jean (John) Weidner.

On our way to Spain we would stay at Robert's father's apartment in the Trocadero Quarter of Paris at the Rue Magdebourg, an obvious great advantage since it would eliminate the risk of booking into a Parisian hotel or boarding house where all guests had to be registered and were regularly checked by German authorities, or for that matter into one of the 'safe' hotels, about which later.

In October of 1943, Albert Starink came over to Amsterdam and when meeting at Mrs. van Exter's flat he outlined our route to Paris. We learned after the War that, as an employee of the Grond Mechanica Laboratorium in Ghent (Belgium) and thereafter of the Societe de la Precontraite in Paris, he had been issued a *Durchlaßschein* (travel permit) which allowed him to travel freely in the Occupied Territories of France, Belgium and the Netherlands.

We were to await a summons from the contact person in Breda, near the Dutch-Belgian border, where a *passeur* (guide) would take us over the border to a 'safe house' in Brussels. Although this border was not intensively guarded it was helpful to be guided by a *passeur*, who often knew the patrolling Belgian border guards. In Brussels we would be provided with counterfeit French identity cards to allow us to cross the French frontier by train.

The call duly arrived on the 4th of December and on the 6th of December we met an 'Eddie' at the Breda Station. He took us to a hotel, which I believe was owned by his family. We were to proceed to Brussels the next day, but at 11 p.m. that evening the courier, who would have escorted us across the border to Brussels, arrived with the news that the safe-house in Brussels had been raided by the Gestapo *"and they are now in a hospital"*, the euphemism for having ended up in jail.

Without the safe address in Brussels and false French identity cards, and not knowing whether Albert Starink had also been arrested, we decided to immediately return to Amsterdam the next morning.

It just so happened that on the day before our departure on 6th December, Fred Braat, a good friend of mine, had suddenly died and my absence at his funeral would have raised eyebrows. As it was, I remember thinking that nobody present could have known or guessed, that sad afternoon at the funeral, that I had barely two hours earlier returned to Amsterdam from an attempt to make my escape to England.

We soon learned that Albert Starink had not been caught up in the aftermath of the arrests in Brussels of the unlucky safe-house occupants and he arrived in Amsterdam a few days before Christmas. Robert and I met him at the cafe of the well-known Hotel Americain on the Leidsche Plein (Square). Busy places full of people are the most inconspicuous places to meet, provided you don't stand out in a crowd; and no one took any notice of a blond man seating himself at a table, where two other young men were reading a newspaper and 'enjoying' a cup of quite awful *ersatz* coffee, after first asking politely whether the empty seat at the table was free.

Our conversation was brief: Robert was to receive a letter from a man calling himself 'Monsieur Henri' telling us when he would meet us at Robert's flat. Monsieur Henri would provide us with falsified *Sicherheitsdienst* (German Security Police) identity cards and travel documents and advise us how and when we were to travel to Paris. With an *"I'll see you in Paris"* Albert left us.

On December 29th, Monsieur Henri, also known as 'Sandberg', duly arrived at the Beethoven Straat and came straight to the point: we were to travel, as Albert had already told us, on *Sicherheitsdienst* identity cards and falsified German travel documents as issued to the military police and officials. The journey would take us from Pau, a city in the south of France, to Amsterdam and return, again via Paris, to Pau. The genuine SD identity cards with a vertical crossed green stripe had been stolen from an SD Office and would be provided with our photos and identical information and signatures as on our Dutch identity cards. The SD card was 'signed' by our Commanding *Grüne Polizei* Officer, an *Untersturmführer*, whose signature had been copied, just as were the various stamps and signatures of German officials stationed along the route from Pau to Amsterdam and return. According to our SD identity cards we were *Vertragsangestellten* (contract employees), ostensibly attached to the Pau-Bureau in southern France of the SD and employed for interrogating Dutch and Flemish prisoners. Monsieur Henri noted the details of our Dutch identity cards and received passport photos from us and the next day he handed us two sets of documents and the SD identity cards with our photos on them. Our cover story, for travelling to and from Amsterdam, was that we had been on a short home leave after delivering documents to the SD Headquarters in Holland. The stamps and signatures of a host of German authorities on our *Sonderausweis* (an official travel order), signed by the officer in charge in Pau, along with the *Bescheiningung* (official certificate) issued on behalf of *"Der Befehshaber Der Sichereits Polizei und des SD für die Besetzen Franzosischen Gebieten,"* attested to this. We received two sets of travel documents. The second *Sonderausweis* showed that on January 3rd of 1944 we had travelled from Pau in southern France to Amsterdam and had reported our arrival at the *Hauptkommandantur* in Amsterdam. It was also provided with a stamp confirming that we had reported our arrival in Paris, on our return journey to Pau, at the bureau of the Kommandant von Gross, Paris on January 12th. The second set we hid inside a talcum powder tin.

On the morning of January 12, we were to destroy the first set, which had different and earlier dates—it showed our date of departure from Pau and having reported at the *Kommandantur* in Paris and our arrival in Amsterdam.

The irony was, of course, not lost on us that we would travel as members of the German Security Police, which worked hand in hand with the Gestapo and after all these years I am still amazed at the thought of travelling on documents of the very people who were hunting for us evaders/escapees. However, to us at that time, it did not appear to be audacious and was just part of the risky endeavour we were to engage in. The Verzet's Museum (Resistance Museum) of Amsterdam at the Gebouw Plancius, Stadhuis K 1388, Amstel 1, now has Robert's set of SD documents, which he donated to them.

Albert Starink wrote in his memoirs about 'Sandberg', aka 'Monsieur Henri'—whose real name was Henry Scharrer—that he was from Ghent in Belgium and, working as a journalist for the *Schweizerische Presse Telegraph*. He had obtained the so-important *Durchlaßschein* that allowed him to travel legally through the occupied countries of Belgium and Holland. [Editor's note: Scharrer was captured by the Germans in August 1944, and on 6 September 1944 he was taken to some woods where he was executed together with more than 300 others by machine gun fire.]

On the day of my departure, Monday the 12th of January, my father, before walking to his office in the Vijzelstraat, slipped into my bedroom and gave me his gold cigarette case for me to sell in case I needed money and said in English *"May all go well"*. We shook hands and just smiled. I still have that cigarette case in which his last words *"May all go well"* have been engraved after the War. Only my father knew about my escape plan and had provided me with the money to pay Sandberg for the counterfeit documents.

"Behave yourself when I am in Eindhoven" I shouted to my sisters Mary and Anne when they left a few minutes later for the Colonial Institute where they worked. *"You'd better look after yourself young man"* the youngest replied. I had told my family that I was going to stay for a couple of days with a friend, Octave Redele, who lived at 56 Parkstraat in Eindhoven. *"Can't you play golf here in Amsterdam?"* my mother asked when I kissed her goodbye. *"That's already risky enough with these frequent razzias (raids) nowadays,"* I said. She would tell me, on my return to Holland in 1946, that she had sensed my leaving that time was different from previous occasions. There surely must be a sixth sense.

In retrospect, it is disconcerting to remember how somehow during the War years it was with little emotion that we could say goodbye to people, even those who were your next of kin who you might never see again. It was the same when leaving friends in London and America and even when taking leave from the girl in Australia you were to marry. Perhaps, ever since the Germans invaded the Netherlands, we learned under the Nazi Occupation not to dwell on things and this made us resist too much emotionalism.

On my way to Robert's flat in the Beethoven Street on that January 5th, 1944, with small suitcase in hand, I met Vlasta Kôkes, sister of my close Czech friend Zdenek. *"Hello migrant"* she laughed pointing to my suitcase. After the War I would tell her how right she had been. In December of 1939 her brother, Zdenek, had gone to London to study at London University and had recently spoken over Radio Orange of the BBC in London.

At Robert's flat, Sandberg gave us our final 'interrogation' and made sure we knew all the particulars and details of our documents and were able to describe the building, the street and the other houses standing in the street where the *Sicherheits Polizei* HQ at Pau were situated. We had an early lunch with Sandberg and Mrs. van Exter, who had arranged for a taxi to take us to the Central Station in Amsterdam. We boarded a German Army train 2nd class compartment for Maastricht in the southern tip of the Netherlands where we had to transfer to the train for Paris the next morning. First class carriages were for high-ranking officials and high-ranked officers, second class for officers and third class for other ranks.

A corpulent German army officer was already seated at one of the windows when we entered the compartment. After we had pushed our small suitcases onto the luggage racks, and after Robert managed to crush a light bulb with his suitcase, we both made sure that, whilst the train was still stationary, our faces were hidden behind the unfolded German newspapers we had purchased at a kiosk in the entrance hall of the Central Station. It would have been quite embarrassing and perhaps dangerous if one of our friends had, perchance, observed us in a compartment of a *Nur Für Wehrmacht* railway carriage.

Quite soon after the train departed, the corpulent *Wehrmacht* Officer started a conversation. He seemed curious about us, which was not surprising since we were in civilian clothes and spoke German with an accent. This being the first time that we ostensibly posed as employees for a German authority and had to conduct a conversation with a German Officer, we were somewhat apprehensive and quite relieved when, only about five minutes later, the train suddenly stopped, quite unexpectedly, exactly on the railway viaduct over the road leading to the Berlage Bridge and just short of the Amstel Zuid Station in SE Amsterdam. This railway bridge is over a main road leading to and in sight of Amsterdam's highest building, the *Wolkenkrabber* (skyscraper), on what is now called Victorie Square. Seconds later the door of our compartment flew open when a *Feldwebel* (sergeant) of the German Railway Police entered the compartment asking for *Ausweisen* (identity papers).

I must admit that I was very nervous when I handed over my *Sicherheitsdienst* identity card and the travel warrant and quite relieved when they were handed back with a *"danke schön."* After returning the documents to my breast pocket, I put my hands in my coat pockets for fear that my hands would tremble.

Thereafter we were fully confident, in fact somewhat over-confident, that our counterfeit documents would pass any routine checks. We were, however, so relieved that we had passed our first test and a subsequent second German *Kontrole* at Utrecht Station that it did not register—until after we had arrived at our hotel in Maastricht—that our corpulent 'friend' had lost interest in inquiring about our activities for the German authorities after he had seen the vertical green stripe of our SD identity cards, which we had handed over to the sergeant. The dreaded SD caused anybody, including Germans, to become very apprehensive and cautious. It is, however, curious how, once the apprehension of possible arrest after the first encounter with the enemy has been mastered, the chance of a future possible arrest and failure had virtually disappeared from one's mind. This over-confidence led to a rather terrifying incident a week later.

In the old city of Maastricht, founded by the Romans on one of the important crossroads of Europe on the River Maas (Meuse), we stayed the night in a small, clean hotel called 'Du Levrier Et De L'Aigle Noir', where Robert managed to burn a hole in his mattress. On the morning of the 6th of January, after turning the holed mattress over, we left hastily for the station to catch the 9 o'clock German Army *Fronturlaubzug* (home leave train) for Paris. We boarded a very crowded officers' carriage and, with difficulty, found two empty seats in a compartment in which three army officers and a civilian were already seated in the four corner seats. To avoid being drawn into conversation we unfolded and started reading Goebbels' Nazi Party newspaper, 'Das Reich', as soon as we were seated and thereafter feigned being asleep.

During the uneventful journey through Belgium to the Belgian-French border, the three officers and German civilian spoke freely about their experiences and observations when back home on leave. They expressed anger for the devastation caused by Allied air-raids and complained about the defeatism of so many at home. *"Those civilians just can't understand that the Führer is waiting for the right moment to use our secret weapons,"* a rather arrogant officer remarked. After the *Oberst* had voiced his opinion, a most animated discourse followed about inside information received and rumours about the secret weapons, purported to be rockets of different types and launching pads that had been or were being constructed along the western coast of Europe.

The conversation about secret weapons and defeatism promptly died out when we had to show our SD identity cards and travel papers to a French conductor at the Belgian-French border. Little did they know that within a few weeks we would retell all we had heard when we were interviewed by a British Intelligence Officer in the British Embassy in Madrid, as well as thereafter by British Intelligence in Gibraltar and London.

Somewhere near Compiegne we passed a badly damaged locomotive lying beside the track. *"Those damned French"* said somebody. However it could well have been shot-up by Allied airplanes instead of having been derailed by the French Resistance, a sabotage act in which the *Maquis* were proficient. It was only then that I realised that our train could be a target for RAF fighter-bombers and I was now, for more than one reason, pleased when our train reached the Gare du Nord in Paris.

We hadn't eaten since a hasty breakfast bought at a railway canteen in Maastricht and, on arriving in Paris in early evening, we spent our 14 French francs at the *Deutsche Wehrmachtsheim* (German Soldiers' Home) in the Gare du Nord, on bread rolls and a glass of cognac.

Since we had no money left for Metro underground tickets to the Trocadero Station, and didn't fancy a long walk, we decided to bluff our way through the entrance to our Metro platform by curtly and authoritatively saying *"Polizei"* to the ticket inspector and at the same time showing our SD identity cards. We were not challenged and for the next few weeks at no time did we buy a Metro ticket, but simply showed our SD card and said curtly *"Polizei"* and thereafter walked around Paris with our recently acquired authoritative look of a German official.

After leaving the Trocadero Metro Station, Robert took me to the terrace of the Palais de Chaillot from where, on a frosty night with a brilliant, starlit sky, I had my first and unforgettable view of the Eiffel Tower. From photos I saw after the War we must have stood on the same spot where Adolf Hitler viewed the Eiffel Tower just after dawn in July 1940.

Robert's father was most pleased to see us arrive at his flat in the Rue de Magdebourg.

13. Paris: Arrest and Escape

The next few days, while waiting for the call from Albert regarding the departure for Toulouse, we behaved like any tourists in Paris, visiting the Notre-Dame, the Dome des Invalides, the tomb of Napoleon, the Eiffel Tower and even attended an evening show at the Folies Bergère, seated amongst hordes of German military. The favourite spot for German military was the Sacre-Coeur at Montmartre where we felt quite safe amongst the hundreds of sightseeing uniformed Germans but, of course, we avoided any conversation that could compromise us if overheard by Germans in mufti or French collaborators.

The general atmosphere in Paris was not as sombre as in Holland and living conditions seemed generally better. A new experience was the nearly daily air-raid alerts during daylight when American planes raided the industrial suburbs or crossed over France on their way to Germany. Like most Parisians we ignored the air-raid warnings and watched the action from the streets of Paris. We could often see dozens of B17 'Flying Fortresses' and B24 'Liberators' flying high in formation. Sometimes the escorting Allied single seaters were being attacked by German fighters. In Holland during 1940-1943 we hardly ever experienced daylight raids. I can only remember witnessing the first daylight RAF raid on the harbour area of Amsterdam in 1940. While I was standing in a crowd on the Rokin near De Dam and Royal Palace in Amsterdam, I saw the crew bailing out.

A friend of Mr. van Exter, Mr. Lahnemann, a Dutch businessman who lived and worked in Paris, lent me 20,000 French francs, trusting time, honour and the course of the war for repayment of my IOU. I needed 12,000 to pay the escape organization to cover the cost of our journey from Paris to the Spanish frontier. Our guides belonged to the

Resistance, but many guides in the Pyrenees were professional smugglers who knew the tracks inside-out and would charge anywhere up to the 12,000 francs for the trip just from the foothill towns to the border. Robert's father, who also provided us with a small amount of Spanish pesetas and two small flasks of cognac, naturally, met Robert's expenses. It was at Mr. Lahnemann's home that I was introduced to the lovely apple-brandy from Normandy called *Calvados*.

Robert's mother had given us the name of a young French woman, Ann Comtesse de Casalette, who we could completely trust, and on the afternoon of January 14th we had lunch together at the 'Beaulieu', a classy restaurant and *thé-dansant* on the Rue du Faubourg St Honoré (it closed its doors quite some years ago). After lunch we had coffee in the crowded cafe section where André Evkian's jazz band was playing. The conversation was mainly in French but, since my command of the French language was that of a schoolboy only—and Ann delighted in speaking English—we did at times resort to English. We were however, so we thought, circumspect not to be overheard, but apparently not careful enough. At about a quarter to seven we decided to leave. I went ahead to fetch my hat and coat from the cloakroom while Robert settled the bill. Before I reached the cloakroom someone tapped me on the shoulder. Turning around I looked into the gaze of a German *Wehrmacht* officer who politely but firmly said to me *"Sie haben English gesprochen."* It was quite unexpected and I was caught off-guard, but had the sense to stay calm and not to deny it, for it was a statement and not a question. Making eye contact with the officer I answered, *"Jawhol dasz stimmt."* The *Oberleutnant* then asked whether he could see my identification papers. Without hesitation I answered *"aber natürlich,"* and reached for the breast pocket of my jacket. *"No, no, not here, over there"* he remarked. *"In a corner near the counter of the cloakroom"*. I handed him my papers. He looked at them briefly, returned them, apparently convinced that the SD employed me and said, smiling, in French, *"merci."* *"Danke schön,"* I replied, realising later that I, as an SD employee, should have added *"Heil Hitler."*

I collected my coat and hat and, for some inexplicable reason, did not wait at the cloakroom for Ann and Robert but went down the few steps leading to the spacious entrance hall adjoining the restaurant-café to wait for them.

I must have been standing about half-way from the cloakroom to the door when another German Officer, a *Hauptmann* (Captain)—whom I had seen speaking with a waiter and who had several times turned their heads in my direction—approached me asking whether he could also see my papers. He looked at them carefully and remarked, *"They may be alright but I want them inspected at the Hauptkommandant,"* and pocketed my papers. That waiter—no doubt being a collaborator—must have overheard us speaking English and reported us to the *Wehrmacht* Officers.

The travel *Sonderausweis* he had looked at was the second one we had received from 'Monsieur Henri' and incorporated the stamp that we had reported two days earlier on 12th of January at the *Gross Paris Hauptkommandant*. On checking their register no entry would of course show up. While I was struggling to catch my thoughts, my instinctive reaction was not to show any sign of fear and without hesitation I agreed to his suggestion and immediately walked towards the exit, thus forcing him to accompany me to the Rue du Faubourg St Honoré. Some 20 to 30 metres to the right in the unlit street, their Corporal driver and a black Citroën *'Quatre Avant'*, parked at the curb, was waiting. I remember quite clearly that amongst the guests, who had also started to leave the restaurant-cafe proper for the entrance hall, somebody said *"Ils disent qu'il est un aviateur Anglais"* (They say he's an English aviator). I also remember seeing that the *Gefreite* (Corporal), on seeing the *Hauptmann* approaching the Citroën immediately sprang to attention clicking his heels. I continued walking towards the motorcar closely followed by the *Hauptmann*.

Just as I reached the Citroën and turned around, the *Oberleutnant* appeared with their overcoats but without Robert. Seeing only me standing next to the Citroën with the *Hauptmann* and *Gefreite*, he exclaimed *"Wo ist ihr freund?"* At that very moment the *Hauptmann* started shouting, apparently at Robert, but turning towards the entrance of the Beaulieu. However, I didn't see any sign of Robert at all.

I have often wondered what would have happened if I had not immediately walked to the revolving doors of the Beaulieu necessitating the *Hauptmann* to stay with me, thus causing confusion between the two officers, because it was obvious that the *Hauptmann* had expected his companion officer to collect Robert. It was one of the crucial moments of our escape.

A week or so later, in a safe house in the village of Cazeres, Robert told me how he had watched the drama unfold. When the *Oberleutnant*, after collecting their military overcoats, had followed the *Hauptmann* and me, Robert decided to grasp the half-chance offered and followed audaciously close behind the *Oberleutnant* through the revolving door, while Ann de Casalette unobtrusively merged into the crowd of patrons watching the goings on. As soon as Robert was outside the front door of the Beaulieu he saw me, in a flash, with the *Hauptmann* near the Citroën, as well as the back of the *Oberleutnant* carrying their overcoats, and promptly turned left and literally ran for his life into the blacked-out Rue du Faubourg St Honoré. Only a second or so later the German officers spotted him and started shouting. It was then that the *Hauptmann* remarked *"Ach, what does it matter, we have you!"*

I was put in the back seat of the low *Quatre Avant* behind the *Oberleutnant*, the *Hauptmann* taking the seat to the left of me; both had their pistols in open holsters on their laps. It is said that nothing clears the mind more rapidly than the knowledge that you are to die and I, having been in that situation, cannot but fully agree. I knew the moment the door of the Citroën closed that if I did not escape I was to die at the hands of the Gestapo or in a concentration camp. Even before the Germans were seated my right hand had already found the door handle and noted that because of the handle's low position, my knees and legs hid my right hand.

"Hauptkommandantur," one of them ordered the driver and we drove off into blacked-out Paris. We had barely driven a few hundred metres when the *Hauptmann* changed his mind and ordered the driver to go to the Gestapo, *"auf Avenue Foch"*. At that time I did not know where the Gestapo Headquarters in Paris was, but I knew that the Avenue Foch was to the left of the Rue du Faubourg St Honoré. He had come to the obvious conclusion that Robert would have stayed with me and not run away if we were indeed *Vertagsangestellten* of the *Sicherheitsdienst*. The driver now had to change direction and while no doubt, like all Germans in uniform, he knew exactly where the *Hauptkommandantur* (headquarters of the Commander of the city) was, he had, as a common soldier, probably never before been ordered to proceed to the Gestapo Headquarters, although he had perhaps heard of the address.

In blacked out Paris, with headlights covered except for a narrow slit,
street signs were very hard to read and the driver was scolded when he
missed the left-hand turn he should have taken. *"Bitte Entschüldigung, Herr
Hauptmann,"* he answered the officer who had berated him. All three
Germans were now trying to read the street names appearing on the left-
hand side of the Rue du Faubourg St Honoré. *"I think it's the next left,"* one
of the officers remarked. The Citroën slowed down, almost to a standstill
to enable them to read the name of the next cross street. At that moment
with all three peering to the left, and thus away from me, I pushed my
hand, which was already gripping the door handle, down, jumped out and
sprinted towards a side street accompanied by shouts of *"Halt! Da geht der
Schwein!"* I looked back only once and saw that both officers had only just
got out of the *Wehrmacht* Citroën and that I had at least a ten metres head-
start.

Because of the darkness in blacked-out Paris—it was just after 7
o'clock in the winter evening of January 14th (a day I commemorate every
year)—and my running on rubber-soled Bally shoes, they could hardly
hear, let alone see me. I disappeared into a side street of the Rue du
Faubourg St Honoré running in the middle of the street to avoid
bumping into pedestrians on the footpaths. I had only heard the sound of
German boots running after me for a few seconds, for it must have been
obvious to them that they had little chance of catching me. I deliberately
did not run into the first side street but thereafter ran into so many more
side streets that I had no idea where I was in relation to the Rue du
Faubourg St Honoré.

After a while, to catch my breath, I had to sit down on the front steps
of an entrance door of a row of houses. Hardly a minute later a car with
blazing headlights approached around a far corner of the street. I quickly
jumped into the wide porch of a house to get out of the lights of the
passing car. It must have been the *Wehrmacht* Citroën—even though there
were plenty around Paris at that time—since the headlamp covers were
not attached and only in an emergency would anybody dare to remove the
compulsory headlamp covers.

After walking aimlessly for a while through virtually deserted streets, I
noticed a wider street with many pedestrians and, plucking up courage, I
approached a simply-dressed elderly lady with a shawl over her head and
asked her to please direct me to the nearest Metro station. My still

somewhat heavy breathing and foreign accent seemed to have alerted her that perhaps I was on the run. She looked at me with what seemed a look of understanding, then offering her left arm she answered, *"Monsieur, prenez mon bras, s'il vous plaît"* (please take my arm, sir).

Walking on the arm of an elderly woman, carrying a wicker shopping basket on her other arm, I could only have been regarded by anyone, and even those *Wehrmacht* Officers, as a son walking with his mother. At the steps leading down to the St Augustin Metro Station I took leave of her by kissing her on the cheek. Nobody heard me say, *"Mille remerciements, Madame."* At the ticket counter I bought a ticket for the Trocadero Station and about 40 minutes after the arrest at the Beaulieu, still not breathing easily, I rang the bell at Robert's father's apartment. Mr. van Exter had, a few minutes before, received a phone call from Robert telling him about the arrest. He realised only too well that everybody connected to me was now in extreme danger. He was in a most anxious state of mind when he opened the front door and was understandably delighted to see me standing there.

Looking back, I believe that I was so scared out of my wits when arrested that it made me dead calm and that saved me. Since then I have studied road maps of Paris and photos of the street junctions of the Rue du Faubourg St Honore and the sidestreets Rue Saussies and Rue Penthieve, and returned to the spot where the Citroën motorcar had come to a near halt at the corner of the Avenue de Marigny , where I had parted company with my *Wehrmacht* captors. I have worked out that I then ran into the Rue des Saussies, past the Palais de l'Elysee, the residence of the French President. After running right and left into various sidestreets, it was on the Boulevard Malesherbes that I approached the lady dressed in black and walked, on her arm, to the St Augustin Metro station

The importance of Robert van Exter avoiding arrest and escaping was vital and cannot be over-emphasized. Robert, after removing himself from the Beaulieu and Rue Faubourg St Honore, and, like me, running for quite a while, had gone to a cafe and phoned his father asking him to immediately alert Albert Starink.

Our French lady friend, Ann, had distanced herself from us during the confrontation in the hall of the Beaulieu, and had gone straight home where Robert soon contacted her. Ann was able to put him up in the vacant flat of a holidaying friend who had left the keys in her keeping.

A much-relieved Albert Starink, for he had not yet heard of my escape, soon arrived at the Rue de Magdebourg No 9 apartment. When I told him about my carelessness at having been overhead speaking English, he made me feel less upset by remarking that I was not the first to have been caught since most downed airmen could only speak one language, especially the Americans, and that he himself often had to resort to English, even in crowded restaurants and cafés.

The decision was made that Robert and I would no longer stay at the Rue de Magdebourg apartment, even though Mr. van Exter's address wasn't mentioned on my SD identity card or travel papers impounded by the *Hauptmann* of the *Wehrmacht*. We all wondered whether and how the two officers reported the incident to their superiors or indeed to the *Sicherheitsdienst* HQ in Paris. Many years after the War I learned that another Dutchman, Victor Swane, a golfing friend of mine and member of the Eindhoven Golf Club, was arrested on April the 10th with a similar counterfeited SD identity card from 'Sandberg' on his person. Vic didn't survive his incarceration and died on October 8th, 1944 in a concentration camp. The falsified SD papers were, however, still used at times without detection by a few others, including Albert Starink.

That evening of January 14th, he and I avoided the Metro because he had noticed increased activities at the ticket inspection gates. By now I had no identity papers since my Dutch Identity Card had also been pocketed by the Hauptmann. That day there had been daylight air attacks over the industrial northern suburbs and airmen of the downed planes had been seen bailing out. As usual, in the German-occupied countries of Western Europe, there were nearly always people on hand to assist and hide the Allied airmen, hence the increase in security checks at the Metro and railway stations.

We walked to our destination, which was the 'safe' Hotel de Medicis on the Rue Monsieur le Prince 56 at the crossing of the Rue Gay Lussac and near the Boulevard Raspaille and Boulevard St Michel in Montparnasse. This very simple hotel was not far from the Luxembourg Gardens and also quite near the local district's German *Orts Kommandantur*. The Hotel de Medicis was, as I later learned, frequently used by the Resistance, but I saw very little of these other 'special' guests whose names, like mine, would not have been entered in the hotel register as required by the German authorities. The French *Gendarmes* and German police would regularly check the registers of hotels. Hoteliers sympathetic to the Allied cause, who would not enter the names of evaders into their register, were vital to the escape lines and the Resistance.

Fugitives were, however, not entirely safe because the police would sometimes enter hotel rooms to check the identity of hotel guests. Hoteliers, being responsible for entries into the hotel's register, therefore ran considerable risks and some unavoidably ended up in concentration camps. After a fugitive was arrested in February and, under torture at the hands of the Gestapo, gave away names and addresses, the Hotel de Medicis was raided by the Gestapo on or about the 5th of March 1944, resulting in everybody present being arrested. Albert, who, unbeknownst to me, also had a room at the 'de Medicis', happened to be away; you needed luck in the Resistance! It's not known by my sources of information what happened to the hotelier or to his employees or to the hotel guests who were in the rooms at that time. It should be noted that a hotelier was in the clear if a person who was arrested was registered under an assumed name or was using a counterfeit identity card.

During my three nights and two days' stay in a narrow, tiny, unheated bedroom, complete with a barred window and a broken window pane, the room temperature barely rose above zero degrees Celsius, even in daytime. During those days I remained mostly in my room during daylight hours since I was not yet in possession of a counterfeit French ID card. Because of the cold I would crawl fully clothed under the blankets. At night it was so cold that I would also put on the dark blue overcoat and French beret which I had received from Albert in exchange for my brown camel hair overcoat and 'Dobbs' hat. I could no longer be seen in these in case the Germans had circulated my description.

Albert supplied me with bread and cheese for breakfast and lunch, but that evening, and the following two evenings, I slipped out of the 'de Medicis' after dark and had a good hot meal in a side street at the 'safe' Chinese restaurant of a Mr. Wong, a man of whom words cannot speak highly enough, both for his food and for the excellent heating in his restaurant. I had no doubt that whilst I was hastily enjoying one of Mr. Wong's lovely rice dishes, seated as close as I could get to the kitchen and therefore the back door, that some of my fellow guests were also keeping a wary eye on the entrance to the restaurant. Long after the war ended, I befriended Sam (Dick) Timmers Verhoeven and learned that he was at that same Hotel de Medicis at that same time and had learned about our escape through Albert. Unknowingly, we may have seen each other at Mr. Wong's Chinese restaurant. Ships that pass in the night!

On the second day, the 16th, Albert provided me with spectacles and I had a haircut at a barbershop, a stone's throw from the district *Kommandantur*. Cut short in the back and the sides, the haircut was a necessity since my identity papers, now presumably in the hands of the Germans, showed me with medium length hair. The barber must have wondered why the man who did not look particularly like a foreigner, but had a foreign accent, wanted a good haircut murdered by clipping it in a short, back-and-sides, military style.

Passport photos were then made at the *Pret a 5 Minutes* photographer on the nearby Boulevard St Michel, just opposite the junction of the Rue Monsieur le Prince. The transformation astounded me and I now felt quite sure that I couldn't be easily recognised from the photo on the SD identity card.

On the 17th, the Dutch artist John Ruys, who lived in Montparnasse, offered me a room in his heated studio apartment at No 12 Rue Victor Considerant. He was a tall, slim aristocrat with thinning hair. He was a most charming and considerate host. This typical well-heeled, educated gentleman and good artist regaled me with delightful stories about Spain, the Riviera and Art. I spent a few most pleasant days at his atelier.

In the evenings he would take me, now bespectacled, to dine at brasseries like 'Le Dome' and the still famous 'La Coupole' on the Boulevardd du Montparnasse, where he would point out interesting guests. The only one I can still recall was Picasso. In spite of not having a valid ID card and with my Dutch identity card being rather dicey to use, John's confidence in our safety put me at ease and enabled me to regain the confidence I had acquired after the first *"Ausweisen Bitte"* inspection on the train to Maastricht. John, divorced from his artist wife who lived in The Hague, had an English lady-friend in London. He asked me to look her up, which I did, and it was she, living in Hill Street, Mayfair, who gave me a photo of him taken on an esplanade somewhere on the French Riviera.

In Australia in 1946 I learned with great sadness from another *Engelandvaarder* that John Ruys had been arrested in early 1944 in the company of a Dutch escapee and had not survived the end of the War.

When, in the Resistance, only pseudonyms were used the damage was limited, but for those who sheltered fugitives, even if they were their own kith and kin, the consequences were fateful for the whole family. For John Ruys, sheltering fugitives in his own home, the risk of being compromised was therefore very great and his name and address was obtained by the Gestapo, under torture, from an arrested member of an escape organisation.

Many years after the war, I spoke by phone with John's grandson, US Navy Commander R. E. Ruys, and told him about the days I spent at 12 Rue Victor (as the street is now indicated on street directories of Paris). It was the Commander who told me that John Ruys had first been transported to Natsweiler Concentration Camp and then to Dachau Concentration Camp.

14. By Train to Toulouse

Robert and I were reunited at his father's apartment in the afternoon of the 21st January, the day we left Paris for Spain. Albert picked me up at John Ruys' atelier with the acquired two stolen original French *Cartes d'Identité* already provided with our pass-photos and stamps on which we had to enter our signatures. Robert became Robert Pierre Van Castel, an *Employé de bureau* born on September 2, 1911.

My alias was Jean Paul Pascal, profession *Dessinateur* (designer), born on December 5th in 1910 in Saigon, Indo-China. My address was 4 Rue le Goff, Montaigu-de-Quercy. Jean Paul was the Christian name of my friend J. P. Perez. December 5th was my father's birthday and 1910 the year of birth of my older brother Torn. All of these particulars were easy to remember if questioned. I chose the occupation of draughtsman. When I asked where the village was where I was supposed to live, Albert told me that it was about 600 kms south of Paris and west of Cahors and that hardly any Frenchman knew of its existence let alone a German.

Albert gave us an anxious moment when he made a mistake entering our particulars onto the ID cards. He managed to erase the mistake but at very close scrutiny it could and can still be seen. Since we were to depart in three hours for Toulouse, there was no possibility of obtaining a fresh set of identity cards with the necessary signatures, duty-stamps and inked rubber stamps.

After an early dinner, Robert's father opened a bottle of champagne to toast the success of our trip to the Spanish border. After the War, Robert learned that Bert, his father, had been an undercover agent for the Dutch Intelligence Service of the Department of Foreign Affairs since 1912 and had also assisted Albert Starink and the Paris-Dutch Escape

Line during the German Occupation of France. We said our goodbyes to him and to Ann de Casalette and seven days to the minute of our arrest we left No 9 with Albert for the Trocadero Metro Station. Albert, consistent with the unwritten rules of those in hiding and their helpers in the Resistance, did not tell us, nor did we ask, the name of the escape line which was to guide us from Paris to the Spanish border.

Albert Starink, as we would only learn after the War, and the Dutch-Paris Escape Organisation had decided to bring our departure for Spain forward because the Gestapo, in possession of my description, would be looking for us. It was therefore, for all concerned, best for Robert and me to be dispatched to Spain, with a number of downed Allied airmen, as soon as possible.

At the Gare d'Austerlitz Albert bought our train tickets for Toulouse and a platform ticket for himself. Ten American airmen and one RAF pilot, besides ourselves, were to be escorted by guides from an escape organisation until we reached Toulouse. We were introduced to the group leader, 'Jacques', and told that we would get further instructions from him on our arrival at the Toulouse Station platform. After the War, looking at illustrations showing members of the Paris-Dutch Escape Line, I recognised the face of an important member of Dutch-Paris: Jacques Rens. He was one and the same 'Jacques' who had led us from Paris to Toulouse.

We had also been given black leather boots, as worn by workmen, a heavy dark blue overcoat and a deep blue French beret, which is a very effective disguise. The Escape Line had similarly outfitted the Americans and the British pilot with dark blue and grey overcoats. Some also carried *musettes* (haversacks) slung over their shoulders or across the chest, the way French peasants, labourers and artisans commonly carry them. Others had rucksacks.

David Delfosse has researched the escape and evasion history of the USAF B-17 "Flying Fortress" called "Sarah Jane" which crash-landed near Vimy in Northern France in 1943. Five of its crew—2nd Lt. Ernest Stock, 2nd Lt. Frank A. Tank, S/Sgt. Russell C. Gallo, S/Sgt. Eric Kolc and Sgt. Leonard H. Cassady—left Paris on the 21st of January for Toulouse as part of our group of 13 evaders, guided by Rens.

Apart from the regular ID card inspections, both at the stations and on the trains, it didn't make us feel any easier that we were able to spot five pseudo-Frenchmen within minutes.

Albert directed us to one of the last carriages because the locomotives and the carriages at the front always suffered the most casualties when the *Maquis* (French Resistance) sabotaged a train. Furthermore, even ending up in a hospital could be fatal by revealing our real identities. Also the chances of being able to 'make a run for it' were infinitely higher from the last carriages. I would not meet Albert again until 1977 although in 1945 we would nearly meet up in Koepang, Timor.

Jacques had distributed the fugitive airmen over several of the other carriages and, as we later learned, told them to pretend to sleep most of the time and to avoid speaking at all, except for *pardon* and *merci*. On the packed train we could only stand or sit on the floor on our small suitcases in the crowded corridor of our carriage.

There was an unpleasant incident when a young woman claimed loudly that her handbag had been stolen and threatened to call the police. To our, and no doubt some of the other train passengers' relief, she managed with the assistance of other passengers to find her handbag, but not before she had pulled Robert's hair and pushed him aside when he did not move quickly enough to her liking. There was very little conversation going on, with most people dozing or sleeping in the dim light, while the train made its way through the countryside, occasionally stopping at blacked out stations or towns, the names of which being instantly forgotten in my apprehension of possible German or Vichy French Police inspections. The knowledge that Toulouse Station was one of the three most dangerous places in Southern France (the two others being Bordeaux and Perpignan Railway Stations), where the Gestapo and their counterpart the Sipo *(Sicherheits Polizei)* as well as the Vichy French Police and *Milice* kept a vigilant eye on the comings and goings, only increased our unease.

Particularly feared was the *Milice*, which Pierre Laval, the Prime Minister of the Vichy French Government created in 1943 and which operated under the tutelage of his German masters. They were all fanatic French fascists and comparable to Himmler's SS. Their uniform was a khaki shirt and black tie, dark blue trousers and jacket and blue beret of the *Chasseurs Alpins*. The 30,000-man strong *Milice* operated like a militarised police and had a reputation worse than the SS. Apart from rounding up Jews, they hunted down the Maquis and evaders and were used for quelling dissent.

What worried me most, as I sat on the floor of the gangway of the railway carriage, was the thought of an inspection of identity papers but, to my great relief, no ID card or ticket inspections were conducted at all by either the French or Germans during the whole 12-hour journey. This was a rare occurrence and most welcome since the arrest of one of our Allied friends would have resulted in a very thorough search by the Security Police.

At 8.30 on the morning of January 22nd our train came to a stop at the Gate Matabiau, situated in a very old part of Toulouse and near the Canal du Midi. We had hardly stepped onto the platform when Jacques passed by and whispered to us to follow a girl dressed in a black and white overcoat and, once outside, to turn right and wait by the canal near the station.

The pretty young woman duly appeared and we followed her at a few paces to her right and, while she drew admiring glances and male attention, went through a barrier handing our train tickets to the railway ticket inspector. We then walked into the big station hall past several pale green uniformed *Grüne Polizei, Milice* and French *Gendarmes* in dark blue. None of them—as we had fully expected—asked to see our papers! We could not believe our luck.

It is still a mystery to me that not one of 'our' Americans, whom Robert and I had easily spotted on the railway platform in Paris, was asked to identify himself. Perhaps the SD and Gendarmes were trying to spot a particular person whose identity was known to them and paid little attention to the other passengers.

Once outside the building we turned right into the Boulevard de la Gare, alongside a canal which was still covered in a light mist. A few men, some alone, were already standing or loitering on the boulevard, amongst whom we recognized three of the five Allied airmen we had spotted at the Gare d'Austerlitz in Paris.

When Robert and I halted and prepared to light a cigarette we were still feeling the tension from passing through the station platform barrier and from the deliberately slow walk through the hall to the exit of the Gare Matabiau. At that very moment, whilst I was holding a burning

match to the 'Blue Caporal' in my mouth, a man of Northern
European appearance approached me and asked in perfect English, as if
we were standing in London's Piccadilly Circus *"Have you got a light please?"*
He was none other than the RAF Navigator (from a shot-down
Lancaster) from our group of 13, Sgt. Harold W. Bailey, who had seen us
talking with Jacques and, having met the ten Americans earlier, had
thought that Robert and I worked for 'the organisation'. It was one of
those unforgettably-curious incongruous moments that stay with you for
the rest of your life. It was also at this very spot that, in 1952, my wife,
Berna, driving our Morris Minor, touched the curb with the front wheel
when she parked the car, which made me exclaim in surprise at the
coincidence.

Jacques and a few other men soon thereafter guided us fugitives, in
groups of three or four, over different routes to a French restaurant called
'Chez Emile' at the Place St George. 'Chez Emile' still exists and is still
patronized by former *Engelandvaarders*. Emile assisted the Paris-
Dutch Escape Line as well as being a member of a *Maquis* group in the
Ariege district to which our guides 'Palo' (also occasionally written as
'Palot') and 'Mireille' belonged. Here, seated in this restaurant in the
centre of Toulouse, we had breakfast, with little conversation, and Robert
and I were then escorted by Jacques to his hotel, possibly the 'Panier
Fleuri' which was, like 'Chez Emile', used by the Paris-Dutch Escape
Line. We washed in the hand basin in Jacques' hotel room and Robert and
I were told to leave our small suitcases behind. We were each given a
rucksack into which we transferred our small flasks of cognac, one set of
underwear, two pairs of socks, a shirt and toiletries. We put on our water-
resistant golf jackets and trousers over our suits and under our raincoats
for the walk across the Pyrenees, for which specific purpose we had taken
them along. I also added to the rucksack my Bally shoes which had served
me so well when escaping from my *Wehrmacht* captors. We were then led
through some ancient streets to a two-storey brick house with boarded up
windows. In one of the rooms we joined four Americans, two of whom
we had met earlier at 'Chez Emile': the small dark-haired Sgt. Leonard H.
Cassady, a waist gunner of a Flying Fortress and the blond Sgt. James
Hussong, who nursed a wounded leg. Hussong was a Liberator tail-
gunner from Hagerstown, Maryland. The other two were Navigator Lt.

Charles 'Chuck' Downe and Lt. Ernest Grubb, a Marauder pilot. All had been shot down over northern France.

At about one o'clock in the afternoon we were fetched by the two guides, one of whom was 'Palo', who spoke some English, and taken back to the station. After waiting for a while in the large busy hall, we were told that seven of our group of 13 would leave immediately by train and that a group of six, including Robert and myself, would follow later in the afternoon. Our destination was not mentioned. It seemed a logical decision since a group of 13 men plus guides would be far more conspicuous than groups of six and seven plus guides.

We all traipsed back to the room in the boarded-up house, which our Yanks decided had to be an old brothel. Their fixation with brothels was perhaps not so curious since many a downed airman had found refuge in Belgian and French brothels, which were so often used by the Resistance as safe-houses.

It must have been about five o'clock when Jacques, Palo and Mireille arrived to take us back to the Gare Matabiau. It had been their intention to minimize time spent by us at the station and particularly on the platform.

Their timing was wrong, however, and the 5 p.m. train pulled out just as we reached the platform!

After a very short conference, the three Escape Line members decided not to take us back to the safe-house with the risk of running into an ID card check which, Palo told us later, was rumoured to take place that evening. Robert and I were taken aside and told to take charge until they returned in time for us to catch a later train. After providing us with a few francs, food coupons, newspapers and magazines, Jacques said *"À tout* à *l'heure"* (see you shortly) and they left.

There we were, literally sitting in the middle of the large cafe and waiting room of the Toulouse Station, completely surrounded, mainly by Germans of all ranks in every different type of uniform and hardly any civilians. Robert and I handed each American a newspaper or magazine and quietly told them to pretend to read or sleep and to only say the words *'pardon'*, *'merci'*, *'oui'* or *'non'* when we said something to them in French, for these were the only French words they all knew and understood. Just before the two of us sat down Robert spotted Ernie reading a French magazine upside down, He quickly snatched it out of

Ernie's hands, turned to me and in fluent audible French made some comment pointing to a photo, to which I replied, also audibly to bystanders, in French. Robert then returned the magazine to Ernie right side up!

I bought beer and bread rolls with the food coupons and money Mireille had given us. This would allow the Americans time off from feigning sleep or pretending to read a French periodical which they couldn't understand. The bread rolls were also useful for giving the Americans an opportunity to say *'merci'* and *'merci beaucoup'* loudly for every passer-by to hear and thus to indicate that they were not deaf-mutes. More importantly they were able to use their hands to eat the rolls, and not a knife and fork. Many Americans have betrayed themselves in Occupied Europe by following their custom of putting their knife down after cutting up their food and then transferring the fork to their right hand to eat with. Meanwhile Robert intermittently kept up a conversation in fluent French to which I replied to the best of my ability.

Luckily for us, seated in the *buffet* of the Toulouse Station for nearly two hours, not a single document inspection took place nor did we spot any SD or French *Milice* types, I was too conscious, however, that we were marooned for a few very dangerous hours in the centre of one of the three most important railway junctions in southern France. These junctions, were regularly subjected to identity checks because most fugitives had to pass through Toulouse, Bordeaux and Perpignan stations.

Maybe there had been some truth in the rumours about raids in some Toulouse precincts and French and German Police had been engaged elsewhere in Toulouse. Or perhaps it proved the dictum that the potentially most dangerous place is often the safest.

We were most relieved, putting it mildly, when Palo and Mireille came to collect us and to take our seats in the dimly-lit carriage of a slow train to St Gaudens, which stopped at all stations. Soon we alighted at the village of Cazeres where, after a walk in complete darkness, we were put up in a new but, as yet, incomplete two-storey house. Being January, it was quite cold and Mireille lit a fire in the large, open fireplace. He left that evening on his bicycle in order to meet with the *passeurs* of the seven airmen from the other group who had travelled from Toulouse earlier and had obviously gone to another town. This town had been the original destination for the six of us. He returned the next evening with the news that we would not join up as they had already left for Spain. Later, in Gibraltar, we learned from the RAF Navigator of the *"May I have a light, please"* fame that their guides had taken a route via Foix to Andorra. The train we had missed at 5 p.m. on January 22 must have been the last one to run between Toulouse and Foix or St Girons.

We spent two uncomfortable nights at the Cazeres safe house, sleeping two to a double bed. During the daytime we passed the time around the fireplace by telling our wartime experiences. Sgt. Leonard Cassady from Tunnelton, West Virginia, waist-gunner of a B17 Flying Fortress, was shot down over northern France on his third mission, a raid to Ludwigshaven. Sgt. James Hussong from Hagerstown, Maryland had been on the same air raid as tail gunner of a B-24 Liberator and had bailed out when Focke-Wolfe fighters from the *Luftwaffe* shot down his plane. He had a bullet wound in one leg and experienced a most anxious moment when, exiting his turret, his foot got caught and it took a struggle to free himself.

The French and Belgian Resistance had helped them evade the German search parties by moving them to various safe houses and they had twice crossed the French-Belgian border before they had been placed on a Paris-bound train at Cambrai.

Lt. Charles 'Chuck' Downe from Orange, New Jersey, a navigator, had also bailed out of a Flying Fortress over northern France and had, only in Toulouse, met up with Lt. Ernest Grubb, who came from the far west town of Onalaska in the State of Washington. Grubb's Marauder had been downed near St Omer in October. He had spent months in hiding in a farmhouse, together with the British Navigator, Sgt. Harold W. Bailey. They had killed two Germans who had entered one of their hiding places, before the Resistance moved them to a safe house in Paris. One evening, while they and other Americans were waiting in a square to be picked up by a truck and transported elsewhere, they were suddenly surrounded by German troops. Harold and Ernie managed to get away in the darkness of the Parisian black-out, but those Americans already in the truck were not so lucky and Ernie saw his whole crew arrested.

They also told us about a street in Paris where so many downed American airmen were hiding that it was known as "Rue Americain" or "Rue Yankee". On that day in Cazeres I became quite friendly with Palo, a typical wiry Frenchman, who proved to be a good cook and who shared my love of jazz music. The chain-smoking Mireille, at first impression appeared a nervous type but he was actually quite the opposite. His courage would have tragic consequences after the defeat of the Germans in 1945. Mireille hardly spoke a word of English and was solidly built, with a face that would not be out of place anywhere in Western Europe.

I remember going to bed in the unfinished house which had no doors or windows on the upper floor and was freezing cold. We only took our shoes off and fully clothed, complete with our French berets, crawled under the blankets. I did not find the tall 'Roberto' the most sought-after person to share a bed with and am sure it was an opinion he reciprocated. Cazeres was the first and last time that either of us shared a double bed with a man! Our guides, naturally, kept quiet about their Resistance activities except to mention that both were Reserve Officers and that Palo had been a POW in Germany. During the time we camped in the Cazeres house Chuck Downe 'sang' "Pistol Packing Mamma" from morning till night, whenever he was not talking, or had food or drink in his mouth.

15. Crossing the Pyrenees

O n the morning of the 24th of January, our guides took us to the Cazeres Station to catch the slow train to Boussens where we had to wait a while for the bus to the village of Mane. When we walked across the wide road outside the station heading for a cafe, Mireille spotted a car that he knew belonged to an officer of the SD in the district, Palo quickly told the very Nordic looking Charles Downe and Jimmy Hussong, to get on the bicycles, which he and Mireille had brought with them from Cazeres, and told them to keep circulating until the bus arrived.

Meanwhile the rest of us spread ourselves out over several tables outside the cafe. After a while, saw a man known to Palo to belong to the SD, dressed in civilian clothes, get into his parked motor car and leave. After about 20 minutes the still circulating Downe and Hussong were called in and we all boarded a rather ancient motorbus through the back door. Petrol being a very rare commodity during the war, the bus ran on coke gas.

Just as we were about to leave, an officer in his light green *Grüne Polizei* uniform entered the bus through the front side door and sat down in the front row, reserved for German officials. After a while he turned in his seat and began to scrutinize the occupants. Having probably been posted to the Pyrenean foothills area for some time he must have felt that those of us at the back of the bus had faces that didn't entirely fit into the 'landscape', in spite of our similar dress mode to the locals.

Palo, alert to the danger, got up and sat in the empty seat next to the *Grüne Polizei* officer and started an animated conversation, gesticulating, laughing and offering him a cigarette, thus diverting the Nazi's attention. When the bus reached the first houses of Mane, Palo stood up and took leave of the SD officer and made his way to the back of the bus where we were sitting. Palo was about to bend over and say something to Robert and me when at the same moment the German turned around to look at us again. Palo, watching our faces and immediately sensing danger, quickly grabbed his rucksack and doubled back to the German in the front seat, extending his hand again in parting, in doing so blocking his view to the back door of the bus where we were seated. We nearly fell out of the back of the bus and Mireille guided us on the double around the corner of the crossroads where the bus had stopped. He directed us across a bridge of the small Arbas River and down some steps leading to a basement café. Palo joined us shortly after recovering the bikes that had been transported on top of the bus.

Apparently Palo, who had picked up some German while a POW in Germany, had pretended to be a French collaborator and told the *Grüne Polizei* officer that he was looking forward to going back to work in Germany in a few weeks' time.

In the dingy basement cafe in Mane, seated at bare wooden tables, we ate a hearty meal of *des oeufs au lard* (eggs and fatty bacon) and *des saucissons* (sausages), which stuck to our ribs. We were then handed provisions consisting of bacon, sugar-cubes and a few slices of bread, which we put in our haversacks or rucksacks. My wristwatch said it was nearly nine in the evening when we began our three days and two nights walk across the foothills and mountains of the Pyrenees to the Spanish border.

Apart from *Sperr-zeit* (curfew), the Germans had created a forbidden area of 15 kilometres adjoining the French-Spanish border where the locals were issued with special passes. The Germans, often with dogs, regularly patrolled the roads, villages and hamlets in the valleys of this *Zone Interdit*, and they were authorized to, and often would, shoot on sight. From observation posts the Germans also scoured the hills and mountains with binoculars, while ski-patrols were employed in the higher snow-bound areas. It had also been decreed that anybody arrested in this zone would not be held in military custody, but handed over to the *Sicherheitsdienst.*

The Pyrenees are made up of a number of mountain ranges running from east to west, from the Mediterranean to the Bay of Biscay, with only a few mountain passes running north-south through them. It is extremely rugged country on both sides of the border and impassable for the most part. Even when travelling up the Garonne River valley through the Val d'Aran on the Spanish side, there is yet another high mountain pass, the Port de la Benaigua. This pass sits at 2072 metres above sea level. It is snowbound in winter and has to be negotiated by foot, or on a donkey or horse to reach the major Spanish city of Lerida. The *passeurs* were therefore forced to guide escapees from mountain ridge to mountain ridge spending as little time as possible crossing the valleys, avoiding the occasional hamlets, farms or woodcutters' huts.

The first stage from Mane was over route D13 to Arbas, an approximately 12 kilometre walk on a bitumen road over gently undulating country. Mireille went ahead on his bike to scout the road. Palo on his bike leading the six of us, who, marching in military step— left, right, left, right—made good time, slowing down only once to silently pass a *Gendarme* Post without incident. Arriving at Arbas, our guides, after crossing a bridge, left their bicycles in the shed of a friend and we left the paved streets of the village and headed south.

Still following the D13, the gentle ascent soon changed as the road became narrower and steeper and was no longer paved. We kept going until about one o'clock before halting at a barn, where, covered with hay to protect us from the cold, we rested for about four hours, finding sleeping difficult.

On the second day of our trek over the Pyrenees to Spain, our guides aroused us from our sleep at 4.00 a.m. in the pitch black of a very early midwinter morning.

Light rain had started to fall when at first light we entered a forested area where the *tonk, tonk, tonk,* of woodcutters' axes slamming into the trees was the only accompaniment to the sound of our feet on the muddy road. We had not gone far when Chuck Downe complained about stomach pains and not feeling well. We thought that the heavy sausages and fatty bacon we had at the cafe in Mane were the likely cause of his distress. After hastily setting off for some bushes and regaling us with some pitiful groaning, he soon reappeared with an expression of great relief and we continued our climb. At a *bergerie* (a sheep-herder's shelter) a little farther on, Palo dug up a cloth-covered parcel containing two pistols and some ammunition for himself and Mireille, explaining that we were entering the *Zone Interdit* and might need them. From there on we kept on climbing higher and higher.

The rain had eased by the time we reached a hamlet, most likely Sarrat De Bouch, where, in the house of an anti-German *gendarme,* we were served a breakfast of bread, butter and sausages by a taciturn elderly woman and where, to protect us from the cold, a cast iron stove glowed warmly in the room. It was here, at breakfast, that Palo told us how only a few weeks earlier, returning from guiding a group of Allied airmen to the frontier, they had run into a German ski-patrol. Before the Germans could unsling their machine pistols they had leaped into a ravine and, because the Germans were hampered by their skis, they had somehow managed to get away. Later they showed us the spot where they had flung themselves over the precipice down, at my guess, at least a six metre drop where the knee-deep snow in the gully must have cushioned their fall.

After that interlude it was still to be another 27 hours of hard-going, with only short breaks, mostly of only a few minutes.

The rainfall had made the narrow mountain track muddy and slippery and it only got worse on the winding, much steeper and narrower path leading to the Pic de l'Aube. Light snow fell and we soon trudged through inches deep snow above the snowline. At about 1500 metres above sea level we crossed a ridge and zigzagged down a footpath through a tree-covered slope to the south. The wind had now abated and the clouds had lifted sufficiently for us to be able to see a row of low mountains to the south. Beyond these rose the massive Pic de la Calabasse. We could also vaguely see the much higher mountains on the Spanish side of the border, which are over 3000 metres high. Below us was the fairly level area of the pass known as Col de Portet d'Aspet, near which stood, and is still standing today, at 1069 metres above sea level, a *cabane* (hut), that is now converted into a holiday house. It became famous in the annals of the Escape Lines, the Dutch-Paris in particular, and is now called *'La Cabane des Evades'.* The *cabane* at that time actually consisted of two huts to shelter sheep and store hay and wine, connected by the walls of a manure trough.

Arriving at the *cabane,* Mireille pointed left towards the east and remarked: *"Les Boches sont là".* Once inside, we ate a piece of bread and fatty bacon, had a swig of cognac and swallowed a few lumps of sugar for energy. After leaving Mane we had ascended from 300 to 1500 metres above sea level and now, at just above 1070 metres, had covered about 13 kilometres since Arbas.

In 1977, at the *Engelandvaarders'* Reunion, I was to learn that at this same hut on February the 6th, just 11 days later, the Germans ambushed Sam Timmers Verhoeven, on his birthday of all days, along with a very large contingent of some 35 escapees and Allied airmen. Some, like Sam, Mireille and Palo escaped after Palo raised the alarm when he spotted the Germans waiting in ambush. What happened to the mainly American airmen is unknown, but all of the evaders who were captured died in concentration camps, except two who managed to jump from a moving train.

Next, we would have to cross the road that we could see some 150 metres down a gentle slope from the *cabane*, and on which road, Palo told us, Germans with dogs patrolled a few times a day. To the right of the crest of the pass I could see a wooded valley. To our left, and only about 300 metres down from the crest of the road, Palo said, was the village of Portet d'Aspet with German and French *Gendarme* stations. The road was and is the Route National D618 with the crest of it being the Col named after the village of Portet d'Aspet.

Palo was the first to go, moving from tree to tree and rock to bush down the slope. The six of us followed one at a time, with Mireille bringing up the rear. He then ran, in a crouched position across the D618 and up the slope to the timber line on the other side of the road. *"It's like playing cowboys and Indians"* one American remarked.

Once we were all across, Palo and Mireille urged us to walk as fast as we could for fear that dogs from one of the frequent German patrols passing over the Col de Portet d'Aspet, would pick up our scent.

After a tiring several hundred metres of mainly uphill walking, we tried to put as much distance as possible between the Col d'Aspet and ourselves. We stopped briefly for a cool drink of water at a beautifully clear stream. Soon after that the weather deteriorated again. Drizzle was falling by the time we saw some houses to our west, most likely belonging to the small village of Couledoux. It was to be our last sighting of a hamlet or farmhouse until daylight the next day. Even these two experienced guides, born and raised in the foothills of the Pyrenees, lost their way at one time in the foul weather and after a reconnoitre by Palo we changed direction.

Drizzle soon changed to rain and the wind had increased, while the temperature dropped. The weather slowly deteriorated further and later in the afternoon and evening we experienced periods of sleet and snow blowing nearly horizontally into us. Our boots, issued by the escape organisation in Paris, could not keep our feet dry any longer and our socks were by now soaking wet. It was of some consolation, but scant comfort to us, that the bad weather ensured that the German patrols would be less active and the observation posts would be blinded by the snow and sleet.

When there was only a light covering of snow, we would climb a distance of 500 metres or so in about an hour, but in ankle or knee-deep snow and slippery mud it could take five times as long,

Since the clear mountain brook after the Col de Portet we hadn't come across any clear-water streams, only very muddy ones. Ignoring the warnings of our guides, we started to scoop up snow and melt it in our mouths to quench our thirst. I clearly remember that the two guides, as well as Robert and I, had a small flat flask of cognac each in our rucksacks, but that nobody carried a water bottle. We simply hadn't thought of it, nor apparently had our guides. Perhaps they were hardier types.

By evening the snow now changed to sleet and the wind had increased in velocity making conditions quite terrible. A more unpleasant and dismal evening and night would be difficult to imagine than this mixture of rain, snow, sleet, mud, extreme cold, wet feet and soaked overcoats. Robert and I, fortunately, wore golf jackets under our raincoats. The Americans, without the extra protection of a golf jacket, were not so lucky. All the while we kept climbing with an occasional break for a minute or so when we were forced to halt and turn our backs to the blizzard to catch our breath.

Nearing the top of the ridge, stumbling over the small rocks and stones, blinded by the blizzard, we finally, at about one in the morning, crested a mountain ridge to take refuge in a hut, which Mireille somehow found without a discernible track to guide him. Totally exhausted, eight bedraggled men, shivering from the icy wind, practically fell into the hut and sank down on the wooden floor with our backs against the timber wall.

Nobody spoke for several minutes. Although now sheltered from the biting wind, at an altitude of some 1800 metres, it was still bitterly cold inside the hut which must have been to the west of the Cap de Gauch and near the disused 'Ancient Mines'. Several of these mines can be found in this area and were already being mined well before Roman times. We took our socks off and rubbed our feet to restore the circulation and, before putting my still wet socks back on (the proven way to prevent frostbite), I noted that the sole of one of my boots had virtually parted company with the upper. I discarded them and put on my Bally rubber-soled, water resistant, but otherwise ordinary walking shoes that had served me so well in Paris and which I had been carrying in my rucksack.

It must have been nearly an hour later when, in darkness and in an icy cold gale, we left the *cabane* and began the most difficult of all descents in the direction of the Col d'Artigascout. The wind was still fairly strong but soon the snow stopped falling and we were also spared the even worse sleet. Shivering from the cold, we stumbled down the bare rocky slope in pitch-black darkness for several hours, often having to walk in mostly dry streambeds covered in stones and small rocks, frequently falling in pain. Many an oath in three languages was often resorted to as we made our way in Indian file, often with a hand on the shoulder of the man in front so as to prevent falling behind or losing the way in the darkness of the night.

Those following Robert's light khaki-coloured trench coat, Ernie's grey overcoat and my bleached-to-almost-white, beige Egyptian cotton raincoat, were lucky. The others in their dark blue and dark brown woollen coats that blended easily into the colours of the rocky terrain were very difficult to follow. Images of that ascent to the 'Cabane du Gauch' and descent in the bitter night and icy cold dawn are permanently engraved in my memory.

By daybreak the gale force wind had abated and we had descended well down the wooded slope leading to the valley of a small river called Maudan. We could hear the roar of the fast-moving water well before we could see it through the trees, way down below us. Fifty years later I learned that we were just west of the small village of Labach.

It wasn't long afterwards that the sun broke through the clouds lighting up the snow on the highest mountain peaks. *"Those mountains"* Palo remarked, *"are in Spain."* It would still take more than a five-hour walk to reach the frontier.

At about 20 metres or so above the Maudan, Palo and Mireille left us to walk ahead and investigate the situation. They returned about 20 minutes later and told us that we would have to cross the river over a stone bridge and, in order to reach the bridge, we would have to walk past a house, the shutters of which were still closed but could be manned by still-sleeping German soldiers or *Gendarmes*. It was vital to get across the bridge since it was dangerous to cross the foaming icy torrent, most certainly in mid-winter, and have to continue in soaked clothes in freezing temperatures.

Proceeding warily we descended to the dirt road (the D44), turned to our left, and one by one, about five yards apart, tiptoed past the closed shutters of the faded yellowish-beige brick blockhouse. We then ran in a crouched position across the bridge and up the incline on the south side of the Maudan, the sound of our running drowned out by the roaring of the water.

A hundred metres past the stone bridge, and well out of sight of the blockhouse, we stopped running and rested for a few minutes in the wet grass amongst the shrubs and trees.

Next we had to climb the slope of a looming dark mountain ridge which, like the Maudan Valley, was still in the shadow of higher mountains and clouds. Soon the sun would shine on its northern slope. *"Les Boches sont la et la,"* observed Palo, pointing in an easterly and then westerly direction into the Maudan Valley. *"We must be over the top before about 8.30 otherwise they can detect us through their binoculars and warn the ski-patrols."* This message from the French-speaking Mireille was translated by Robert for the benefit of the Americans.

The going soon became very difficult over muddy and at times very slippery and steep ground. It was a struggle to keep up with Palo, while the *Gauloises* chain-smoking Mireille kept urging us on from the back of the pack. Hussong, whose wounded leg was troubling him, had picked up a bare tree-branch to steady himself.

On the very steep, slippery parts we often had to pull ourselves up by grasping bushes and tree branches and, at times, we had to crawl on our hands and knees. Mireille had hardly finished pushing the last of us over the edge when the sun started to break through, illuminating the hill we had just crested.

It was after this strenuous climb that Ernie Grubb broke down. Literally grey from exhaustion and trembling from fever, he collapsed in the snow. Mireille quickly poured some cognac over several lumps of sugar in an empty Capstain cigarette tin and helped Ernie to drink this concoction. It worked like magic. After about ten minutes a revived Ernie was hoisted to his feet and, assisted by Palo and Mireille, started walking again, while Leonard Cassady, being the toughest of us all, carried their rucksacks. Robert and I also took a turn at supporting Ernie until he was able to walk unassisted. Cognac with sugar is a marvellous reviver!

Many a downed Allied aviator sometimes had to spend many weeks, and in Ernie's case months, hiding in barn lofts and garrets of houses or cooped up in attics of safe houses in towns or cities, causing their physical condition to deteriorate. Ernie had kept on going, in spite of his distress, not wanting to jeopardize us all by not reaching the shadows of the safe area beckoning ahead of us. Robert and I were both, despite years of food rationing, physically the equal of our American friends and certainly better prepared mentally for this strenuous trip. Besides, we knew that detection and arrest meant that we would be shot on the spot or be 'interviewed' by the Gestapo. If we survived, we would end up in a concentration camp. For the Allied airmen it should mean (as they all believed) ending up in a POW camp. I wrote 'should' because it has become known that—in spite of the Geneva Convention rules regarding the treatment of prisoners of war—the SD and the *Waffen SS* had shot captured Allied soldiers and escaped POWs. After the War I read stories of those incapable of continuing being left behind in a makeshift hiding place or—if they could cause serious danger to others—being shot dead. Those left behind were sometimes recovered by the *passeurs* and able to make a second attempt to reach Spain, but skeletons discovered in these rugged mountains attest to those stragglers and other unfortunates who died lonely deaths. Our fatigue, combined with fear of running into a German ski-patrol, made us forget our hunger, even though by now we had eaten very little for the past 26 hours and had hardly slept at all.

The continuous *tonk, tonk, tonk* sound of woodcutters at work in the Mandan Valley receded as we negotiated a narrow path alongside a deep gully in the forest that brought us to a clear, slow-moving brook partially covered with ice at the edges and bordered by pine trees. We stopped for a drink of the ice-cold water and it was at this beautiful brook that I took off the sheepskin-lined glove of my right hand to scoop up water, I then forgot to put it back on, and lost it there or soon thereafter. Later at the frontier I gave my left-hand glove to Palo and expressed the hope that he would find the other one on his way back. Fifty years later that lost glove would play an important role.

Once beyond the Mont Gaubach forest and on the snow-covered plateau, it became slow-going. The snow-covered peaks of the granite mass of the Spanish Maladetta Range could now be seen above the Gaubach Ridge. Except for the guides, we all were now desperately tired and our swollen feet made walking difficult. Palo kept on encouraging us by saying *"Allons mes amis, only ten more minutes."* He repeated this encouragement many times while we struggled, in the mental fog of exhaustion, through the knee-high glistening snow, until well ahead of us he stopped, planted his walking stick in the snow, turned around and, in English, announced: *"This is the frontier."* Almost to the minute, it was half past twelve on the 26th of January 1944.

16. Spain – We Made It!

Palo, pushing his walking stick into the snow and announcing that we had reached Spain, remains a vivid, exhilarating and unforgettable image engraved in my memory and no doubt in the memories of all others present. I recall the sense of exaltation and the deep awareness that overcame me with the realisation that we had made it. Palo and Mireille had their hands vigorously shaken and there was much joy, backslapping, shouting and general horsing around in the relief and elation of the moment.

Palo had already told me at the house in Cazeres that he and Mireille had been officers in the French Army and that he had been a POW in Germany for nearly two years. On his return to St Girons he had joined the *Maquis Patriotique* in the Ariege district where he, among others, guided fugitives over the Pyrenees. The word *'Maquis'*, by the way, means shrub-wooded upland. It was, at first, used to describe those in the French Resistance who operated from armed camps in the woods and mountains. Its numbers increased greatly in 1943 when young men called up for *Arbeidseinsatz* in Germany went into hiding and joined local *Maquis* in droves. They were called *Maquisards*.

In Ariege, another resistance group, the *Maquis Communiste,* was also active. Shortly after the War, Mireille, while having discussions at their headquarters, was killed by a pistol shot from behind. There is no doubt that the Communists planned to usurp power in the West.

It was at the border that Palo told me his real name was Pierre Philippe Treillet and that Mireille's real name was Henri Marrot and that they were permanent members of the Dutch-Paris Escape Line. He also told me that the *Mairie* (town hall) of St Girons would always know his whereabouts.

It was perhaps only ten minutes after reaching the frontier that our guides made ready to leave, but not before instructing us to walk in a westerly direction down the fairly steep slope until we reached the village of Canejan. When asked whether they weren't too tired to make the return journey, our guides smiled and said *"No, it will only take a day and a half."*

After *"au revoirs"*, the wiry, friendly Palo and quiet, sympathetic Mireille commenced their return to Arbas to collect their bicycles and prepare to guide another group of fugitives and airmen across the Pyrenees. This next group would be the unlucky group with Sam Timmers Verhoeven.

After the emotional parting, the possibility of being spotted by a German ski-patrol made us descend about 30 metres down the southern snowbound slope of the 1700-metre high mountain ridge into Spanish territory, where from extreme fatigue we simply flopped down in the knee-high snow. We opened Robert's only tin of corned beef, which he had brought with him all the way from Amsterdam, divided the last four slices of bread and took a last swig from the nearly empty flasks of cognac. It was only then, in a heightened state of sensitivity and awareness, that we began to notice the spectacular views and appreciate the majesty of the Pyrenees. We revelled in the wild beauty of the chain of mighty snow-capped peaks and rugged ridges stretching as far as the eye could see, both to the south and to the eastern and western horizons. We were also able to see a valley to the south, and kilometres away, a large village, but no sight yet of the village of Canejan.

Fugitives and escapees caught by the Germans in the forbidden zone along the frontier were often shot on the spot or, if they did not manage to escape, were unlikely to survive the Nazi concentration camps. I have not learned how the Germans treated escaped Allied POWs or downed Allied airmen whom they captured in the *Zone Interdit*. In 1943, the Germans had issued a warning that all Allied Military Personnel caught in a border zone with Switzerland would be considered spies. The death penalty would then immediately follow. One must presume that this also would apply to the Pyrenean frontier. We realised that we had better get a move on—the actual border was after all now an invisible line where not even a marker could be seen in the snowscape. There was still a risk of being detected and arrested by a German ski-patrol.

In the highest of spirits, we made our way down slowly, on our sore ankles and swollen wet feet along the Spanish south side of the snow-covered slope to the west of the 2034 metre Cap de la Pique and in the direction of Pont du Roi, the frontier post on the Garonne River. We could now see for miles into the Aran Valley, one of the very few north-south valleys in the Pyrenees. It is at the Pont du Roi, about 600 metres above sea level, that the Garonne emerges from the Spanish Pyrenees and flows into the valleys of the lower mountains and hills of southern France to finally empty into the Bay of Biscay.

Before we reached Canejan, we passed a farmhouse where a two-wheeled cart loaded with stones and pulled by oxen was being unloaded by two weather-beaten Spaniards. They were our first human contact in Spain. One of our Americans greeted them with a *"Buenos dias"* to which, with a smile, they similarly replied.

Not long after we passed the snowline, we saw the first houses of Canejan and spotted a footpath running into a narrow, cobbled street. We asked a curious bystander *"Policia?"* and were told, presumably in Spanish and with hand signs, to follow the middle-aged woman to the *Guardia Frontera* situated in a brick house with faded reddish-coloured plaster walls.

The reception at the police bureau by the two *Guardias* in their green uniforms was not unfriendly. An elderly woman, who had silently appeared, was asked by the *Guardia* to put more logs on a burning pile in a huge fireplace to dry our clothes and socks and brought us water and hot coffee. We must have had four glasses of water each.

Robert and I stripped off our raincoats followed by our golf-jackets and trousers, which soon after the second day couldn't keep the rain out any longer. Then we took off the damp grey flannel trousers, to reveal our dry business suits and pullovers. The *Guardias* and others gathered around us were highly amused.

Meanwhile, a *Guardia Civil* chap wrote down our names and particulars and, after having made us empty our pockets, a policeman in civilian clothes relieved us of our pocket-knives, some French money and our cigarette lighters, on the pretext that they were forbidden imports. Others have experienced the same curious predilection for cigarette lighters by the *Guardia Civil*. However, both Robert and I had managed not to empty all pockets, which wasn't too difficult to get away with and prevented having some *pesetas* and personal items impounded. 'Our' Americans, apart from giving their rank and numbers, only stated that they had been shot down over France. Both Robert and I had hidden our French ID cards (I still have mine) and gave our true names and other particulars, stating that we wished to go to the Dutch Colonies of Surinam in South America or Curacao in the West Indies. Later we were to learn that the Spanish Government considered men who were 18 to 36 years to be of military age and until November '42 had refused them transit visas. After Germany occupied Vichy-France, exit visas were not granted to men of military age, at least not until late 1943. When asked the question of where we had crossed the border, "*somewhere to the east of Canejan*" seemed to satisfy them.

Our arrival must have been an important occasion for officialdom in this outpost of their country. Once our clothes were quite dry the *Guardia Frontera*, after much discussion of the necessary details to be entered into the register, completed the required forms.

After the ranking officer had phoned and likely spoken with the *Guardia Civil* Commanding Officer of the area, we were told, in a mixture of Spanish and French, that he had been instructed that we were to stay in *residence forcée* at an hotel in the nearby village of Les. Having expected to be locked up in the local jail, the six of us, sporting three-day old beards and quite exhausted and looking forward to hotel beds, now set off for Les in the highest of spirits preceded and followed by *Carabinero* in their three-cornered, black-lacquered hats, accompanied by the shouts of "*Adios*" and even "*Viva Forteleza Volantes*" by some of the locals.

A steep road led down to the Toran River, a tributary of the Garonne, after which, for the rest of the way to the small town of Les, on the Garonne River, it was fairly level going. Nevertheless, it was still some six kilometres to the Hotel Franco-Espagñol.

For the first time in two days our socks were dry but most of us had great difficulty walking on our badly swollen feet and sore ankles. When we reached the main road along the Garonne, Ernie Grubb and I had difficulty keeping up with the others and the *Guardias*, noting our discomfort, didn't urge us along. One of them stayed with us two stragglers.

Upon reaching the Hotel Franco-Espagñol, the *Guardia Civil* left us in the care of a very friendly, stout, middle-aged woman who said to us in French that she was the proprietress. *"Allez pauvres garçons,"* she exclaimed, ushering us into the lounge room of the hotel where we were warmly greeted by her daughter. We told her, when asked, that we hadn't had a warm meal for several days. *"Pauvres garçons,"* she exclaimed again and assured us that she would serve us a proper meal in half an hour. During that half hour, Robert, Leonard Cassady and I finished a bottle of port and enjoyed a Camel cigarette, which we hadn't smoked since 1940 and which the daughter's fiancé offered us. We were also warned not to talk about *"quelque chose d'important"* because there were some Fascists present in the main dining room.

The Spanish Civil War started on 13th of July 1936 at Melilla in Spanish Morocco after the assassination of the monarchist leader Calvo Sotelo. The Val d'Aran, as a part of the Republican-held part of Spain, held out for many months after most of the province of Lerida had fallen to the Nationalists in March 1938. The heavily French-influenced Aranais population remained mainly anti-fascist, hence the friendly attitude towards illegal arrivals from non-fascist counties.

By the time we were asked to come to the dining table, which was large enough to seat six, and which must have been in the owner's own dining room, our feet were so badly swollen that we all had discarded our shoes and in socks hobbled painfully to the dining table. We must have smelled quite 'high' by the time we sat down for dinner since we had not had a bath or been able to brush our teeth since leaving Cazeres three days earlier.

After some lovely hot soup our hosts presented us with three large dishes heaped with rice, meat and herbs, which we wolfed down much to the delight of the happily smiling proprietress. My final memory of that meal, fit for the gods, was the arrival of oranges, which we hadn't seen in Holland since the summer of 1940. The next thing I remember was waking up in the morning in my hotel bed. I had quite simply and quite suddenly passed out before I could drink my coffee. Robert, Charles Downe and Ernie Grubb had carried me up the stairs to my hotel room and Ernie, who didn't feel too well himself, had crawled into the other bed. Robert told me that at the frontier he had felt a little queasy and feverish and had taken some aspirin tablets and ascribed my 'collapse' to my having partaken too much of port. However, a few weeks later in Madrid, Robert was himself to experience a very nasty reaction, so severe as to cause a heart-rhythm disturbance.

Not surprisingly, after hardly sleeping and with only short rest periods over the previous three days, nobody rose early the next morning. After breakfast Charles Downe and Ernie Grubb were able to get through to the American Consul in Barcelona thanks to Robert's command of the French language, which many Catalans spoke or understood and through a sustained effort by the elderly lady at the archaic Post Office Telephone Exchange. Ernie reported the arrival of the four Americans, giving their names, ranks and serial numbers. Robert also asked their Consul to contact the Dutch Consul (who I believe was the Catalonian agent for the Phillips conglomerate) and report the arrival of Robert Piet van Exter and Pieter Rudolph Zeeman, and to please take the necessary steps with the Spanish authorities.

The American Consul told Ernie that patience was required since it would take some time to get the approval for travel to Madrid, and for the Hollanders to be released to the Netherlands Diplomatic Service. For the time being we were under the authority of the *Policia Seguridad* and in the custody of the *Guardia Civil*.

I should mention that information about the reception and treatment by the Spanish authorities of 'illegals' who crossed into Spain had, over the grapevine, filtered through to Holland. It was, by the summer of 1943, known that we would most likely see the inside of a Spanish jail and/or be put behind the barbed wire of a camp for illegals until our Dutch Government's representative could bail us out. Logic therefore told us how important it was to get through to our diplomatic service as soon as possible.

We knew by the end of 1941 that Swiss frontier guards would hand over those illegally crossing the border, when caught in the border area, to the Vichy French police or the Germans at the German-occupied French border with Switzerland, but it was only after reaching Spain that I learned that those who crossed illegally into Spain and were caught near the frontier—at that part of the French-Spanish border under German Occupation in 1940-1942—were handed back to the Germans.

The questioning by the *Guardia Civil* who were the Spanish Government police in Canej (as distinct from Municipal/City police) had not presented any problems. Thereafter the general attitude of the authorities towards us was not unfriendly. However, we had the distinct impression that our being two Dutchmen amongst a large group of American airmen caused us to be treated differently than other illegal entrants.

We spent two happy days at the Hotel Franco-Espagñol where the kind proprietress looked after the welfare of her *"pauvres garçons"* as if we were her own sons. When we weren't eating or sleeping, which on reflection must have been most of the time, we would, in daytime, sit opposite the hotel on the grass bank of the Garonne River. On the first day we dangled our swollen feet and ankles in the fast-flowing, ice-cold water while basking in the winter sun. Passing locals often stopped for a chat, sometimes offering us tobacco and occasionally a cigarette, which was greatly appreciated even though the quality of the Spanish tobacco left a lot to be desired. Most only spoke a local dialect and some Spanish. Our conversations with these passers-by were therefore confined to sign language and the few words of Spanish we knew. When they spoke a little French, an exchange of pleasantries could take place. Quite a few would mention *"Forteleza Volante"* ("Flying Fortress") followed by the universal thumbs up sign.

It was only after the War that I learned that, apart from Castilian Spanish and Catalan, some few thousand inhabitants of the Aran Valley speak the ancient Occitan language, which they call Aranais. Occitan is still spoken in southern France (from the Limosin across Auvergne, Provence and Languedoc to the southern part of the Italian Alps) by perhaps 10 percent of the population, and is still understood by millions.

The Aran Valley has been a part of Spain since the 13th century but was isolated from the rest of it until the road over the Bonaigua Pass was completed. Supplies for the Aran Valley before 1925 and thereafter during the winter months came in via French ports, in sealed trucks from Marseille, to the valley via the Port du Roi on the Garonne River which is only a few kilometres from where we crossed the frontier. It was only after 1925 that the Val d'Aran could be reached from Spain in winter via an unsealed road over the 2072-metre high pass of Port de la Bonaigua, between Vielha and Esterri.

The performance of a human's natural functions is seldom mentioned in literature or shown in movies, but it has played on my mind ever since the Pyrenean sojourn. How did we cope with the calls of Mother Nature? We were spared the diarrhoea that struck down those who drank water from one of the streams and brooks in the Pyrenees. Perhaps it was the simple fact that cattle and sheep were kept in stables during the severest winter months and were not roaming the high country in January that spared us the agony of this affliction. Anyhow, it is something of which I have no recollection at all during our crossing of the Pyrenees except for Chuck Down's heroic efforts after Arbas. Yet I can still remember clearly the simply awful rows of toilets, without any partitions, on the troopship from Gibraltar to England and some of the primitive latrines in New Guinea.

It was with great regret that we had to leave the motherly care of the kind proprietress and her daughter at the Hotel Franco-Espagñol in the afternoon of January 28th, escorted by two *Guardias*. Soon after arriving at the Hotel Antonio Serrano at Vielha, which was situated on the main road and very near the bridge crossing the Rio Negre, a tributary of the Garonne River, somebody mentioned a Hollander being treated in Vielha's hospital.

Amongst the *Engelandvaarders* who fell sick during the trek over the Pyrenees, and were carried half-frozen over the border by their companions, was Harry Wins, whom we found in the small, grubby hospital in the village called Vielha (also written as Viella.)

A sallow-skinned, puffy-faced, Spanish doctor directed us to Harry's bed, which was next to that of a Frenchman with an amputated leg and not far from a man coughing his lungs out and who obviously didn't have long to live. Harry was understandably glad to meet Robert and myself and to speak with compatriots. After a nasty fall he had lain for five hours flat on his back in the snow and had been carried across the border into Spain, ending up with frostbite. He had languished in the hospital for about two months. His knees and back would trouble him for the rest of his life.

Somehow Harry had acquired the affection of the telephone operator of the Vielha Exchange, a pretty young girl by the name of Maria, and it was she who told him of any news of interest she overheard at her job. It was through Maria and Harry that we learned that another group of

Americans were expected to arrive in Vielha late that afternoon, having crossed into Spain from the west through the Maladetta Range. The nine Americans, announced by Harry's Maria, duly arrived late that afternoon. They were Harold K. Lockwood, Owen Scott, Edward L. Knapp, James E. Nacy, Robert H. Martin, George M. Bertholdt, George Jasman, Meredith H. Rueff and a 'character' called Tiger Hicks.

In Vielha, having nothing better to do, a few of us would sometimes 'drape' ourselves over the parapet of the bridge over the Rio Negro and watch the passing traffic. Again, like at Les, the population was friendly and at one time someone pointed to an approaching motorcar: *"Alemànes"* (Germans), he remarked. An open *Wehrmacht* passenger car with two men, one of Germanic appearance with a monocle in his right eye seated behind the driver, came into view. When they crossed the bridge, the stern-looking Germans were greeted by the broadly smiling faces and 'V for victory' hand signs from some six or seven of us. This unexpected encounter surprised me because this was 1944 and not 1940-1942. It indicated that, as late as 1944, Spanish authorities still supported the Nazis and that their presence in the frontier area was known to the local population.

After the War, I read Sam Timmers Verhoeven's account of his Pyrenean adventure. At dusk one evening in early April, Sam writes, sitting on a bench in the village square of Vielha with Han Langerer, they saw a door of a tavern open and, to their astonishment, a *Feldwebel* in German uniform appeared. Not only did the Sergeant confirm the rumour that *Wehrmacht* motorcars had arrived in Vielha, but it was the very same *Feldwebel* who had arrested Han Langerer near the border one year earlier! Han, who had escaped after that arrest by jumping out of a moving train, was naturally shaken by this totally unexpected encounter. Sam T. Verhoeven had also felt great unease at the totally unexpected appearance of a German in uniform well inside Spain, for he had been on the run for his life after the ambush at the Col de Portet d'Aspet on the 6th February. After many adventures, Sam had been guided over the border west of Vielha by the *Maquis* in a group of escapees and American aviators on the 28th of March.

We, at that time, did not know that an arrangement had been made between General Franco's government and the Nazis allowing uniformed members of the German Military and their motorcars to enter a 20 kilometre-wide border zone provided they did not carry any weapons. German Intelligence therefore operated freely inside this Spanish border zone. They were briefed by the Spanish *Policia Seguridad* about escaped members of the Allied Forces, as well as other evaders and escapees who had entered Spain.

17. Over the Bonaigua Pass to Lerida

In the early morning of the 21st of February, two *Guardias*, with heavy winter capes over their uniforms, collected us at the Hotel Antonio Serrano and loaded us all, 15 Americans and two Dutchmen, into an open truck and drove us, in brilliant sunshine, from Vielha up the valley on the unpaved route C142 past the granite-walled houses and a Romanesque Church with a tall belfry in the village of Salardu. Just before reaching the snowline, at about 1300 metres and about 12 kilometres from Vielha, we began our climb to the Port de la Bonaigua, the gateway to Spain. The snow covering was knee-deep well before we neared the 2072 metres high pass from where, surrounded by a circle of snowbound jagged mountain peaks of 2500-3000 metres above sea level, the view was utterly spectacular.

The concise description of this impressive, mysterious and seemingly endless primeval mountain range, with its many granite peaks of over 3000 metres (over 10,000 feet), was made by Sam Timmers Verhoeven when he wrote: *"Switzerland is a park and the Pyrenees are a collection of rockeries."*

I vividly recall a granite building with a pointed, snow-covered roof in the fairly flat area on top of the pass. I recall descending behind the leading *Guardia Civil,* and the intrepid Leonard Cassady with the winding road leading to and following the Rio Bonaigua. Several times the road crossed over stone bridges in the rocky gorge before passing the snowline and reaching the small village of Esterri d'Agneu. We were now 46 kilometres from Vielha.

The walk up to and descending from the Bonaigua Pass to about 1000 metres lower than Esterri d'Agneu was an energy-sapping walk totalling some nine hours. It was also a reminder of our journey over the French Pyrenees, although this walk lasted only some nine hours and not nearly three days.

Dog-tired as we were, an open truck awaiting us at the small village of Esterri was a most welcome sight. It took us through the by now gloomy gorge to our destination for the night. Dusk was falling as we arrived at brightly-lit Sort in winter's early darkness and were taken to a large cafe in the narrow main street where a representative of the US Consulate was awaiting us. He promptly handed out cartons of American cigarettes and bananas to our American friends and, to my and Robert's delight, did not pass over those two *Hollanders* who had arrived with the 15 American aviators. It sometimes pays to be in an absolute minority. Robert and I had not seen a banana since 1940. We were by now used again to seeing streetlights and the lighted windows of houses, which in German-occupied Europe had been extinguished since May/June 1940 and even earlier in Denmark and Norway.

We were billeted in separate buildings. Robert and I were in the 'Fonda Pessits' where I remember that at dinner the soup tasted like varnish. The next day we were woken up too early by the noise reverberating in the narrow medieval street. After breakfast we just lazed around the village where the *rubios,* light blond chaps like Charles Downe, were the centre of attention of the female population.

In the morning of the 4th of February, an empty milk delivery truck took our party from Sort towards Lerida. The scenery was wild. On either side of the blue/grey and white boulder and rock-strewn beds of the Rio Bonaigua, we gradually made our way up the limestone cliffs. Quite soon we drove along the evergreen shores of the Rio Noguera and along blue lakes and curiously-shaped hills, cliffs and low mountains. Short of Lerida, near a hamlet somewhere past Tremp, the truck suffered a punctured tyre. This brought the truck to a halt. The truck's only spare tyre was back in Sort being repaired. We all walked to the nearby hamlet and, alongside the River Noguera, patiently waited for our escorts, the two *Guardias,* to solve our transport problem.

A small truck was flagged down, but could not carry any more than eight of us under its canvas-covered loading tray behind the driver's cabin. One of our Americans had a pack of cards so we drew cards to decide our immediate fate. Robert belonged to the nine losers and would, with one of the *Guardias,* have to wait for another vehicle. It did not prove to be a calamity for they arrived quite shortly after us in Lerida seated on sawn timber at the back of a truck.

In Lerida we were taken to a police station situated in an old, fortress-like, jail building and put in medieval-looking jail cells with walls and floors of granite blocks, an iron door and small, iron-barred windows with a wooden bench, straw mattress and a tin bucket. The poor sods who must have been 'interviewed' by Torquemada's henchmen in times long past would have been thrown into this cell after being tortured and before being burned at the stake or transferred to dungeons under this old jail. Going by the construction of my cell, this jail must have had dungeons. Since I had been treated courteously by my jailors, my only discomfort was the hard seat and straw mattress in this medieval cell. While in jail I was not without 'entertainment.' I could intermittently hear screams and the dull sound of something connecting with a softer object. This "object" must have found the interrogation methods quite painful. It was an experience which the others, particularly Leonard Cassady, would never forget. He commented on this when he wrote me in 1986.

Later, in Madrid and afterwards, I have often wondered why Robert and I were released from the Lerida jail into *residence forcée* and not sent to *El Campo de Concentration Miranda de Ebro.*

Up to D-Day most, if not all, Hollanders and other illegal entrants were sent to this, far from pleasant, internment camp in which, in 1939, International Brigade soldiers had been locked up. By 1942 the soldiers had moved on and been replaced by larger numbers of illegal entrants who had to share the vermin-infested buildings, cramped quarters and shocking sanitary conditions with Spanish criminals.

Although I never discovered the reason for our lucky break—or indeed why we were never handcuffed—I believe that it was the sheer luck of us arriving with a large contingent of Americans.

Robert van Exter had indeed managed to alert the Dutch Consular Service the day after our crossing the border, but so had Sam Timmers Verhoeven's group of Dutchmen after us. Yet, after two days in Lerida's jail, they were, with their hands fettered, transported to the internment camp Miranda de Ebro, where they would spend more than a month before being released to the Dutch Diplomatic Service in Madrid. Earlier *Engelandvaarder* arrivals, in particular those who arrived in Spain between 1940 and 1942 spent well over a year in the Dark Age conditions of Campo Miranda.

It was here in the *Comisaria de Policia* of Lerida that further evidence of continuous assistance given by the Phalangists to German Intelligence and Security authorities showed up. In late July of 1944 the Dutch Secret Service Agent and *Engelandvaarder,* F. M. Beukers, who left Holland in May, was arrested and detained in Lerida the day after having crossed the frontier. Fred, who had asked for consular assistance, was visited in the jail by a representative of the Dutch Embassy, Captain Eddie Hertzberger, a member of the Dutch BI (Intelligence Bureau). Fred managed to slip a receptacle containing micro-photos of intelligence reports. When Hertzberger informed him that nothing could be done by the Diplomatic Service to speed up his release, Fred decided to complain to the jail's Governor that he, posing as an Army Officer ostensibly taken prisoner at Dieppe during the failed landing in 1942, should be treated as befitted his rank and released from jail. The Governor most courteously agreed but indicated that the Provincial Army Commander, a General, wished to speak with him. The General wanted information about the *Maquis* in the parts of France that Fred had travelled through. Realizing that he had to 'buy' his release he provided plausible information and also indicated incorrect areas where the *Maquisards* were active on the maps they showed him. Two days later he was released.

The next day after Robert and I were released from our cells at Lerida's jail, we were taken from the *Comisaria de Policia Seguridad* to the Hotel Mundial, which was to be our *residence forcée* in Lerida as arranged by the Dutch Consul in Barcelona or the Dutch Embassy in Madrid. Our American friends, irrespective of rank, were put up in the Hotel Palacio, the best hotel in Lerida, as befitting the military of the richest nation. The Dutch and Brits stayed in second class hotels and the French, Poles and Walter Breuer, the only Czech we met in Spain, had to accept accommodation in a third-class hotel or *casa de huéspedes* (guest house), some of which were quite seedy. Many Frenchmen would pose as Canadians who had been shot down or escaped from POW camps in the hope of facilitating their release from Spanish custody.

Recalling Erik Michielsen's postcard to me from Switzerland indicating his having arrived safely in Switzerland in 1942 and which had passed the German censors, I sent a postcard (in the Dutch language) to my parents in Amsterdam to announce my safely reaching Spain. It read:

Dear friends,

How are things? I have not heard from you for ages. Hopefully you are all well. I am fine, although I still have a sore throat, caused by a cold I caught last week. My work is progressing well. Yesterday I finished a painting and I am now busy with a city view of Lerida. I think I'll go to Madrid, or Barcelona in a few weeks' time. I would like to spend some time in a large city again. Lerida is not what you would call a large town although we have seven cinemas here. They show American and German movies dubbed in Spanish. Meals in my hotel are good and my favourite fruits, bananas and oranges, are in plentiful supply. Comparing Spain with Holland, according to your letters, we do not notice much of the war. My dears, I am going to light a 'Lucky' and have a nip. Do write. Adios. 'Rudy'.

On second thought, Robert and I then decided to also send a telegram, reasoning that if mail from neutral countries was duly delivered to addresses in the Occupied countries then why not a telegram. Beside our postcards could well get lost or be destroyed in a bombing raid or lost in the mail. My carefully worded telegram (in the Dutch language) on that 5th day of February read:

HEARTIEST CONGRATULATIONS WHY DON'T YOU WRITE BACK HOTEL MUNDIAL LERIDA HOPE ALL WELL GIVE MY BEST GREETINGS TO ALL—RUDY

Both passed the German censors and duly arrived at No 96 de Lairessestraat in Amsterdam, embellished with German Eagles and Swastika stamps. It was one of those silly things that happened during the War. Some services just carried on as before.

My father would write later that while happy with the good news, it did cause much apprehension and worry of a visit from the SD to enquire about the identity of the sender of the telegram. The feared visit by the SD did not come but I should have thought of it, the more so since I was myself fearful that the Germans, in possession of my Dutch papers, would search my parents' home in Amsterdam and perhaps arrest my father. The thought had worried me greatly at first but later, on second thought, I doubted that the Gestapo would believe that the name and address on my documents, impounded by the Herr Hauptmann, were real. Furthermore, the two German Officers may well have never reported having let a prisoner escape, whilst the Corporal would, as a loyal and true German soldier, never have gone behind his superiors' backs. A doubt, however, kept lingering in my mind until, in June 1945, I received news that my whole family in Amsterdam had survived and had not received a visit from the SD.

That morning we met Tom Bright, a British RAF Sergeant and a "jolly bloke" with whom, from the start, we got on famously. Tom suggested we change from the Hotel Mundial to his hotel, the 'Fonda de Agramunt,' and to our surprise the Dutch Consul from Barcelona, who arrived that afternoon, readily agreed. He also gave us the 90 pesetas weekly 'spending money', provided by the Dutch Government in London. The Dutch Government-in-Exile paid for the accommodation of all Dutch fugitives during their stay in Spain.

We promptly moved into the hotel of Señor Juèlès Ribès where we had a pleasant room overlooking the Plaza d'Espagña. There we shared a dining room table with Tom. We loved the food and were particularly taken with the Spanish custom of providing diners with a *media botella de vino tinto* or *blanco*.

At the behest of the Dutch Consul (in Barcelona), a Spanish general practitioner, Dr. Bordalba, gave *los Subditos Holandèses* injections against Typhus and provided us with the required certificate. In Lerida and in Madrid we were given new clothing paid for by the Dutch Government. My striped, cotton pyjamas must have come from pre-civil-War stock for they soon split straight across the back. I repaired them expertly in Gibraltar by holding the two sides together and simply stitching them up. My expertise provided much amusement to many before the pyjamas fell apart at Lake Sentani in New Guinea a year later.

Already in Julius Caesar's time, there was a citadel built on a mount near the Segre River and Lerida was occupied by the Moors from the 8th to the 12th century. The same Moors, who in 778 A. D. breached the Port de Roncevalles, situated north east of Pamplona in the Pyrenees, were not defeated until they had reached Poitiers just 110 kilometres south of

Tours on the Loire River. The Lerida citadel was partially destroyed by French artillery fire in 1812 and totally destroyed in 1936 during the Civil War. 'Sue Anti', the old cathedral built on the site of a mosque, stands out and dominates the town. It was badly battle-scarred from the Civil War when I saw it in 1944. At that time, it did not occur to me to visit it as our interests were centred on sleep, talk, listening to music and having group photos taken by the street photographers. These photographers had a golden time with the regular arrivals of escaped or fugitive Allied Servicemen from France, Belgium, Holland and Poland as well as the occasional Czech or other nationality. Watching the girls go by while lounging on chairs on the sidewalks on the Plaza de Jose Antonio or Avenida Blondel was a daily, pleasurable pastime.

In Spanish cities, cafes can be found virtually on any street corner, many with tables and chairs on the sidewalks or pavement, and are an indispensable part of everyday Spanish life, as are *tapas* bars. We knew about *bodegas* and *tabernas* in Vielha and Sort but now we discovered the *heladeria* (ice cream parlour) and *pasteleria* (pastry shop), where we spent most of our allowance on *nata con chocolata* (chocolate and cream), pastries, *yogur con mermelada* (a completely new experience) and enjoyed the taste of real coffee again. A favourite haunt was the Café Rialto, although I am not sure whether it was their good-tasting coffee or the waitresses, Carmen and Mercedes, that made this café so popular with us all.

Our American friends left Lerida for an unknown destination before us and so did Tom Bright who gave me his address in London at 105 Varley Road, West Ham and who I would meet again in 1952 while we were walking towards each other on a very crowded Shaftesbury Avenue in Central London. Our unexpected meeting was literally one chance in 8 million!

We were still in Lerida when a party of four older Dutch fugitives arrived, who were (unknown to us at that time) important evaders, whom the Dutch Government-in-Exile needed in London to help prepare with the reconstruction of the Netherlands after the War. They were the police officer Klysingh, Father Leo Laureyssen (a Dutch priest wanted by the Gestapo for his activities in the Paris *Maquis)*, Harrie Guyt (a pilot) who had been in action during the German invasion of the Netherlands, and GJ van Heuven Goedhart (who became a government minister in London). The first three had been spirited away by the Dutch-Paris

Escape Line to Spain, while van Heuven Goedhart, an important Resistance man, had left Holland in the care of another escape line on orders from London.

The Dutch Government, through the Embassy in Madrid must have made urgent representation to the Spanish, for they were moved on to Madrid after only a few days in Lerida, while Robert and I were held for 13 days in this provincial capital.

18.   Escorted by Guardia Civil to Madrid

On the 16th of February we left by a local bus service from the Plaza de Jose Antonio at the ungodly hour of three o'clock in the morning on a pitch-dark night. We were escorted by a good-natured *Guardia Civil,* who nonchalantly carried a rifle, to Zaragoza on the Rio Ebro, some 150 kilometres from Lerida.

We could see little of the countryside and, while I forgot the names of the towns and villages where the bus halted, I still recall the images resembling parts of paintings by Goya and other Spanish artists. I however never forgot the one town called Alfajarin, because the 'Alfa' reminded me of the famous Italian racing cars. The bus also carried goods, apart from baggage, on top of the roof and sometimes we halted for quite a few minutes for produce, cases and bags to be loaded and unloaded. It was therefore not until midday that we arrived at the station of Zaragoza. Our *Guardia* reported our arrival at the bureau of the *Policia* at the station, where we were kept, guarded, in a waiting room. We saw very little of this historic city, where Napoleon's Army in 1808-1809 had to fight from house to house to overcome the courageous defenders.

I should mention that neither Robert nor I (nor any of our Americans) were at any time handcuffed when escorted from town to town, contrary to many *Engelandvaarders* I spoke with or who subsequently wrote to me about their experiences. Other Engelandvaarders were often fettered when arrested after crossing the frontier or after having been 'processed' in Lerida when moved to Campo Miranda and Madrid. I have no satisfactory explanation why Fred Beukers, Robert and I were not thus treated. Here in Zaragoza, Robert and I, again probably because being only the two of us and not in a big group of men who had entered Spain illegally were not, like Sam T. Verhoeven and others, locked up in the city's jail for a whole week. Neither were we transported in handcuffs to Campo Miranda.

Our train for Madrid, which city is, by the way, the highest capital in Europe, left Zaragoza that evening at 20 minutes past nine. Robert, our *Guardia* friend, and I slept the best we could, seated in our first-class compartment. How did I know it was a first-class compartment? I still have the train ticket.

I could not see any war damage from the Civil War of 1936-39. But it was during the attack on Madrid in October 1936 that the Nationalist's General Mola spoke of his Fourth Columns and a Fifth Column in Madrid. Ever since then the expression "the Fifth Column" has come to mean the enemy within.

It was exactly 8.30 a.m. when our train came to a stop at the Egad de Atocha in Madrid. We took leave, most cordially, from 'our' *Guardia* with his three-cornered hat, after he had handed us over to the police station's duty officer.

The Security Police issued us with an identity document, dated the 17th of February, stating that we had entered Spain *clandestinamente* (illegally). It was signed on behalf of the Director (Superintendent) *Policia Seguridad*. At that time the *Policia Seguridad* was the equivalent of the Nazi's *Sicherheitsdienst*. We were instructed to report every Saturday to the *Direccion General de Seguridad* on the Puerta del Sol and released into the custody of the Dutch Diplomatic Service.

The Dutch Intelligence Officer at the Dutch Embassy in Madrid, Captain Hertzberger, interviewed us, individually of course, before we left for the Hotel Internacional, Arenal 19, where a great number of *Engelandvaarders* were already accommodated, some already for quite some time.

Radio Oranje had broadcast that *Engelandvaarders,* soon after their arrival in England, were received for afternoon tea by Queen Wilhelmina. So when Captain Hertzberger's first question was why I wanted to get to England, I was so taken aback by what I considered an idiotic question that I nearly replied: *"Because I want to have tea with Queen Wilhelmina."* However, realising that he was required by his superiors in London to ask this question, I gave him one of those answers which many evaders, before and after me, must have given.

It is of interest to mention that Captain Edmond (Eddy) Hertzberger was a recognisable Jew, who, with his half-Jewish wife, Lore, had made their way via a safe house (an Antwerp brothel) to life-saving freedom in Switzerland, then to later reach Spain via Andorra. In his group of evaders was also Jan Sorrier, a KNIL (Royal Netherlands Indies Army) Officer, who became the Chief of BI, the Dutch Intelligence Bureau in London. Another was Willem Anthonie Mayer who, only a short time before his execution was to take place, had been freed from his death cell by the *Ondergrondse* (Dutch Resistance).

While brothels proved to be good safe houses, and would seem to be so for male evaders and escapees for obvious reasons, Mrs. Eleonore Hertzberger's sharing a room in a brothel with her husband showed otherwise. The *bordellos* swarmed with Germans who had something quite different in mind than checking identity cards and arresting the male population of these venerable establishments and, one must assume, any females that they encountered.

I am not aware whether many *Engelandvaarders* made use of *bordellos* as safe havens, but there is no doubt that the *Maquis* did use them frequently to hide Allied airmen.

The next day, we had to report the story of our trip and escape to the Intelligence Officer at the British Embassy (and repeat it all over again twice more in Gibraltar). Then we had to tell our story several more times after our arrival in England where we were temporarily interned at the Battersea Grammar School and Royal Victoria Patriotic School in London. The reason why everybody had to repeat their story so often was obviously to spot discrepancies in the re-telling of our escape. The fact that I had been arrested by the Germans and escaped from custody within ten minutes and Robert somehow had avoided arrest, although we had been together at the time, caused MI5 to interview us very closely. Although the only three people who could corroborate our reports were Albert Starink, Ann de Casalette and Robert's father in German-occupied Paris, real spies would surely not have thought up such a story. Later in London, the man who wrote the Spymaster books, Lt. Colonel Oreste Pinto (a Major when I met him), would play his part in the interrogation saga.

The day after our arrival in Madrid, we were issued with a certificate, signed by the Consul General, which stated our (new) Dutch passport number. Mine was No 33676, dated 18-02-1944. They were, however, only handed to us on the day of our departure from Madrid. We were handed a visa for Portugal stating *"Bon pour le voyage destination Surinam 23/2/1944"*.

While I cannot but praise the assistance that Robert and I received from Dutch diplomats in Madrid, this—with a few exceptions—was not the case in the early years of the War. This rather shameful episode in the history of Dutch consular officialdom in the early years of the War is mentioned in personal accounts of *Engelandvaarders*. Early arrivals discovered to their astonishment that some consular individuals had no intention of assisting in a speedy departure for England. These fossilized types who had not experienced any hardship, having had the good fortune to be posted to Spain and the Vichy-governed part of France before the German invasion of Holland on the 10th of May 1940, showed conspicuous indifference to the plight and aspirations of compatriots who had escaped from German-occupied Holland and wanted to join free Dutch forces in England. Their attitude was more or less along the lines of: *"These people have no valid papers. All decent citizens possess the required documents and do not cross borders illegally. Besides we do not want any trouble or to disturb our official relationship with the Spaniards and French. Anyway, they are all a gang of irregulars; all whipper-snappers with plenty of 'lip'."*

As unbelievable as it may seem, the following comments were made to *Engelandvaarder*, Herman Speyer, in 1942 by a Dutch Honorary Consul: *"What do you intend to do here? We suggest that you return to the Netherlands by the same route."*

I must presume that when this unacceptable state of affairs became known in London, Queen Wilhelmina instructed her Government to take "necessary steps". Later arrivals, like Robert and I, found a different attitude prevailing from the moment we contacted the Consulate in Barcelona.

The atmosphere at the Hotel Internacional, where we were put up, is best described as a holiday hotel for young men who had just passed their university or high school exams, and larrikins. Amongst the high spirited but amiable group there were, however, also a handful of men who I and others felt 'did not belong'.

After dinner on our second or third night in Madrid, Robert van Exter caused a small panic when he had what seemed to be a heart attack.

Luckily there was a young doctor or medical student, also a fugitive, staying at our hotel. The student, Fred, wrote a request in Spanish on a slip of paper and I set off in a taxi to find an all-night pharmacy. It took some searching by the taxi driver to find an all-night *pharmacia* while Fred (neither Robert nor I can recall his surname) attended to Robert and he recovered completely from his heart-rhythm disturbance.

As to 'Doctor' Fred, who had been in Madrid for some time, the rumour was that he was suspected of being a German agent. We never found out the truth, but were glad he was there that anxious night and hoped that the suspicion was groundless. Robert, in fact, a month and a half later, in April, passed the RAF medical and became a wireless operator after spending a short period with the *Bureau Bijzondere Opdrachten* (SOA equivalent). He subsequently resigned from the Bureau after having received a warning from a friend of his father, the then Minister of Defence, Jhr OCA van Lidth de Jeude, about too many men being lost on secret missions. Only towards the end of 1943 was it revealed that the *Abwehr* (German Military Intelligence) had infiltrated the SOE's Netherlands operations in the Netherlands.

One day we were invited to the British Embassy to view our first English-speaking movie since 1940. It was 'Mrs. Miniver', a famous movie of that time, about the 1940s and the Dunkirk evacuation of British, French, Dutch and Belgian troops. It was also at this Embassy that a secretary was to meet and marry an *Engelandvaarder* called Dolf Mantel, who had crossed the Pyrenees in Sam T. Verhoeven's group of March 1944. In August 1945, Dolf and I would meet and serve as Supply Officers in Merauke, a settlement which is situated in, what I can only describe as, the swampy badlands of Dutch New Guinea. Like so many *Engelandvaarders,* Dolf revisited the Pyrenees several times after the war and on his last visit, accompanied by his daughter, suffered a fatal heart attack. His grave is in Auch at the foothills of the Pyrenees.

I must mention a delightful prank pulled by a few *Engelandvaarders* in Madrid in 1942, which J. J. Hommes described in the periodical De Schakel of April 1998. This magazine is published by the *Engelandvaarder's* Association. Allow me to translate:

> *Every week we presented ourselves at the British Embassy where, free of*
> *charge, we received a ration of English cigarettes, which were a lot better than*

the Spanish rubbish. We became very friendly with the staff at the Embassy, where we were treated as one of their own. The Embassy seemed like paradise to us. Anything you wanted you could get there. Food, drinks, tobacco, clothes—you mention it, they had it.

When we expressed our amazement about it the Brits admitted that their lifestyle in Madrid was very comfortable indeed. The only thing they lacked was good, drinkable beer. It was too bulky to transport and not considered essential and they were therefore dependent on Spanish beer and that was undrinkable, lousy stuff at that time. The only people who had good beer were those at the German Embassy. They received, every month, a special consignment from Dortmund and München through their regular Spanish wine and beer importer.

A week passed and it was by then already July 1942. We decided to take the risk and took a taxi to the importer where, once inside, we asked them what was happening with the monthly German beer order. Well, the consignment had arrived, they told us. It would be delivered to the German Embassy in a few days. We explained to the importer that there would be a big party at the German Embassy that evening and that we had been instructed to ensure that there would be enough beer for the guests. Would the importer therefore please load the consignment into the waiting taxi. We would, of course, sign for receipt of the beer. No sooner said than done.

The beer was loaded into the taxi and we signed the invoice for receipt, whereupon we drove straight to the British Embassy and delivered this special consignment. The Embassy staff thought it was a marvellous trick and were 'over the moon'.

We were of the opinion that we owed the English that much and that it was the best thing we could do in return. That it wasn't legal did not impress upon us at all, nor on the Brits! After all, we had fooled the Germans and that was good enough for us.

The Dutch Ambassador, Jonkheer (The Honourable) Schueller tot Peursum, and his wife also had a number of us to lunch at their residence. No silverware went missing that day and I say this ironically and not jokingly. There were, namely, some rather unsavoury types—four or five youngish men who we suspected had not made their way to Spain to fight the Nazis for "Queen and Fatherland" nor to avoid being arrested for their activities in the Resistance but rather for breaking and entering. They were nick-named '*de Rotterdamse roeiploeg*' (the Rotterdam rowing gang). When they had been for a Saint Nicolas dinner at the Ambassador's residence on the 5th of December, various items of gilded cutlery and other Embassy silverware went missing. These no doubt passed into the hands of fences to supplement their pocket money because it was known that they had also sold furniture from their Hotel Internacional bedrooms and clothing provided to them by the Consulate, at the local flea-market. Although food and drink were available in pre-war abundance, there was a profitable market for clothing, and of course valuable items in Spain.

A fellow *Engelandvaarder,* however, told me an amusing anecdote about *de Roeiploeg.* It appeared that their exploits even extended to having "bills for services rendered" at high class brothels to its 'diplomats' presented to the Embassy of the Netherlands.

Mrs. Schueller tot Peursum was quite active looking after the welfare of escapees during their stay in Madrid, but the Ambassador was quite clearly not in good physical health. He walked with difficulty and appeared old for his age. It was fortunate, therefore, that Consul General DLA Gastmann, who had not long ago been posted to Madrid, seemed energetic in pursuing the interests of us escapees.

Madrid stands at the nearly exact centre of Spain, where in winter the sun, at times, can be deceptively warm on the face and yet you need a heavy overcoat to shield you against the dry, crisp, icy air. The stylish woollen overcoats, paid for by our Government, were therefore most welcome when venturing outside the Hotel Internacional.

In the six days that Robert and I spent in this beautiful city, there was not enough time, nor was our allowance of 90 pesetas a week sufficient, to enjoy all its beauty and cultural life. However, many a time we visited the Calle de Alcala, Avenida de Jose Antonio and especially the Calle de Chichilleros which can be reached by descending covered stairs from the delightful Plaza Mayor and where you could (then) find a great number of small *tapas* (savouries) bars and eateries serving *Jerez* (sherry) for only one peseta.

In Madrid the evening meal is eaten even later than in northern Spain and sitting down at the dinner table at 10 p.m. is not unusual but not easy to quickly adapt to. We could not, of course, afford to eat at *Madrilenos* restaurants but the food at our second-class Hotel Internacional was, to our unspoiled tastes, superb compared to the rations under German occupation in Holland.

The visit to the famous Museo del Prado, one of the great museums of the world, was memorable, not only for the paintings of Velasquez, Goya and El Greco, but also to see so many works of Dutch masters, some perhaps purloined by the Spanish during our 80-year War of Independence of the 16th and 17th centuries.

Spain was 'officially' neutral during World War II, but the sympathies of Dictator Francisco Franco and the Phalangist (fascist) Party were for Hitler's Germany which had rendered valuable assistance to the Nationalists during the Civil War, and a Spanish division was fighting with the Germans on the Eastern Front. However, after the battles of El Alamein and Stalingrad, the Spanish authorities became more compliant and by the end of 1943, if not earlier, they would issue exit permits even to men of military age. Previously it was necessary on *Engelandvaarders* passports issued in Madrid to declare one's age. Now one could write in an age which the Spanish did not consider to be eligible for Nazi military service. There must have been some old-looking youngsters of 16 to 17 years of age and young-looking oldsters of 40 years and over leaving Spanish territory for Portugal in the early War years!

Robert's and my true ages, 22 and 24, were stated on the new Dutch passports issued to us in Madrid and our destination on the transit visa was the Dutch West Indies/Surinam via Portugal.

19.   Leaving Madrid for Portugal

On the 23rd of February we were told that our departure from Madrid, for our journey to England, would take place the next afternoon. We all celebrated the news in style but a few thought that the occasion called for a last BIG party. Among them were Boel van de Ende, Rend de Vries, Harry Wins and Jack Bottenheim, who caused some anxiety when they had not returned to their hotels by the morning of the 24th. The anxiety turned to alarm when they had not showed up by the time we were all collected by bus and transported to the station. I was particularly worried because Boel van de Ende had borrowed my new, Spanish, grey flannel suit to leave a lasting impression on his Spanish girlfriend on their last evening together.

At the very last moment, perhaps only five minutes before our train was to leave, a flustered Jack Bottenheim, accompanied by a consular official, ran towards the carriages and boarded our train. It appeared that some of his party, in drunken revelry, had, among other things, like Tarzans, been swinging from the overhead telephone lines of the Department of Foreign Affairs. When arrested by the guards, Jack, who spoke Spanish, had been their spokesman and had talked his way out of detention. He told us that he had accompanied the others but, while having had quite a few drinks himself, had refrained from their antics and was not playing 'Tarzan' when the guards had appeared. The arresting officers could corroborate his account of events at the interrogation and he was released. I cannot recall whether Jack mentioned at what time he was set free, apparently into the custody of a Dutch Consular official. The official had tried to secure the release of all four of them Harry wrote me, long after the end of the War. After an initial booking procedure and interview, Jack Bottenheim, who acted as their spokesman, was released. Harry did not say at what time Jack was released, but stated that at 4.00 a.m. in the morning the three of them were brought before a military judge and his staff to be interrogated. Since none of them spoke Spanish, a female interpreter was called to assist. She spoke clear Dutch, but Harry noted a faint German accent. She explained that they would all be freed that same morning to join their already-released friend if they signed the statement presented to them. Most unwisely, believing it was the same statement that Bottenheim—who knew the Spanish language—had signed, all three of them, without being able to read a word of it, duly put their signatures to the document.

They had then been incarcerated in an indescribably filthy prison with some 400 prisoners, all dregs of society, and had only been able to find room next to the toilet block where six flooded toilets forced them to stand for the rest of the night. It had taken four weeks before the Dutch Foreign Service representative had been allowed to meet them and learned that they had signed a document admitting entering Spain to spy for a foreign power, to commit acts of sabotage, and a whole string of other offences against the Spanish State. They had actually signed their own death warrant.

There was little or no doubt that the Phalangist-controlled Military Police had intended to get a conviction and knew that they could not fool the Spanish-speaking Bottenheim and therefore purposely let him go. The three others fell into a trap to obtain a confession for spying, if only for propaganda purposes. Perhaps this was a way to vent their fascist anger at the Allies.

They all did eventually reach England after the Normandy invasion, but only after four months in their hellhole among murderers, pickpockets, rapists and other low life, and not before the Dutch Consulate managed to get them transferred to the jurisdiction of a Civil Court which passed a 'not guilty' verdict. They were, however, not released until the Dutch Embassy had paid 100,000 pesetas for each of them at the end of August 1944.

Harry posed the question: *"How was it possible for Jack Bottenheim to get away that easily in a couple of hours and we were charged with God knows what?"* He added: *"What did he tell the police to get himself free?"* Regrettably, Harry did not get an opportunity to meet Jack Bottenheim again, for it would have put Harry's mind at ease to have heard the facts from Jack.

Not surprisingly my new, grey flannel suit did not survive Boel's ordeal. The last time Harry Wins saw him again was in Batavia in 1946, when Boel recounted how in 1945 he had been dropped by parachute in, or near, the Japanese internment camp where his mother had spent three years of her life in most miserable conditions.

Because of the commotion caused by the arrest of the four *Engelandvaarders* on that 24ᵗʰ day of February 1944, we saw very little of the countryside after leaving Madrid Station at 5 p.m. In the early winter darkness, and under overcast skies, we were also deprived of getting an impression of Toledo and its surroundings. Robert and I shared our railway compartment with the future Chairman of the *Engelandvaarders'* Association, Frans Th. Dijckmeester, Theo R. W. Valck Lucassen, Hugo 'Tip' Visser, and, if I remember correctly, van Rossum Schiff and Jan Onderwater. I cannot recall what we had for dinner that evening, but I can remember clearly the uncomfortable night we spent sitting in our compartment trying, as best we could, to get some sleep while leaning against one of our neighbours like canned sardines.

20. A Surprise Destination Awaits Us

In the course of the next morning, after crossing the Sierra de San Pedro, the train halted at 8.15 a.m. at the railyards of Valencia de Alcantara and remained stationary for nearly four hours waiting for a Portuguese locomotive to take us over the border into Portugal. Our train crossed the Portuguese frontier at about 11.30 a.m. Portuguese time and halted for a few minutes at Marvao-Beira before it resumed its slow journey through extensive cork tree groves on both sides of the frontier. To our surprise, it steamed along in a southerly direction, by-passing Lisbon which we had expected to be our destination.

After another most uncomfortable night we finally, on the morning of the 26th of February, noticed the welcome smell of sea air and shortly thereafter we disembarked at Villa Real de San Antonio, a small fishing town on the Rio Guadiana which river marks the border between Portugal and Spain. In later years, some *Engelandvaarders* would occasionally be reminded of this small fishing town by sardine cans sporting the words "Villa Real de San Antonio" on the label.

At the station in Madrid I had already noted a large contingent of Poles but no escapees from other countries. It would be much later that I learned that through the personal connections with the Polish Secret Service of the BI (Dutch Intelligence) Chief, Major J. M. Somer, the Dutch were allowed to use the semi-official route established between the Poles, the Spanish and Portuguese Governments to travel in a secured train from Madrid via Portugal to Villa Real de San Antonio. We were not allowed to leave the train anywhere and it did not stop at any station. I believe that the Spanish preferred 'not to know' that the train would be diverted from the final destination of Lisbon to Villa Real, the Portuguese port nearest to Gibraltar. Major Somer, already in his forties, was in the Resistance before escaping to England.

Our escorts from the Dutch and Polish Consular Services led us from the railway station to a nearby quay alongside the river where a small ship, of less than 1000 tons, was moored. The main deck hardly rose above the level of the quay and we therefore did not notice at first that its hull and funnel were painted grey, while what looked like deck cargo was covered with tarpaulins. A not unfriendly but uncommunicative crew, dressed in plain dark blue jerseys and trousers, directed us to various parts of the small ship. We were no sooner aboard when, just before midday, it cast off and, hardly three miles off the coast, the canvas covers were removed to reveal a small cannon and anti-aircraft guns, while simultaneously the crew shed their jerseys to reveal Royal Navy Uniforms. This Royal Navy ship was a corvette or similar patrol vessel called the HMS 'Tenterfoot'.

Quite soon after leaving Villa Real de San Antonio, the weather deteriorated and by late afternoon we were buffeted by ever-increasing waves. The wind blew up to a gale.

In view of the very restricted sleeping accommodation, we would have to split up into two groups, each being allowed only four hours of rest on bunks. Robert and I, as well as most of the second group, decided to spend the night in the fresh air on deck. The rough seas forced us to tie a rope across the front deck from the starboard to the port-side to help secure ourselves against the upper structure on the deck of the pitching ship. The only faint lights on the coast of Spain that we could see, when darkness fell, were those of Tarifa near the cape of the same name. At dawn the wind eased and the sky cleared from black to dark grey, enabling us to see the coast of Spain and, after sailing into the Bahia de Algeciras, the large bay on the western side of Gibraltar, the waves decreased. Quite soon we saw the silhouette of 'The Rock' as well as merchant ships and war ships lying at anchor, obviously waiting to be moored in the harbour or to be formed up into convoys. It was a true display of military might, especially with the many aeroplanes circulating The Rock or taking off and landing on its airfield.

While describing the approach to 'The Rock', I must mention an outstanding feat of courage and determination that took place in 1942 when the 18-year-old *Engelandvaarder*, Bart Bredero, crawled undetected under barbed wire fences at the Spanish town of La Linea, which were swept by a searchlight and guarded by Spanish frontier police, to swim across the bay to one of the merchant ships lying anchored off the main harbour. Besides Bart, the only other man ever known to have attempted this feat was Louis Remy. Airey Neave wrote, in his book *Saturday at MI9*, about this young Belgian Air Force Officer who, like Neave, escaped from the famous and notorious Colditz internment camp. Louis Remy tried to swim the 20 kilometres from Algeria, west of La Linea, to Gibraltar and very nearly drowned. He was rescued by the Royal Navy.

Martha Gellhorn, the American journalist and wife of the famous author Ernest Hemmingway, wrote a sympathetic and quite extensive story in the March 1944 issue of the American magazine Colliers about *Engelandvaarders* and 'Oranjehaven', the club in London created by Queen Wilhelmina for *Engelandvaarders*. Bart's story was included, but Bart the young Dutchman became "a Dutch girl who swam the mined [sic!] waters from La Linea to an English ship at anchor just off the harbour of Gibraltar."

At around nine o'clock in the morning of the 27th of February, the HMS Tenterfoot entered the inner harbour and moored at a quay. We were the second batch of *Engelandvaarders* to reach Gibraltar within a matter of weeks and brought the total number up to about 130. It was to be the largest group of *Engelandvaarders* to assemble until annual reunions after the War. The first group had left Madrid over the same route and had already organised various activities, an important one being field hockey.

After the 'Tenterfoot' had tied up at a wharf and we descended the gangplank, a small British reception committee was awaiting us on the quay. Our names were checked off against the Tenterfoot's passenger list and then we had to hand in the two English pounds we had each received in Madrid in exchange for two Gibraltar pounds. We were issued with British uniforms; a woollen battle dress, embellished with a shoulder patch showing the Lion of Orange emblem with the letters *'Nederland'* and other standard issue items, including a tropical khaki outfit to complete our military dress. The woollen material was so rough and itchy that it caused me to always wear pyjama pants under my uniform until I was issued with an American uniform.

On military raincoats, as worn by British Officers, it is hard to notice the rank insignia. In the evening, Robert and I would sometimes don ours—which had survived the Pyrenees sojourn and had been dry-cleaned in Madrid—and the sentries at Government House would, to our amusement, invariably spring to attention when we walked past. We in turn would smartly, but nonchalantly, return the salute.

During the daytime we would roam through the narrow streets of Gibraltar town where one would seldom see civilians or a woman, for it was truly one large military gathering-place. As a consequence of this virtually all-male society there were only all-female orchestras playing in the bars of wartime Gibraltar. These bars did a roaring trade for it was about the only place where men, starved of female company, could at least look *at* girls. One of the world-famous tunes of that time was *'Besame Mucho'* (kiss me often) which invariably caused a vocal reaction from the bar's patrons when sung by the pretty singer.

Ritmeester (Captain) Pahud de Mortange, also an *Engelandvaarder* and a famous Olympic horseman, was appointed our Commanding Officer and, during daylight hours, those with military experience tried to introduce military bearing, discipline, drill and the art of saluting correctly to those who had not yet served in the military in Holland. When not thus involved we were free to find our own amusements. On this small peninsula there was of course, to Robert's and my regret, not only no room for a golf course but also no space for a full-size hockey pitch. The six-aside matches against British teams, held on the asphalt parade grounds, were invariably won by the *Engelandvaarder* team. Two of the hockey-players were Jaap Jongeneel and Herman van Nouhuys who would represent the USA at the 1956 Melbourne Olympics. Jongeneel described the playing areas—cordoned off by wooden barriers of about one-foot height—as resembling an asphalt surfaced ice-hockey rink.

We were interrogated twice by British Intelligence Officers and no doubt their notes, and those from Madrid, were forwarded to MI6 in England to be compared with notes to be taken on our subsequent interrogation after arrival in Britain.

Gibraltar was conquered by British and, as is not generally known, by Dutch Naval forces in the 18th century. To be exact, it was conquered on the 4th of August 1704. It was not blacked out since it would have stood out as a black silhouette against the lights of the Spanish mainland.

A number of us were housed in a white-painted stone building called the Moorish Castle, which was some distance above the town and up the western slope of 'The Rock'. It was not far from the edge of the sheer cliff on the Spanish side, from where we had a superb view over the isthmus on which the airfield is situated. Every evening—and sometimes during the day—we would enjoy the sight of the fully-lighted Spanish Coast and the town of Gibraltar and airfield, where planes waited in rows to take off, or circulated at various heights above The Rock area waiting their turn to land. The time lapse between take-off and landing must have been in the space of three minutes, a truly unforgettable spectacle. That an accident could and would occasionally happen seemed unavoidable, if only by the law of averages. The Commander of the Free-Polish forces, the Polish General Sikorski, was killed when his plane crashed on takeoff. The runway is built on partly-reclaimed land between The Rock and the Spanish border. Its eastern end runs into the Bahia de Algeciras and on the west to a stretch of beach on the Mediterranean Sea. There was also a strong searchlight mounted on top of The Rock which would at irregular intervals sweep its beam over the ships at anchor in the bay, from the La Linea border area across the bay into the Straits of Gibraltar.

It was in Gibraltar that we met up briefly with the RAF Navigator of our original group of 13, who had started out at the Gare d'Austerlitz in Paris on the 26th of January. He and the six American aviators had, after we had been separated in Toulouse, crossed into Andorra and then Spain. The British, he said, had permission from the Spanish Government to transfer their sick or wounded countrymen, from anywhere in Spain, by ambulance to Gibraltar. The *"May I have a light please"* Navigator had thus journeyed to Gibraltar. I have little doubt the Spanish authorities were aware of this, but it served them well to retain a cordial relationship with Britain whilst at the same time appearing not to work against their old friends, the Nazis. Another way of spiriting men to Gibraltar was by hiding them under the mailbags in the British Embassy's mail-van before reaching the Spanish frontier at La Linea de Conception. After a perfunctory check by the Spanish and as soon as the vehicle had crossed the airstrip into Gibraltar proper, the traveller re-appeared from his uncomfortable hiding place under the mailbags.

We also learned that the American Air Force fugitives and escapees received a most friendly reception from the Spanish Air Force and were bussed from Spanish Air Force bases to Gibraltar. Leonard Cassady and James Hussong confirmed this in correspondence after the war.

On the 7th of March we were told to pack our kitbags and personal luggage and to be ready to leave the next day for England. The SS 'Orduña' was moored at the quay on the southwestern arm of the pier protecting the harbour. We noted several other cargo and passenger ships being boarded. There were also a greater number of ships at anchor out in the roads. The SS 'Orduña' was full of Montgomery's 'Desert Rats' and other Allied servicemen returning home from the battlefields of North Africa, Sicily and the Italian peninsula. We were accommodated in the bow area of the ship, three decks down in the hold. This is the worst place to be if the ship were to strike a floating mine. We would also be the last to reach the open deck in the event of a torpedo attack. I was glad it was 1944 and not 1941. To our disappointment, we did not depart for England until about midday of the 9th of March and during daylight read the 'Gibraltar Chronicle' (cost one penny), played cards or spoke with some of the 130 *Engelandvaarders* we had not yet met, and discovered friends from school days in Java and in Holland. In the evenings we wished we could have gone to the Royal Navy cinema to see a movie (for only one shilling). We found the reverberations of the explosions of depth-charges being exploded in the seas around Gibraltar most annoying, causing someone to remark that he would have even preferred *"to look at the bl---- monkeys for three days on end"* than hang around on the 'Orduña', a sentiment shared by many.

The oppressive heat and poor ventilation in the hold made most of us spend the nights on deck, even when at sea, until the convoy reached deep into the Atlantic, well west of the coast of Ireland, where the colder Atlantic nights drove us back down below. The indescribable latrines where we had to sit in rows of some 20 toilets facing each other, and without partitions, were more degrading than the most primitive latrines in New Guinea.

Our convoy, which was quite large but not huge consisted, all in all, of 19 troopships, with the battleship 'Warspite' in the centre, escorted by a host of minesweepers, corvettes, destroyers and a cruiser. The 'Warspite' had been damaged by enemy fire near Salerno off the Italian coast and was returning to Britain for repairs.

One of the first evenings, sailing over a smooth ocean, was unforgettable for anyone who was on deck when thousands of men on our and other ships, sailing near us, spontaneously burst out into song. It pulled at your heart strings to listen to "It's a Long Way to Tipperary," "Over There," "My Bonnie Lies Over the Ocean," while the convoy sailed under the clear, bright night sky.

Once out of sight of the Spanish and North African coasts and sailing into the darkness of the Atlantic Ocean, the need to extinguish all lights became necessary again to avoid attracting the attention of U-boats. However, during our whole trip into the Atlantic and around Northern Ireland no U-boats appeared to have spotted our convoy. The escorting RN warships dropped no depth-charges.

Once deeper and more northerly into the Atlantic, we were in range of and shadowed by the coastal patrols of RAF's flying boats and other long-range aircraft. Some poor souls found the Atlantic swells too much to endure. As a result, one of my youth-time friends, Co Vink, spent most of the six-day voyage with seasickness, wrapped in a blanket, on deck. Most of us, sleeping in the holds, silently prayed or kept our fingers crossed that no U-boat would aim a torpedo at the SS 'Orduña'.

Six days after leaving Gibraltar, and sailing in a wide arch around Ireland, and just after a cold dawn on the 15th of March, our convoy arrived in the roads off the Mersey River. A short religious service was held very early that morning to give thanks for our safe passage and arrival, and we were welcomed by the tooting of ship's sirens— the traditional, exhilarating welcome for a convoy reaching safe harbour. The troopships then made their way from the Irish Sea up the river to Liverpool's wharves.

I must dwell for a moment on the naval victories at sea which were as vital, if not more so, than any land battle of World War II. By the end of 1943, the "Battle of the Atlantic" had been won by the Allies, but in the first quarter of 1943, German U-boats had torpedoed and sunk over 600,000 tons of Allied shipping. In 1942 over 6 million tons had gone to the bottom of Neptune's domain not only because of the increased number of U-boats but also because of the protection afforded the U-boats by the huge concrete pens in St Nazaire and Brest situated on Occupied France's Atlantic Coast. In 1944 the U-boats were fitted with a *Schnorkel*, which enabled them to 'breathe' fresh air when submerged. This air-ventilation apparatus, which stuck out above the periscope, allowed the U-boats to remain under water for many weeks and made detection far more difficult. This resulted in a slight increase in the number of Allied ships torpedoed.

To illustrate the bravery of merchant seamen during World War I and World War II, let me quote from an article which appeared in the quarterly publication of NESWA, the Dutch Ex-Servicemen's and Women's Association in Australia:

Who could forget the horrors of the Atlantic Convoys, in ships which in most instances were unable to defend themselves, and were at the mercy of a ruthless enemy day and night for anything up to a month at a time. In the so called 'Battle of the Atlantic', just under 3,000 Allied and neutral Merchant ships were sunk by enemy action between 1939 and 1945, with heavy losses of life.

Those nightmare trips to Archangel and Murmansk, fighting the rigours of an Atlantic winter, while under continuous enemy attack, to see that essential war equipment, supplies and food-stuffs got through to our Russian Allies. Those hard-fought convoys to the little but gallant island of Malta in the Mediterranean, on which so much of the War in the Middle East depended.

One of the greatest sea battles was 'Operation Pedestal' fought by 14 Merchant ships and a large fleet of Naval ships over five days of continuous warfare, from under the water, over the water and in the air, trying to get essential supplies to Malta in 1942.

In the Indian Ocean, the south Atlantic and in the Pacific, the threat of surface raiders and submarines were ever present and in Australian home waters 55 Merchant ships were sunk by enemy action.

Wherever the War was located, Merchant ships were there, taking troops and essential supplies to the heart of the action. The traversing of these supply lines by Merchant ships was an extremely hazardous occupation. The whole maritime world was their battleground.

From the moment they left port, the Merchant ship and her crew were at war, not knowing when they might be blown up or disabled in some fashion. A look at some figures of the cost to the Merchant Service deserves some contemplation: 4,996 ships lost; 48,500 Merchant Seamen killed in action; 4,000 Merchant Seamen wounded and 5,000 taken as prisoners of war. It has been estimated that the Merchant Service losses amounted to one in six, compared to the combined armed forces of one in 33. It is also interesting to note that of the total casualties of Merchant Seamen, only 8.25 per cent were wounded, and 91.75 per cent killed, compared to 79 per cent wounded and 21 per cent killed of the combined Armed Forces.

21. The Royal Victoria Patriotic School

In sharp contrast to brightly-lit Gibraltar, a black-out, was still in effect in Great Britain. When night fell, we watched darkness overtake the city of Liverpool from the deck of the 'Orduña'.

Early the next morning the large contingent of evaders and escapees from several countries were herded by a handful of British soldiers onto a train bound for London which left a little after midday. Reaching the outskirts of London in the early winter twilight, the row upon row of adjoining homes with their minute back-gardens backing on to the railway lines reminded me of my first visit to London in 1938 when arriving on the 'Harwich boat train.'

Nearer the city centre there was evidence of bomb damage dramatized by the grimy black soot of untold years of coal-fired smoke deposits on the buildings. The smoke was also the cause of a true London 'pea-souper' which I had experienced on my first visit to the city. The pea soup had, by the late afternoon, come down quickly while I called on motoring magazine sports editors for discussions and to deliver drawings for illustrations in The Motor and Speed magazines. It was so thick that in the gloom one could not see anything beyond ten feet on that October afternoon in 1938.

On arrival at Euston Station we were loaded into army trucks and transported through Central London to the Battersea Grammar School, which had been converted into a holding camp. Driving through the streets of London, across the Thames into Wandsworth, we could clearly see the recent bomb damage caused by air attacks of the previous month.

I can't remember much about our stay at this holding facility, except for us playing football or cards and talking about our escape from Holland to Spain. Many had spent time at the notorious Campo Miranda de Ebro, crowded not only with refugees from German-occupied Western Europe but also murderers and rapists. They were housed in wooden barracks provided with only three badly-functioning water taps and, what one chap described as *"an international latrine."* Dysentery was, consequently, rife. The situation at the other internment camp, not far from Bilbao, called Uberuaga de Ubilla, seemed no better. Most had also experienced a spell in a Spanish jail and all for much longer periods than Robert and I. Nearly all I spoke to had at one time or another been handcuffed. Here at the Battersea Grammar I was also, but only once, interviewed by an officer from MI5.

On the 30th of March, we were moved to the Royal Victoria Patriotic School, situated on Wandsworth Common and not far from Wandsworth Prison. The building had been requisitioned early in WWII and at first was used as an internment and interrogation centre for refugees from Europe. The Royal Victoria Patriotic School was a dreary place with stone-flagged corridors and a gloomy atmosphere but, for me—and especially those who had been inmates of camps like Campo Miranda—it was a sombre but not a particularly unpleasant place.

The RVPS building is not far from Clapham Junction in Wandsworth and was bought in 1950 by the London City Council for a school and later, when in disrepair, sold to an enterprise which transformed it into 29 luxury apartments, 25 studios, a drama school and a restaurant called 'le Gothique.' My British nephew, Jim Connor, and his wife, Pauline, were married there in 2002. He wrote to me: *"Rudy should know that the venue was chosen in his honour as he was imprisoned in this building for questioning after his great escape."* Times change! The food served at their wedding party was a far cry from the disgusting meals served to us internees by the appointed caterers, Lyons Tea houses. I have ever since, in spite of their good reputation, avoided Lyons establishments.

Another unpleasant memory of the RVPS was vermin. I can still see the red creepy crawlies and some of the indistinct dark coloured forms crawling on the walls.

Quite soon after our arrival *Engelandvaarders* received a parcel containing reading material as well as a most useful pack of cards and a welcoming letter from the 'Welfare Committee for the Netherlands Fighting Forces.'

Among the internees of many nations, during my stay at least, the Dutch were the largest contingent, closely followed by the French and Poles. Apart from Belgians, there was a solitary Russian, whom we called Boris, although that wasn't his real name. It was likely that he had, like other Russians, joined the *Wehrmacht* after having been made a POW on the Eastern Front and deserted when stationed in France. After interrogation at the RVPS, Soviet citizens would be handed over to the Soviet Embassy in London. Their fate, which we only learned long after the War ended, was very grim. Stalin had Soviet POWs either shot or sent to a *gulag* for five months hard labour if lucky, more often for many years. Poor 'Boris' must have awaited a most unpleasant fate.

The daily routine was similar to the Battersea Grammar but at the RVPS there were no football pitches. I did not mix much with other nationalities and while I admired the Poles, I nearly came to blows with one most annoying individual.

When it was not raining we would frequent the yard or the barbed-wire-fenced garden, which partly adjoined the green expanse of Wandsworth Common on which the RVPS bordered. We would watch the trains pass by and enjoy the view of grass and trees under the watchful eye of the sentries walking their beat. I did not get the impression that we were very closely guarded. After all, making a get-away would condemn you as a likely spy.

At night we heard strange noises in the Gothic schoolrooms where we slept but our common sense told us that the noises were not those made, according to legend, by poor Charlotte Jane Bennett who perished in an 1862 fire while locked up for unmentioned reasons in solitary confinement.

After dark we were now, for the first time since Holland and Paris, regaled by the racket of bursting anti-aircraft shells. In early 1944, the *Luftwaffe* had resumed bombing London. They attacked in strengths not experienced by Londoners for some time, but no bombs fell on Battersea or Wandsworth. These raids lasted through April, by which time all the 'Gibraltar *Engelandvaarders*' had been released with the exception of one Dutchman who was transported to the Isle of Mann, where enemy aliens and people considered unreliable were interned. A few loyal patriots were however jailed when wrongly suspected to be, or deliberately treated as, double agents.

Little did we know at that time that two *Engelandvaarders*, Pieter Dourlein and Ben Ubbink, were secret agents of the SOE Dutch Section involved in the *'Engelandspiel'* espionage drama. They had managed to escape from the high security Gestapo jail at Haaren in South Netherlands and had returned to England via Switzerland and Spain.

British Intelligence had arrested and kept them incommunicado until after the D-day landing in order to make it appear to the Germans that they were believed to be German double agents.

The real reason for this charade (unknown to the Dutch and their agents) was the great deception strategy behind SIS's 'Plan Holland', for which the lives of 54 Dutch Agents and untold Resistance members were sacrificed. This was done to make the Germans believe that the D-day landing would take place somewhere south of Antwerp and tie down sizeable German military in Belgium and the south of Holland.

At the interrogations—which began at once and were repeated every two to three days—we were subtly but intensively questioned about our escape and activities in the Netherlands and asked to recall anything we had seen or heard which could be of assistance to the war effort.

On the 17th April, Robert was released but not I and it was obvious to me that they intended to put me under pressure. Three days later I called on my interrogator, Captain Campbell, and told him that I was aware of the reason why I had not been released at the same time as Robert. British and Dutch Intelligence would surely by now have contacted Erik Michielsen, who had hidden in my bedroom for several weeks while on the run from the Gestapo. Michielsen could vouch for me. If, furthermore, I had later changed sides and become a collaborator, ingratiating myself with Robert in order to get to England to spy for the Nazis, then surely it was straining credulity too much to think that German Intelligence could have 'arranged' the arrest at the 'Beaulieu'. I assured Captain Campbell that I had no intention of absconding although it would not be too difficult to do so. The Captain was amused when I added that I would be most grateful if I could be spared further discomfort, boredom and the punishment of having to eat the terribly bad food provided. The next day, in the morning of the 22nd of April, I was released.

I cannot, for the life of me, remember the place where the Dutch Government representative took me. As soon as I had dumped my kitbag at the reception I made my way to Brompton Road in Kensington to give the Perez family the latest news about their son Jean Paul in Amsterdam. I had stayed at the Perez villa in Beckenham in 1938 and knew Mr. Perez and his French wife quite well. They had not heard from 'JPP' (as his friends often called him) since the German invasion of The Low Countries in May 1940. I was greeted warmly by Mr. Perez at his business address. He was to hear that his son was all right and, as the Managing Director of the Perez branches in Holland, was exempted from labour in Germany.

Mr. Perez insisted that I stay in the guestroom at his No 53 Melbury Court, Holland Park, apartment near Kensington High Street. Most gratefully accepting the invitation, I doubled back to collect my baggage and, since I was still a free agent, informed the person in charge that I had been given a room at the home of friends and gave him the address and telephone number.

After dinner that evening I received the key to the front door and was told I was free to come and go as I pleased. I shall forever remember the kindness extended to me by Mr. and Mrs. Perez. They treated me like a son. Regrettably I did not meet up again with their daughters Simone and Paulette who had both joined the Services and were posted 'somewhere' in Britain.

The next day I made my way to 'the City' to call on Mr. W. van de Stadt and Mr. A. A. Pauw, directors in London of the same bank as my father's in Amsterdam. Mr. Pauw had been on business in London when the Germans invaded Holland. Both men were old friends of my father ever since the days they had joined *'De Factorij'* (as the *Nederlandsche Handel Maatschappij* was known in the Netherlands East Indies) as youngsters at the beginning of the 20th century. Mr. Pauw was also my brother Tommy's father-in-law.

The London into which I was released from the confines of the RVPS had, of course, changed dramatically since October 1938, when I last visited this city on the Thames River. From the upper deck of a red painted London double-decker bus I could observe the desolation caused by the German air raids in and around the part of London called 'the City'.

St Paul's Cathedral however stood relatively unscathed, surrounded by damaged or totally ruined buildings. I got off the bus in the middle of the financial district at Threadneedle Street near the Bank of England and walked down Lombard Street to the Netherlands Trading Society Office at No 28 Clements Lane.

I had telegraphed them from Madrid and also phoned them the day before and Messrs. Pauw and van de Stadt were expecting me. After listening to part of my story and the situation in Holland, 'Willy' (as he was called by his friends) declared that I needed a loan of £7 a week because he knew that my pay was insufficient to ensure a pleasant stay in London! He promptly arranged with the Bank's accountant, to provide me, every Friday, with the seven pounds sterling out of his personal account until further notice. This was a loan which my dear father had paid back by the time I returned to Amsterdam in October of 1946.

'Willy' had remained a bachelor all his life and had, apart from a deep understanding of the financial needs of young men, a love for horse-racing and some other pleasant pastimes. He was also, as I knew, a gourmet. To my delight he thereupon invited me to have lunch with Mr. Pauw and himself and, henceforth, to have lunch with him every Friday after collecting my seven pounds. All the time I was in London, a typical London taxi would convey us every Friday to the Savoy Hotel and smoked salmon, which he and I both loved. It was always our first course. I shall always remember our arriving at this famous London hotel. Mr. van de Stadt, who nearly all the staff knew by name, would make his way to the restaurant while handing out, from his waistcoat pockets, small silver coins to the staff, from the doorman onwards and ending with the *maitre d'hôtel*. The latter received the largest tip, and would always seat us at one of the best tables. 'Willy' was also great fun to be with and those Friday lunches remain unforgettable to this day.

In 1952, Mr. van de Stadt invited my whole family to stay a weekend at St James' Apartments in Westminster, where he lived. My parents, my sisters Mary and Ann, and their husbands Rory Connor and Dick Saunders, as well as my wife, Berna, and I were put up in separate apartments. The dinner party he gave us was to be the only time and the last time the whole family was together. 'Willy' is remembered with great affection and I cannot but always think of him when I eat smoked salmon. In the London of 1944, we could not get whipped cream, as in Spain, and there was food rationing but bread, potatoes, flour, milk and cigarettes were not rationed and there were plenty of taxis and thousands of buses still running on petrol. I did not once see any coal or wood-fired gas apparatus attached to a vehicle, as in German-occupied Europe.

On leaving the RVPS, I had been given a voucher to purchase a suit at a selected store and decided on grey flannel trousers and a sports jacket. This was a most welcome addition to my dark brown suit in which I had left Amsterdam. Since I generally did not wear a uniform, hating the rough British Army woollen battle-dress material, I could go about London in mufti because I was considered to be on leave from the NEI Air Force until the day I had to report for departure to Australia.

After release by the British Counter Intelligence at the RVPS, we were investigated by one of the security services of the Netherlands Ministry of Justice: the PBD *(Politie Buitendienst)*. They wanted to make doubly sure of our loyalty and, especially, to glean information about the conditions in Holland. The interrogations by MI5 were primarily conducted to detect enemy spies, but were also providing an important source of information about German fortifications and other intelligence of value to the Allied command.

I duly reported to Major Oreste Pinto at the PBD in 82 Eaton Square. After the War, by then promoted to Lieutenant Colonel, he became well known for his *Spycatcher* books which were based on his wartime experiences. Pinto had, by the time I was interviewed by him, unmasked a number of spies. One story I heard was that a Dutch pseudo *Engelandvaarder*—who turned out to be a German collaborator and spy— had a message (or code) tattooed on his head which was concealed by his hair and he had not been unmasked at the RVPS.

During this interview I was questioned not only (yet again) about my escape from Holland to Spain, but also about my activities in German-occupied Netherlands. The names of people—favourably or unfavourably commented upon—were carefully noted. I did not find Major Pinto a particularly pleasant person—an opinion shared by more than one *Engelandvaarder*. He was, no doubt, a very capable intelligence officer and skilled interrogator, but he was also obviously pleased with himself. This trait did not sit well with many.

Quite soon after I left Eaton Square I noticed (or thought I noticed) I was being shadowed and I realised that Pinto still considered it prudent to keep me under surveillance. After a few days of being tailed I remember being bemused that my loyalty was still in question and, at the same time, amused about the incompetence of my 'shadow'.

Major Pinto took it in good grace, I must say, when I expressed my surprise at being shadowed and added the suggestion to henceforth assign a more competent member of his staff. He did not deny that he had had me followed and I was thereafter left alone. Major (Lt. Col.) Pinto, I should mention, had been instrumental in the establishment of the interrogation centre for European refugees at the RVPS after the collapse of the Allied Front in May and June of 1940. Later on, British Military Intelligence used the facility for interrogation of Allied evaders and escapees.

22. Queen Wilhelmina and Oranjehaven

Queen Wilhelmina had bought, or rented, a house not far from Marble Arch at number 23 Hyde Park Place to house a club for *Engelandvaarders* and most appropriately called it "Oranjehaven" (Orange Harbour), *Oranje* being synonymous with the Dutch Royal House of Oranje-Nassau. A memorial stone has been cemented into the brick front wall of the house stating:

ORANJEHAVEN
This building served as a club
endowed in 1942 by
HER MAJESTY QUEEN WILHELMINA OF THE NETHERLANDS
for Dutchmen having escaped from their Occupied country
to join the Allied Forces

I remember 'our club', Oranjehaven, as a gathering of spirited (highly critical of the London Government's officials), humorous, youngish men. Several ladies, one married to a RAF Officer, ran the club on a voluntary basis, bless their souls, and the club had the added attraction of serving simple but tasty Dutch-style food. The coffee was free. The ladies running the club would be assisted by one and all. The food was brought into the large living room and everyone helped themselves. I can't remember what our financial contribution for the food was, but it was a modest fee.

It was also here at No 23 Hyde Park Place that I ran into Hugo 'Tip' Visser, one of the 'sardines' in the train compartment from Madrid to Portugal. Graduating from the Colonial Agricultural College in Deventer in 1942, he applied for and got a job as a chemist in a sugar factory at Lieusant near Paris. Climbing over the roof of a friend's attic, he entered the Deventer *Arbeids Bureau* through an unlocked top-floor window, liberated a certificate for exemption from labour in Germany and typed his particulars on it using their typewriter adding their rubber stamps and a scrawled signature. The *Ortskommandant* in Amsterdam, a high-ranking German officer, would, after interviewing Hugo, personally approve a one-way ticket for travel to Paris. At the head office of the factory in Paris a German lady provided the chemist (a highly respected profession in Germany) with accommodation in the first-class Hotel de l'Europe on the Place d'Opera. To Hugo's shock and dismay, he found himself among highly-decorated senior German officers, who at breakfast eyed the young civilian with disdain and suspicion. He promptly checked out a day early and made for the sugar factory in Lieusant. A few days later he learned that, on the day he left, the French Resistance had set fire to the kitchen of the Hotel de l'Europe but did not succeed in burning down the building. The Gestapo was called in to investigate but, to his relief, they never paid him a visit at the sugar factory. Tip considered his decision to immediately check out of the hotel as one of those lucky breaks so necessary for survival. Had he not checked out the Gestapo would have investigated and discovered his falsified papers which exempted him from work in Germany. He would have ended up in a Gestapo concentration camp.

After the sugar harvest and completion of production, Tip contacted an address in Paris which had been given to him by Frans Kouwenhoven—an *Engelandvaarder* who had joined Dutch Intelligence in London and been parachuted back into Holland—and whom he had per chance met at a friend's place in Deventer. To cut a long story short, he was put in touch with an escape line, received a falsified French identity card, travelled by train to Toulouse, experienced some anxious moments and adventures followed by a walk to the west of the Garonne River, and over the Pyrenean Mountains to reach Vielha in Spain's Aran Valley.

On the 10th of May 1944, the anniversary of the day in 1940 that the Germans invaded the Netherlands, Queen Wilhelmina unveiled a polished wooden memorial board at Oranjehaven. It showed the names of those who, as far as was known at that time, had perished attempting to reach England. There were then only some 30 names, a small percentage of those who did not make it. It is now part of the triptych in the War

Memorial Hall in Loenen in Central Netherlands. The triptych shows 317 names.

Engelandvaarders, with only a few exceptions, had made their way there singly or with few companions. It was therefore not surprising that many had never met before. Here I encountered old school or sports friends from Batavia and Holland, just as I had met up with a few in Gibraltar and on the SS 'Orduña'. Apart from meeting many a 'Gib-*Engelandvaarder*, it was here at Oranjehaven that I met up again with Eddy Le Grand, a school friend from our boyhood years in Batavia in the early 1930s.

Oranjehaven was popular and a focal point for *Engelandvaarders* in London and a place where news and rumours, leaked from Government Departments, circulated freely, which was not very surprising in view of the animosity and jealousy prevailing even in peacetime between governments and bureaucracies, let alone here in the small wartime Dutch community.

Holland, not having been involved in a European war since 1830, had bred complacency, indifference and lassitude in our Government officials. Dutchmen who had worked overseas had always found their compatriots 'back home', and particularly Government officials, to be stuffy and narrow-minded. It was, therefore that there was rancour between the Government officials evacuated hastily from the Netherlands on 14th and 15th of May, 1940, on the one hand, and the new-comers from the Colonies and the *Engelandvaarders* particularly.

Soon after my release from the RVPS I was warned about the strained relationships and to steer away from any friction with officials. At Oranjehaven we listened—gleefully I may add—to the leaked stories from various 'London' Government departments and the perceived stupidities of the dead hand of bureaucracy and the inter-departmental rivalries.

The disgraceful behaviour of our Prime Minister at the time of the German invasion still rankled and was felt by some, if unfairly, as a blot on the whole 'London' Government-in-Exile. Mr. D. J. de Geer, a weakling and defeatist, absconded and returned to the Occupied Netherlands—a story that was milked by the propaganda machine of Herr Goebbels. De Geer died disgraced soon after the end of the War.

Someone at Oranjehaven once remarked with a derisive tone: "Bear in mind that a Government in exile, like ours, has nothing to govern except themselves." This was largely true—and certainly in the early war years with respect to the hundreds of minnows housed in several buildings like Arlington House in Arlington Street, 4 North Row and Stratton House in the street of the same name where the Dutch Prime Minister had his office. It also applied to some ministers as well but not to the Prime Minister, or rather the second Prime Minister, Mr. Pieter S. Gerbrandy. Small in stature and with a walrus moustache, he was highly respected by many, including Sir Winston Churchill who called him "Cherry Brandy" behind his back.

The reason for the great difference in mentality between *Engelandvaarders* and most of the 'London' Dutch, both military and civilian, was that there had not been any political or social upheaval in the Netherlands, nor a war fought, for over a hundred years. Consequently, the ingrained 'rank and social standing' attitude amongst those born and raised in the Low Countries and transplanted, on the 13th and 15th of May 1940, from the typical hothouse atmosphere of a country's seat of government in The Hague, could not but lead to friction with the cosmopolitan 'colonials' and other overseas Dutch who had joined the war effort in London.

Into that 'London' arrived the *Engelandvaarders*—energetic 'doers' with scant regard for authority. They viewed the hierarchical goings-on with amusement and derision. There was, for instance, a colonel who ordered that, even in the corridors of the building of his department, lower ranks had to salute higher ranks. This caused great hilarity amongst the *Engelandvaarders* who wondered out loud whether it also be required in the men's room.

Many an *Engelandvaarder* would not apply for or accept a Government post and disappeared into one of the military services, no doubt to the relief of those who considered *Engelandvaarders* too aggressive and lacking due respect. The Interim Minister for War, van Boeien, described *Engelandvaarders* as *"over-excited adventurers"*. This view was heartily endorsed by most of the 'old guard' of the 'London' Government but, I must stress, not by all and most certainly not by our Queen Wilhelmina who had been 'my/our' Queen all my life and, to most Dutchmen and most certainly the *Engelandvaarders,* was the Netherlands personified.

Queen Wilhelmina had a high regard for the men and women who had made the dangerous journey from German-occupied Holland to England to serve their country in the fight against Hitler's Nazis. In a speech the Queen had described us as her *'Schakel'* (link) with her people in German-occupied Netherlands. The quarterly magazine of the *Engelandvaarders'* Association was consequently called De Schakel and it is truly the link between the *Engelandvaarders,* who now live all over the world.

Queen Wilhelmina would interview some of us about conditions in the Netherlands and about our escape when receiving us at an informal audience for afternoon tea. A few would be asked later to present themselves several times for further questioning, occasionally in private. As a further token of her appreciation, Her Majesty demanded from her Government Ministers that all deserving *Engelandvaarders* be decorated, Over-ruling some ministers' objections, she was instrumental in the creation of the *Bronze Kruis* (Bronze Cross) to be awarded to those who had crossed to England by sea and the *Kruis van Verdienste* (Cross of Merit) to the overlanders and some who came over the North Sea. It was also thanks to Queen Wilhelmina over-riding objections from traditionalists in the Military that a few *Engelandvaarders* received the highest Dutch decoration for valour in combat, the MWO *(Militaire Willems Orde),* for exceptional bravery during secret service missions.

One day in May, I and another 10 or so *Engelandvaarders* were fetched and delivered by motorcar to Queen Wilhelmina's office and occasional residence at No 77 Chester Square. Upon entering the mansion, we were received in the hall by Major Beelaerts van Blockland and a Lady in Waiting who instructed us on etiquette. One "no-no" was to reply in the negative to any remark of Her Majesty and a *"yes Ma'am"* or *"yes Your Majesty"* was to precede a positive reply.

After the Queen, on entering, had greeted us with a slight bow and seated herself behind a large low tea-table, we formed a close circle on both sides of Her Majesty, who now, assisted by her Lady in Waiting, poured the tea. Queen Wilhelmina was quite small and somewhat pear-shaped, with bright eyes and a motherly face; yet there was no doubting that she was her Majesty the Queen. After the tea, sandwiches and cookies were passed around and the Queen spoke briefly to each one of us. All went well until one chap—with an agricultural degree, who would be engaged in the rehabilitation of rubber plantations in the Netherlands East Indies after the defeat of the Japanese—was asked what his task in the NICA (Netherlands Indies Civil Administration) would be.

He, obviously in awe of being addressed by the Queen of the Netherlands, answered nervously and inadequately: *"In rubber, Ma'am."* Hereupon, the Queen observed: *"and where are you going to manufacture rubber tyres?"*

This caused surprised guffaws by some, which most fortunately went unnoticed by our Queen, while Mr. "I am in rubber", after a pregnant pause, stuttered; *"Yes, Your Majesty, I will be involved in the rehabilitation of the rubber plantations in the Netherlands Indies."*

When, after the informal audience, we were driven home again, one chap remarked; *"It feels good to receive recognition from one's Queen, particularly after the indifferent or lukewarm reception from some of the officials."* (He actually used a derogative ending, which I have omitted.)

Queen Wilhelmina had a country house in Maidenhead but conducted the Business of State at 77 Chester Square, situated behind Buckingham Palace in Belgravia. The most important member of her staff was her personal advisor and private secretary, Francois van 't Sant, who had the titular rank of Major General and the trust of most *Engelandvaarders*.

Prince Bernhard of the Netherlands was also someone we could turn to. This slim, elegant and charming prince I had the pleasure of meeting a few times when visiting Holland. Prince Bernhard would, when he could, attend the *Engelandvaarders'* annual reunions and monthly *borrel* (drinks) in the officers mess at the Frederiks Kazerne (barracks) in The Hague.

The Prince, of German origin, had at first not been generally accepted by the Dutch population at large who felt that the Germans had blackened their copybook with their ruthless invasion of neutral Belgium in 1914. In a country that had still not forgiven the Spaniards for their rule in the 15th through 17th centuries, Holland's neighbours were known as *Moffenjongens*—the Dutch equivalent of *Les Boches,* Krauts and The Huns.

Prince Bernhard's courageous behaviour during the Nazi invasion of May 1940, and his openly taking the side of his adopted country and the Allies, made him become 'one of us'. His war effort would seal his place in the hearts of the Dutch population and especially the *Engelandvaarders*.

Long after the War, I read a report of a Dutch historian (if I am correct, Dr L. de Jong) that, in London during the War, Queen Wilhelmina was of the opinion that the high-ranking Dutch officers had calcified arteries and had become useless! What a marvellous woman! She overruled some of their decisions regarding awarding the MWO, the Dutch VC, to some deserving recipients, because they had based their decisions on the provisions of a law drawn up in 1815. I know that it was, in one or two cases, more likely that they did not appreciate the attitude, lack of respect shown or reports written by these *Engelandvaarders.*

Once released from the RVPS, the various Dutch Government Departments were however keen to enlist us. Chaps with agricultural diplomas ended up in the section for the rehabilitation of the diverse plantations in the Netherlands East Indies. We called them the 'rubber boys'. Those who had studied *Indologie*—i.e. the languages, culture, history, races and tribes of the many islands stretched out over an area of more than 2500 miles or 4000 kilometres along the Equator—logically joined the Netherlands Indies Civil Administration or NICA for short. A few brave souls, like the future Chairman of the *Stichting Engelandvaarders,* Mr. L. B. Frans Th Dijkmeester, joined the Dutch Intelligence. He was parachuted into the Netherlands and did sterling work in organising resistance groups into the BS *(Binnenlandse Strijdkrachten)* to assist the Allies after D-Day. It is worth mentioning that more than 50 per cent of Intelligence agents dropped into the Netherlands during WWII were *Engelandvaarders.*

On my release from the RVPS, I was most disappointed to learn that the RAF training scheme for pilots had very recently been suspended as, in the opinion of Allied Command, the war would be over before we had gained our wings. I could have joined the 'Princess Irene' Brigade but after the walk across the Pyrenean Mountains I did not have any desire to become a slogging infantry soldier. Since I had studied at the Colonial Institute and spoke Malay, which had been my second language (English being the third) before I was eight, they talked me into joining the NICA. There and then I was promoted to sergeant.

Not a week later I learned from others at Oranjehaven that the KNIL (Royal East Indies Army) had an aircrew training arrangement with the RAAF in Australia and were looking for recruits. Yet the Government Representative who interviewed me chose not to make me aware of pilot training for the NEI Air Force with the RAAF. I passed the required RAF medical test and was accepted for pilot training and promptly handed in my sergeant stripes to become an officer air cadet.

It would be another two months, nearly to the day, before I got called up to present myself for embarkation to our final destination; Australia. Meanwhile, I spent pleasant hours at Oranjehaven and thoroughly enjoyed the Friday lunches with Mr. van de Stadt at the Savoy Hotel. I visited the sights in London town like any tourist but this time among a multitude of Allied soldiers, sailors and airmen from 12 nations and not, as four months earlier in Paris, among Germans from the *Wehrmacht*, SS, *Luftwaffe* and *Kriegsmarine*.

I had also met a nice English girl called Pat Port with whom I would grace the dance floors of The Embassy Club and other dance halls. Thanks to my £7 from 'Willy', I could also afford to take her for drinks at one of the most pleasant British pubs and for dinner at 'The Chinese', or restaurants like Hatchetts. I also became a member of the 'United Nations Forces Club' and the 'Queenberry All Services Club' (on Old Compton Street, W1), on the membership card of which was printed *"Valid up to December 1944 or the termination of hostilities with Germany, whichever is the earlier."* A less optimistic and more accurate prediction of the end of the War was mentioned on my membership card of 'The Netherlands House' (at 16 Charles Street, W1): *"Valid till 1-5-1945."*

At that time in London I had not even bothered to check the validity dates of my membership cards since I expected to leave England within a few weeks. However, its import some 60 years later has registered the stronger, for it revealed the opinion prevailing among the 'Top Brass' and governments about the likely duration of the war.

23. My Last Meeting with Erik Michielsen

Shortly after my encounter with Major Pinto, I received a phone call from Lt. Erik Michielsen, on leave in London from his RAF base, inviting me to meet him at The Cumberland Hotel near Marble Arch. It was three years after parting at De Lairessestraat 96, in Amsterdam, that I knocked on his hotel door. He was sitting in his striped pyjamas on his bed and was busy clipping his toe nails when I entered his hotel room. It was one of those silly moments you always remember. After bringing each other up to date, I mentioned the criticism I had heard about the 'London' government and the friction between the early arrivals in May of 1940 and the newcomers. His comments were along these lines: *"That old Dutch mob only indulges in self-interest. Queen Wilhelmina has a soft corner in her heart for all Engelandvaarders and if you want to get anything done or have serious problems then there are only three people you can count on: Her Majesty, Prince Bernhard and General Van 't Sant. The latter is the Queen's advisor and has her confidence"*. That evening Erik took me to the Wings Club in Chesterfield Street for drinks and we had dinner somewhere—'Odeninos' if I remember correctly.

I mentioned earlier about Erik Michielsen having hidden in my bedroom when the Gestapo were looking for him. He had become involved in the espionage affair of the secret agent and Dutch Royal Navy Lt. L. A. R. J. van Hamel in September of 1940. Van Hamel, a courageous and highly intelligent person, was the first Dutch secret agent parachuted into German-occupied Holland in August of 1940. Lodo van Hamel's contact address had been 54 Rapenburg in the university town of Leiden, where his friend, a medical student called Hans Hers, had rooms.

Having learned of Erik's involvement in, among other things, the successful escape of his brother Karel to England, Erik was asked to assist in the preparation for van Hamel to be picked up at the Tjeuke Meer, a lake in the northern province of Friesland. Erik from then on assisted with intelligence gathering, coding and de-coding messages. Erik had been promised a place in the plane if there was room for him. There was not, but he and Cal Kranenburg, another Leiden University student, nevertheless accompanied Lodo and the others to the province of Friesland.

To cut a long story short, the seaplane pick-up went wrong when the presence of van Hamel and three of his companions was reported by a farmer's wife to the local county constable who in turn phoned his superior, a pro-German Police Kolonel. When the seaplane, a Fokker T-VII-W piloted by Dutch Navy Lt. H. Schaper who knew the area well, arrived over the Tjeuke Meer, it could not land owing to ground mist. The Germans having been tipped off, and waiting in ambush, thereupon arrested the occupants of the small rowing boat on that fateful 15th of October 1940. All ended up in the hands of the Gestapo and were jailed in the notorious SS jail at Scheveningen which the Dutch population dubbed the "Oranje Hotel". It had this name since all the inmates had been arrested for their activities against the Occupiers and for their Queen of the Royal House of Orange, and for their country. Although Lodo van Hamel and his right-hand man, Hans Hers, were savagely interrogated, neither gave anything away. Lodo was executed on the Waalsdorper Dunes on the 16th of June 1941 and Hans Hers received a life sentence. Jean Mesritz got three years in jail and died at Dachau Concentration Camp from typhoid. Prof. Dr. L. G. M. Baas Becking and Miss Marion Smit, the two other passengers, were very lucky and were acquitted.

The same Hans Hers, at that time a medical student at Leiden University, was to become the physician, Dr. J. F. Ph. Hers, who examined ex-Resistance persons at the Leiden Academic Hospital. The Dutch State awarded a pension to those who, because of their wartime Resistance activities, suffered serious physical and/or psychological health problems which are generally manifested later in life. If anybody was qualified to pass medical judgement on ex-Resistance members, then it surely was Dr. Hans Hers who himself had experienced the extreme trauma of espionage resulting from Gestapo interrogation and incarceration. When I visited Dr. Hers at his home in the

Koningsweg in Oestgeest (a virtual suburb of Leiden), he told me about some of his disgusting and gruesome experiences in a Nazi jail.

Erik and Cal had watched the drama unfold at the Tjeuke Meer and managed to extricate themselves but the others had been observed in the area by a collaborating county constable and locals who had warned the SD.

From that moment both, of course, had to go underground and during the next eight months or so Erik frequently changed from one hiding place to another. He arrived at my parent's apartment in early November of that first year of German Occupation. My father had, without a second thought, agreed to offer shelter to Erik when Mr. Michielsen Sr. had approached him. They were old and close friends since their days in Batavia in the early Thirties and no doubt Erik's father would have done the same for me. In fact, in 1943 I also once or twice slept at their villa on the Van Alkemadelaan in The Hague when tipped off about planned raids in Amsterdam. Sheltering friends was a risk honourable people like our parents took without hesitation. However, if detected, the occupants of the house, and particularly the father of the family, could expect no mercy and many paid with their lives for helping or sheltering those wanted by the Gestapo.

Soon after Erik had moved into my room at my parent's home, on a winter morning on the 23rd of November at half past seven, in pitch darkness, a large SS van arrived at the Michielsen Villa on the Van Alkemadelaan. Two armed SS soldiers jumped out while a third guarded the entrance. Two Germans in civilian clothes made for the front door, rang the bell and shouted *"Geheim polizei! Aufmachen!"* In Erik's book the encounter between his parents—who both spoke fluent German, Erik's mother being of Austrian origin—and the two Gestapo Officers is described in detail. The interrogation and house-search lasted 13 hours. Half an hour after they had all left, one Gestapo officer called Sgt. Stowe returned to renew the interrogation but left a few hours later none the wiser. The Michielsen Villa was kept under Gestapo surveillance well into 1941.

That November in 1940 was not the first time that Erik had arrived at our house. He slept in the spare bed for he had been a regular guest at our previous home in the Viottastraat, No 37. At that time, he was doing his one-year military service in the Horse Artillery and was commissioned a Reserve Lieutenant before enrolling for Law studies at Leiden University. It was because of his desire to first gain his Law degree that he had not joined his younger brother Karel, Kees van Endenburg and Freddie vas Nunes on their successful attempt to cross the North Sea to England.

Erik, after taking his Law degree, had resumed his efforts to get to England but, as I found out myself a year later after having matriculated, escaping over sea had become more difficult because the Germans had strengthened the coastal defences. To find an overland route which presented a reasonable chance of success was far from easy either. He made several unsuccessful attempts, one with Erik Hazelhoff Roelfsema, who was to become famous in Holland for his war exploits and his book, *Soldaat van Oranje*. On another attempt disaster struck. Erik, Cal Kranenburg, Jean Mesritz and Anton de Haseth Moller had hardly got their small boat through the breakers when they lost their outboard motor. The boat was swamped. All they could do was to crawl back onto the beach. Soaked to the skin, they clambered up the dunes where Cal remarked: *"Let us put on record that there is absolutely no doubt that if WE cannot succeed now or later, one thing is certain: the 'Moffen' [Germans] will never get across to England!"* It was this experience of Erik's which made me strongly favour the land route to Spain.

Later, in January of 1942, after the Gestapo had ceased their close surveillance, Erik, through the Resistance, came into contact with an escape line to Switzerland. He left The Hague on the 30th of January with Peter Tazelaar and Gerard Dogger, two outstanding *Engelandvaarders*, for Bergen op Zoom. A bus took them to Putte on the Belgian border where they spent the night at a farmhouse. After staying a night with a Dutch family in Antwerp they took the train to Montbeliard, not far from the Swiss border, travelling on forged Belgian identity cards. They climbed the Jura Mountains, walking through knee-deep snow and crossed the border on the evening of the 2nd of February. Travelling with a Swiss police convoy through Vichy-France on the 26th of March to Spain, Erik finally reached Gibraltar on the 12th of April from where he wrote his first report, dated the 21st of May, for the Dutch government in London. After his arrival in the British capital, he delivered personal messages from an associate in Holland to Prof. Dr. P. S. Gerbrandy, the Dutch

Prime Minister, and wrote several reports for the government. He was received several times in audience by Queen Wilhelmina.

When we parted that evening in May 1944, it was like saying goodbye to an older brother who, over the years, had given me many a wise word of advice. Little did I know that I would never see him again for Erik was killed on a night training exercise above Thornhill Airfield near Shrewsbury in Wales. The Wellington Bomber he piloted was rammed from behind causing the tail to break off. Three Canadian crew members also perished.

At his funeral in Brookwood on the 31st of August, Her Majesty Queen Wilhelmina sent her adjutant and so did Prince Bernhard. Others who attended were representatives of the Dutch War Office, the RAF, the Chaplain to the Forces, Father Monchen, and Mr. W. van de Stadt Jr., an old and close friend of Erik's father, representing the family.

Queen Wilhelmina had also asked the Reverend van Dorp, the RN Chaplain, to hold the funeral oration at his grave site. Wreaths from Queen Wilhelmina and all those mentioned above graced his grave.

The Queen's high opinion of Erik was based on personal interviews and the reading of his reports and essays written for the Government when in Gibraltar in May of 1942 and in London. The last one was dated May, 1944 and was published at the end of *Tegen de Vlagen Van De Oostenwind* (Against the Gusts of the Eastwind).

As mentioned earlier, Erik had commenced writing his book when hiding from the Gestapo at my parent's home and, before he left, we had hidden the completed pages in the double-walled cavity of the sliding doors leading from the dining room to my father's study. He and my father had retrieved the manuscript after the liberation of Holland.

It was when writing his book that Erik asked me to draw a few illustrations and I remember clearly the one depicting Cal Kranenburg in jail. I do not know what happened to those drawings but I mention this anecdote to illustrate how confident we were in the ultimate victory of the Allies even in the darkest days of World War II. It was the same kind of confidence that you had that you would survive the War.

24. D-Day, the V-1, and Crossing the Atlantic

It was in the very early morning of the 13th of June, when it was still dark, that I awoke in my bed at Melbury Court to the loud sound of a single, very low-flying aeroplane and bursting anti-aircraft shells. I did not hear any bombs drop and, thinking nothing of it, I went back to sleep. It was to be my first of many encounters with Hitler's first V-weapon, or *Vergeltungswaffen,* and the start of the second London Blitz.

The news on the 6th of June of the Allied landings on the Normandy beaches and the good news that followed had filled the newspapers but the V-1 Flying Bomb had, on the 12th of June, come as an unpleasant reminder that the War was still far from over. It made me recall the conversations in the *Wehrmacht* train from Maastricht to Paris of our German fellow train-passengers about secret weapons.

The Allies had known of new weapons being developed by the Germans, hence the air-raids on Penemunde and other sites which had helped delay but not prevent the V-1 and later V-2 attacks. The steady stream of V-1 'doodlebugs', the noise of which could be heard for miles, became a part of life in London to which everybody adjusted. It however did not make me stop enjoying life in wartime London, which was much enhanced by the weekly £7 allowance. I simply ignored the danger presented by the steady stream of V-1s and I was not the only one.

Once, I was crossing the entrance hall of the Regent Palace Hotel near Piccadilly in the company of my old friend F/O Zdenek Kokes when a V-1 hit the building with a tremendous bang. We had not heard its approach, or the tell-tale engine cut-out, but instinctively both of us hit the floor. After picking ourselves up and dusting the chalk, glass fragments and pieces of rubbish from our jackets and trousers, 'Steve' remarked dryly *"I think it's time for a drink."*

Zdenek, the son of the Honorary Consul of Czechoslovakia in Amsterdam, had become my first close friend after my family had returned to Holland in 1934. That's when my father became one of the managing directors of the NHM Head Office in Amsterdam. Steve had, in 1939, gone to London to study Economics at London University and, after the German invasion of Holland, he had joined the RAF. On leave from his RAF Coastal Command base, he had driven to London in his beat-up 'ninth-hand' open, two-seater MG sports car, the left-hand passenger door of which was secured by a piece of string. He picked me up at Melbury Court and we drove to Soho. Where he managed to park the car I can't remember. But I do remember the girls looking at the handsome blond RAF Officer in his MG. After London, Steve and I would, in 1947, play golf at the AGC. We played on the same team in competition matches on most of the golf courses in the Netherlands but thereafter did not see each other again until 1961 when my wife and I, on home leave from Hong Kong, visited him and his American wife, Louise, at his home near Washington DC.

Although there had been fewer German air-raids after 1940-41, until the V-1 flying bombs started dropping on London, the Underground stations were nevertheless still used by many to bed down in at night. After the 13th of June, however, the population of London, with typical British resilience and the stoicism displayed during the London Blitz, took the flying bomb onslaught in their stride and returned in far greater numbers to the shelter of the Underground stations. During the day they went, as before, about their business, keeping an ear open for a nearby V-1's engine cutting off and, in the deafening silence that followed, running for shelter. Yet the damage and death caused by the V-1s and V-2s was, in such a short time-span, far greater than in all the years before. It was also a relentless 24-hour attack that did not cease until the Allied advance across Europe wiped out the V-1 launching pads and forced the V-2 launchers out-of-range.

The V-1 and V-2 carried one ton of explosives and razed more than 17,000 houses to the ground and damaged another 800,000 or so in Southern England in the space of seven weeks. I read once, in a newspaper I think, that in four years German bombs wrecked or damaged 2,750,000 houses in England and Wales. The V-1 and V-2 onslaught alone claimed the lives of nearly 9,000 people.

My friend Pat and I would stay where we were until or near closing time and, since I would always escort Pat to her widowed mother's home, it meant that I missed the last tube of the Piccadilly Line to Knightsbridge which was the nearest station to Melbury Court. I would instead catch the last tube on the Central Line from Oxford Circus Station to Notting Hill Gate Station, which left some 40 minutes later. Notting Hill Gate is the deepest London Underground Transport station and its platforms were always lined with people sitting, reading or sleeping on mats, mattresses, folding beds or chairs along the walls, leaving only a narrow path on the railway track side of the platform. One had to carefully avoid, and on the narrower platforms step over, legs or bodies sleeping tightly packed.

Walking from Notting Hill Gate along Kensington High Street to the Perez apartment, I was often accompanied by an American Captain and a Polish Sergeant. We often saw the whitish to reddish flame flaring from the exhaust pipe of a passing V-1 and would dash into a portico or down basement steps of homes when the engine cut off, thereby announcing its drop to earth.

In all my time in England I somehow not once sought refuge in a bomb shelter. In Holland and Paris we did not expect to be bombed in residential areas, although it did happen once disastrously in The Hague and Nijmegen when a navigational error was made. In London, like all young men, I totally disregarded danger and, without a worry, crawled into my bed every night, V-1 or no V-1 roaring past. After all, I was sufficiently protected, I hoped, by the two or three floors above my bedroom if a V-1 should dive into the Melbury Court apartment building.

One day in early July I received my travel order for departure from London's Euston Station. Now that I was to leave, those last few days in Britain's capital I spent in greater awareness of the familiar sight of air defence balloons slowly moving in the breeze on cables to which they were attached and I noted that the number of uniforms on the streets had not much decreased since the Normandy Landing. The V-1s still came over regularly and at night people returned to the Underground stations which they had vacated early that morning. I packed my kitbag, had a last dinner and dance with Pat Port and said my goodbyes.

On the 10th of July at Euston Station, Lt. van Kregten, in charge of our party of KNIL personnel bound for America, introduced me to four officers and three air cadets. I had not knowingly met Sgt. Henk Baxmeier, Jaap (Jim) Jongeneel and Herman van Nouhuys before, although the last two had been part of the large Dutch contingent of *Engelandvaarders* in Gibraltar and on the 'SS Orduña'. We must also at one time or another have been together at the RVPS and Oranjehaven. It was for me a fateful meeting for, thanks to Jimmy and Herman, I was to meet my future wife and Henk would become my best man.

After an uneventful train journey to Glasgow, our KNIL Air Force party was taken by army truck to Greenock and by motor launch down the Firth of Clyde, past a number of navy and merchant ships towards a large passenger ship painted in war-time grey. Even before we saw the name of the over-painted escutcheon, we recognised the Cunard Line's famous passenger liner, the RMS 'Queen Mary' by its shape and her three funnels. This time we were not put up in the lowest cargo hold without portholes at the bow, as on that rust-bucket the 'Orduña, but on the top A-deck in a large pre-War, first-class stateroom with a window and en suite bathroom. All the beds (not bunks in 1st class!), furniture and fittings had been removed and four metal bunk stands each with three-tiered folding bunk beds had been erected. Although quite spartan, we each had our own tier of three bunk beds and only shared a large cabin and bathroom between the four of us. Our five KNIL officers had the same accommodation. I would not travel in such style on a troopship ever again. The 'Queen Mary' was not filled to her about 15,000-man capacity. On this voyage she carried 8,000 German POWs from the Normandy front destined for POW internment camps in the USA and Canada and perhaps only a few hundred Allied troops. No sooner were we installed in our No 21 stateroom, than we had to report to Lt. van Kregten. Interpreters were needed to accompany the four senior officers in charge of the four separate POW quarters on the daily inspections. Since we four had all matriculated we were expected to know the German language and the more so since we had recently left German-occupied Holland.

I found it an interesting experience to do the rounds with the Colonel I was "seconded" to, and walk through throngs of *Heinies* (as the Americans called them) on inspection of a particular POW compound on the 'Queen Mary'. Their sleeping quarters were on the lower (passenger) decks, with portholes and the same as those for Allied troops on other voyages but the POWs were confined for most of the day in these areas and only aired once a day. In spite of the ventilation and portholes, the foul smell of the unwashed uniforms in which they had been taken prisoner was not pleasant, but noting their demeanour towards their captors was interesting. Their attitude was generally polite or indifferent but some, usually the *Unteroffizieren* (petty officers) in the dark blue uniform of the *Kriegsmarine,* would give us a look of disdain or hatred. When these men would deliberately try to hold up proceedings during the daily airings on the open or promenade decks, particularly when descending the companionways to their quarters, the British guards would use a firm push or the butt of their rifles.

Noting the embroidered letters "Netherlands" below a Dutch Lion on my shoulder patch seemed to surprise some at first but they very quickly came to know that I, the interpreter, was one of the four *Hollander* aboard who had escaped from German-occupied Europe. Their source of information was no doubt 'our' German POW steward, serving our table in one of the ship's dining rooms. The original furnishings of the dining room had been removed and replaced with simple, long, wooden tables and benches.

I did enjoy the special attention we received from 'our' German steward who obviously had been a professional waiter and/or the batman of a *Wehrmacht* General. He was always correct and polite and never failed to enquire whether *"die Herren'* would like a second serving of eggs and bacon. My reply was invariably in the affirmative.

Fast ships like the 'Queen Mary' would cross the Atlantic and other oceans unescorted. Their speed, and zigzag course, made them safe from U-boats. However, earlier in the war, when Prime Minister Winston Churchill made his three crossings of the Atlantic Ocean, there was nevertheless always an escort of cruisers and/or destroyers. The zigzags were executed at different intervals. Only a puff of steam, and shortly thereafter the blast of the ship's siren, would announce a change of direction. A close watch by the escorting ships was therefore necessary as the C-class cruiser 'Curacao' learned to her grief when she was run down by the 'Queen Mary' in 1942.

By the time we reached 'The New World', we four air cadets had learned much about each other.

Jaap (Jim) Jongeneel had crossed the Spanish frontier north of the small town called Orbaiceta on the 7th of November, 1943. After being escorted by heavily armed *Guardia Civil* to Pamplona, the capital of the province of Navarra, he and his companions were interrogated in the Pamplona Jail.

Co Vink, with whom Jaap had made the journey all the way from Holland, was one of those transported to the concentration camp at Uberuaga de Ubilla near Bilbao and spent time there amongst fugitives from the Nazis, as well as rapists, murderers and thieves. From descriptions I heard, it was worse than the notorious Campo Miranda de Ebro.

Jaap, having been tipped off by a female bystander in Orbeiceta to say that he was 18-years-old, was released into *residence forcée* at Banos de Besancoin and thereafter in Leiza. Before being released into the custody of Dutch Consular Officials in Madrid, he was locked up for 36 hours in the catacombs of the *Policia Seguridad* Headquarters on the Puerta del Sol, the so-called Piccadilly Circus of Madrid. It illustrates once again the difference in treatment we 'illegals' received from Spanish authorities. One was jailed, the other not: one was put in a concentration camp, the other not.

Jaap (called Jim ever since London), Herman and I, like most *Engelandvaarders* (and many a Resistance fighter) who went overland, were awarded the *Kruis van Verdienste* (Cross of Merit) but Henk Baxmeier, having reached England by crossing the North Sea, received a higher decoration, the Bronze Cross, from the hands of Queen Wilhelmina herself.

In their book, *Vrijheid Achter de Horizon* (Freedom over the Horizon), Jan Bruin and Jan van der Werff write about a number of voyages by *Engelandvaarders* across the North Sea during the war years 1940-1945. Theirs is, however, a rather bravado account of the crossing of the five men in their seven-metre flat-bottomed boat and in which the two men, without whom the enterprise would have failed, were hardly mentioned. The true and more sober report of their hazardous sea voyage in this *vlet* (as this small boat is called in Holland) can be found in the diaries of Henk Baxmeier, the navigator on the voyage, which he donated to the Dutch War Documentation Archives. Instrumental in the planning of the trip were the electro-technical engineer, Ir. Edzard Moddemeyer, and John Osten, who had bought the *vlet* in 1943 through the

intermediary of the brothers Piet and Joop Meyer. Both had been of great
help in previous escape attempts and successful escapes.

After preparing the *vlet* for the open sea voyage across the North Sea
the original engine was removed and a stronger 70-horsepower Chevrolet
petrol engine installed at the wharf of the Thijssen brothers in Leiden.
Through Vice Admiral Osten, John's father, sea charts and a compass
were acquired. Meanwhile the 'crewhands', Hein Fuchter and his
friend Flip Winckel (curiously, both were old school friends of mine) had
transported tens of litres of petrol in jerry cans stolen from the *Wehrmacht*.
These were put into large so-called Shanghai (wicker) suitcases, and sent
by train from Dieren, a town near Arnhem, to Puttershoek, a village to the
east of the medieval city of Dordrecht on the Oudemaas River.
Dordrecht is situated in the midst of a tangle of waterways, created by the
Rhine and Meuse Rivers, south of Rotterdam in south-west Holland. On
the 18th December '43 the *vlet* had been loaded in Leiden into the hold of
the inland navigation freighter of Skipper Panjer and transported to
Dordrecht, where it was unloaded in the Niewehaven and towed
to Puttershoek for engine trials. After effecting several most necessary
repairs to the Chevrolet engine, their first attempt on the 17th had to be
aborted when they got stuck on a sandbank in the Haringvliet. They
managed to dislodge the *vlet*, move upstream and hide in the Bernisse
Creek of the island of Voorne-Putten, not far from the village called
Zuidland, on the Spui River without having been spotted by German
watch posts. After fresh preparations and repairs and taking on *boerenbrood*
(home-baked bread) and sausages, given to them by a local farmer, they
sailed from the inlet down the Spui and then over the Haringvliet in the
early evening darkness of the 22nd of February. The tension would
be momentarily broken when they heard music on a radio or a broadcast
from Radio Calais while gliding past German watch posts. At one of the
most dangerous spots, when passing the Kriegsmarine E-boat base at the
old Dutch harbour town of Hellevoetsluis, the silence was broken by a
radio loudly blaring *"Das Oberkommando der Wehrmacht gibt bekannt"*
followed by Hitler's strident voice. It took five hours to reach
the relatively calm North Sea. Since the *vlet* started leaking soon after they
had departed, Hein Fuchter and Flip Winckel had to remain down in the
bilge of the flat-bottomed hull manning the pumps. With Henk navigating
the small boat in a generally north-westerly direction and several times

changing course to avoid sandbanks and German patrol ships which they spotted on the horizon, they were intercepted 40 miles east of Great Yarmouth by an RAF rescue launch and taken aboard at about 12.30 p.m. on the 23rd of February. As far as I have been able to ascertain, theirs was the last successful crossing by sea from Holland to England in WWII.

Henk, when telling his story, emphasised that without the technical and practical skills of Edzard Moddemeier in repairing the motor, which broke down several times, even while still on the inland waterways, they would surely have fallen prey to German patrol boats or perished at sea.

My French Identity Card showing the transformation after the new haircut and glasses (including loss of hair since 1941).

The falsified Sonderausweis (Special Travel Warrant) issued by the SD Office Feldpost N2 24393P (at Pau) for the contract-employee Robert van Exter travelling on the 3rd of January 1944 to Amsterdam via Paris and Maastricht on SD business. My Sonderausweis was the same and the stamps similar—a good example of the art of forgery. The rubber stamps on this document show, amongst other things, that on Robert's return journey he reported at the Gross Paris Kommandantur on the 12th of January 1944, and that he received cash from the Reichskreditkasse in Maastricht as well as food and tobacco rations for the period 7-11 January 1944.

A Citroën Traction Avant similar to the one from which I parted company with the German officers. (Photo from Pixabay.com.)

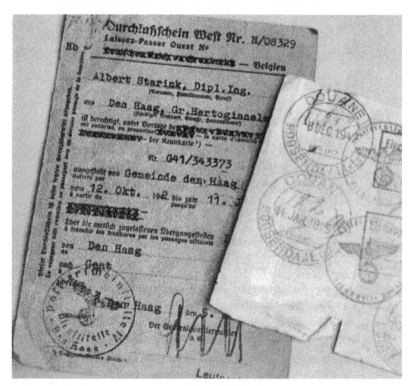

Albert Starink's Durchlaßschein (certified travel document) and a "LaissezPasser".

Jean (John) Henri Weidner, founder and leader of the Dutch-Paris
Escape Line. The Line grew to include more than 300 rescuers. It
sheltered or escorted to safety an estimated 3,000 Jews, downed
Allied pilots, *Engelandvaarders*, and other persecuted people in
Nazi-occupied Europe. (Photograph courtesy of the John Henry
Weidner Foundation for Altruism.)

Jacques Rens, our group leader from Paris to Toulouse and one of Weidner's chief lieutenants.

Pierre Treillet, our guide over the Pyrenees, who was also a member of the Dutch-Paris Escape Line.

Pierre "Palo" Treillet's forged identity card.

Restaurant Emile in Toulouse.

Rue Croix-Baragnion, Toulouse, where we stayed in a "safe house" on 21 January 1944.

15 August 1943: Albert Starink, second from right in a cable car near Lourdes.

The back of the cabane on the Portet d'Aspet Pass. On 25 January 1944 we approached this cabane from this west side.

February 1944: Evaders in Lerida, Spain. Back row: myself, Meredith H. Rueff, Charles Downe, Robert van Exter, Harold Lockwood, George Jasman. Front row: Tiger Hicks Ernest Grubb, Edward Knapp, James Hussong and Leonard Cassady.

February 1944: Left to right: Leonard Cassady, James Hussong, Charles Downe, myself, Robert van Exter and Ernest Grubb in Lerida.

El extranjero de nacionalidad, **Holandesa**,

Don **Pieter Rudolph ZEEMAN**,

de **24** años, de estado **soltero**,

profesión **contable**, domiciliado accidentalmente en **Madrid**
(Población)

Arenal 19
(Calle)

H.Internacional
(Pensión, etc.)

entrado en España **clandestinamente**
(Clasificación de la forma en que ha entrado)

ha comparecido en el día de hoy procedente de **Lérida**,

_____ tríptico núm. **s.colectiv**
(Presentado o siéndole asignado)

Hasta que por la Superioridad a quien se da cuenta del caso, resuelva sobre la situación de dicho extranjero, este viene obligado a presentarse en esta Comisaría todos los **sábados**, no pudiendo cambiar de domicilio sin previa autorización de la misma.

Madrid, **17** de **Febrero** de **1944**

El Comisario Jefe,
P.O.

El Inspector, Jefe del servicio,

(Véase a la vuelta)

My Policia Seguridad Identity Card issued in Madrid on 17 February 1944 and ordering me to report every Saturday at the Comisaria on the Puerto del Sol in the centre of Madrid.

My Zaragoza to Madrid 1st-class railway ticket.

The artist John Ruys on a visit to the French Riviera. Ruys gave me shelter in his Montparnasse apartment. He was later arrested for aiding another Dutch escapee and died in Oranienburg concentration camp in Germany.

Mr W van de Stadt, a banker and friend of my father who helped to support me when I first arrived in England.

My close friend, F/O Zdenek (Steve) Kôkes, with whom I narrowly survived a V-1 attack in London

The Hotel Franco-Espagñol in Val d'Aran, Spain. The Hotel was a welcome sight to escapees and evaders who made it safely across the Pyrenees Mountains. It opened its doors to many fleeing refugees and Allied pilots. These photos were taken by Ian and Sandie Schagen in 2015 as they retraced the steps of Ian's father, Pieter, who was also a Dutch evader. The Hotel was in disrepair and not in use at the time. (Photos courtesy of Ian and Sandie Schagen.)

My postcard to my parents written on 5 February 1944.

February 1944: Tom Bright, Robert and myself in Lerida.

De Lairessestraat 96. Our family's apartment was on the 2nd floor (the third row of windows from pavement).

My father at his desk in his study at no 96 de Lairessestraat, Amsterdam. A drawing of his good friend Karel Michielson Sr. hangs on the wall above the desk.

Part III:
Around the World in 1014 Days

25. New York and San Francisco

On the early morning of the 14th of July, 1944, we could see a dark outline on the horizon of the continent which would not be named after Columbus but after Amerigo Vespucci who had sailed under his command on the 1492 voyage of discovery. Amerigo would discover the North American continent on a later voyage and the name America is the latinization of his name.

We hastened down to the dining room and I had 'our' German POW steward serve me my usual double helping of eggs and bacon. He was the first German, since my 1939 visit to Germany to watch the Eifelrennen Autoraces on the Nürnburg Ring near Adenau, from whom I took my leave with a friendly *"Auf Wiedersehen."*

From our A-deck vantage point we watched our mighty ship enter New York Harbour. In lower New York Bay we could already see the very tops of its famous skyline. Moving between New Jersey and Brooklyn and entering Upper New York Bay, the view was just as I remembered from newsreels. It was quite unforgettable. Sailing towards the Hudson River, the New York City skyline loomed higher and higher to our starboard side, the Empire State and Chrysler Buildings easily recognisable. Passing the Statue of Liberty to portside, the RMS 'Queen Mary' reached the Hudson River and, after gliding past Battery Park and more than 40 piers, three tugboats eased the big ship into the Cunard Pier 86 dock. We could see the grey-painted RMS 'Queen Elizabeth' and other large troopships moored further up the Hudson River but not the burnt-out and capsized 'Normandie' of the French Line.

It was well past noon when we left the ship at a forward starboard gangway and descended a gangplank to the quay where, without further ado, we were marched past immigration officials. This group included a few American Army MPs and a perspiring gentleman in a business suit and hat who was obviously a Dutch Consular Official. We were led to a nearby waiting military bus. It was like getting off a ferry and walking to a bus-stop. Such was travel in uniform from continent to continent and country to country in wartime.

Dressed in our British khaki tropical uniform, with shorts and knee-high socks, we immediately drew the attention of bystanders because, in the USA of 1944, no grown-up American male would go about in shorts, not even in humid 40°C heat! Shorts were for kids or were only worn by the Boy Scouts. Humorous remarks followed us wherever we went but nothing could stop the four of us from hitting town after we had checked in at a second class, but third rate, 42nd Street hotel just off Broadway and Times Square and in the heart of New York's entertainment precinct.

Our five officers were booked into the superior 'Cumberland Hotel', also situated on 42nd Street, where Lt. van Kregten, (according to my 1944 Spanish notebook) had room 1122, telephone Murray Hill 6-6000. While we were free to go as we pleased, we had to notify him when out of town since our orders to leave for San Francisco could arrive any time.

My single bedroom, as were those for the others, was wide enough for a bed and left enough room to open the built-in wardrobe doors. The bathroom was shared with the occupant of the room on the wardrobe side, and from the window one had a view into other buildings and, below us, the wire mesh grating covering the balconies. The practical purpose of these wire mesh coverings was instantly appreciated for it caught anything thrown out of the hotel windows, which were mainly a large number of condoms. Jim Jongeneel thought we were most fortunate to have a room without a balcony and Herman found it necessary to make lewd remarks about the sound of windows being opened at all times of the day and night, the trajectory and the effect of these items when landing on the mesh gratings covering the balconies below us. While we made fun of it, and used the very small rooms only to sleep in, it was nevertheless not a particularly uplifting sight.

That first evening we made our way in our British khaki shorts, bush-jacket and beret, through the evening crowds of giggling girls and bystanders with amused looks. It was quite an experience to be the centre of curiosity and attention on Times Square in New York City of all places.

According to Jim Jongeneel, some girls tried to pull the hairs from his legs, an experience that did not befall me or Henk. That first evening we discovered the Pepsi Cola Centre for "enlisted men in uniform" on Times Square where we only had to pay five cents for a big glass of milk and 10 cents for excellent hot dogs, while cold Pepsi Cola was free of charge. We could also escape the torrid heat in this air-conditioned amenity. Another free, marvellous amenity for the GIs (and us) was the 'Stage Door Canteen', an entertainment nightclub. On entry we received a small pack of five 'Chesterfield' cigarettes, while soft drinks were free and we were entertained by artists before, after or between their appearances at shows, cafe-bars, restaurants and dance halls. At cinemas and other entertainment centres, soldiers in uniform were, furthermore, offered concessionary rates.

In the morning after the day of our arrival, we were taken to Brookes Brothers by our CO and outfitted with American tropical and winter uniforms and, of course, provided with KNIL insignias and 'Royal East Indies Army' shoulder patches. We also exchanged the British beret for a cap. The difference in quality of the materials used in American and British uniforms was notable and much appreciated by me.

I did not see much of Henk, Herman and Jim during our stay in New York. Herman and Jim had a few very wild nights on the town but most of the time were entertained by the Dutch community in 'the Netherlands Club' and at their homes, while Henk, like later in Australia, would meet and make lifetime friends.

Soon after my arrival in the city founded by the Dutch in the 17th century, and which they called "*Nieuw*" Amsterdam, I phoned, as I had promised, Charles Downe's parents who lived in the town of Orange, New Jersey. They were keen to learn all about our trip from Paris to Lerida and invited me to their home which, for reasons which I can no longer remember, I regretfully could not accept.

When in London, I had written to my old friends Ata and André Ceurvorst—whose address I had been given by Mr. Pauw, Ata's stepfather—that they could expect me to arrive sometime after June.

Ata and her sister Hetty had been close friends of mine ever since we, as children, met for the first time in 1928 at Ata's birthday party in Soerabaja, Java. There we were treated to *es poeter*—vanilla ice-cream prepared in a wooden tub—a great treat in those days. Eleven years later

Hetty would marry my brother Tommy, who in 1928 was at high school in The Hague and staying with his grandmother.

Ata, born in San Francisco, applied and was granted US citizenship during the first year of the German Occupation of Holland. This allowed her to leave German-controlled territory to join and marry her fiancé in the USA. André Ceurvorst had been stranded there in May of 1940 while on a visit to the Chrysler factory for which the Ceurvorst firm were the sole importers in the Netherlands. He had however secured a Chrysler dealership in Poughkeepsie, north of New York City, but an accident left him a semi-invalid with serious back trouble. The car sales came to a virtual standstill when the USA went to war. Ata worked at Bergdorf & Goodman and it was therefore André who showed me the sights during the day, foremost being the 102-story Empire State Building, *"the nearest thing to heaven in New York City"*, with its fabulous view over the city.

Travelling the length and breadth of New York's Manhattan Island, mostly by bus and on foot, showed us a metropolis where life went on as before the War. The traffic was hectic and the shops displayed an abundance of luxury goods, in sharp contrast not only to occupied Europe but also to England. Only the large number of uniformed men everywhere indicated that there was a war on somewhere in which the Americans were also involved.

During the evenings when we did not enjoy the slightly cooler air on the terrace of their apartment above the Grammercy Park Hotel on Grammercy Park, near 21st Street, Ata and André would take me to shows, music-bars, restaurants like the '3 Deuces' on 52nd Street (minimum charge $3) where the great jazz pianist Art Tatum performed. They also made sure to take me to a piano bar where the African-American pianist Freddy Johnson was playing. All three of us had many a time listened to him tickling the ivories at the 'Negro Palace' just off Rembrandtsplein (*"plein"* means square) in Amsterdam where Coleman Hawkins, one of the greats amongst saxophone players, had enraptured the jazz aficionados in the pre-War days. Freddy Johnson gave me a most friendly welcome and questioned me about Amsterdam under German Occupation.

One morning I made my way to the Lane Studios on 1480 Broadway where servicemen could have a message recorded on a gramophone record. I sent a record to Mr. van de Stadt in London for him to pass on to my family in Amsterdam as soon as Holland was liberated.

We had arrived in an honest-to-goodness July heat-wave and I could not recall ever having anywhere—even in the tropics—experienced heat and humidity that made one perspire as profusely while just sitting quietly in a chair in the very city praised in Frank Sinatra's ballad 'New York, New York'.

The worst of the heat-wave had blessedly passed when we spent a weekend in Poughkeepsie on the Hudson River, north of New York, where André had his Chrysler dealership and where they still had a house.

At the Saturday evening baseball game, to my acute embarrassment, it was announced that "a war hero from Holland" was present. I was made to stand up in the stadium and acknowledge the applause of the crowd. Young men in my day, and most certainly *Engelandvaarders,* did not consider themselves true heroes. Chaps with guts, yes. Since then times have changed and now many totally undeserving persons, including sportsmen, are called heroes.

For the last two days of my stay in New York I moved out of the, shall I say unforgettable, 42nd Street hotel into a single room at the Grammercy Park Hotel. This hotel occupied the lower floors of the Ceurvorst's apartment building, enabling me to spend the last days enjoying the balmy air on the terrace of Ata and André's apartment high above the city. After a farewell party at the 'Downbeat Club' on West 52nd Street, it was with regret that I said goodbye to Ata and André who had given me such a marvellous time and, with a last embrace, I left them at the entrance to the platform for the train to Chicago on the morning of the 8th of August. At that time, I did not know, and could not have guessed, that the spinal injuries, which André had sustained in a car accident back in Holland a few years earlier, were seriously aggravated later by the mishap in America. They would be the cause of his death only two years later.

At about 10 o'clock the next morning the train pulled into Chicago Station where we had a four-hour stay before departure for the West Coast of the USA. Jaap and Herman decided to have a look at the town made famous by Al Capone and his gangster friends, while, for some inexplicable reason, Henk and I decided to stay in our compartment instead of exploring at least a small part of this city.

Jim and Herman returned hardly 10 minutes before the train's departure. It was an anxious Lt. van Kregten, Henk and I who saw the twosome unsteadily walking up the incline of the passage to the departure platform. Jim has ever since strenuously denied that they had far too much to drink, but we could not and would not believe that in at least two hours (but probably three) of being entertained in a bar by well-heeled citizens of Chicago they had only consumed "one or two" drinks.

As in New York, they had experienced a most friendly welcome from the inhabitants of this city on Lake Michigan. Upon entering a bar, for a soft drink no doubt, the saloon's patrons noted their NEI Army shoulder patches and they were promptly 'shouted' drinks. Further libations were ordered when it was learned that they had recently escaped from German-occupied Western Europe. In spite of their inebriated state, Jim and Herman contended, to Henk's and my disbelief, that they were 'as sober as judges' and tried to convince us by telling some outrageous stories.

In a letter to me of January 1996, Jim wrote yet another defence of his Chicago escapade which would do an Attorney proud:

Incidentally, as to van Nouhuys and me "getting into alcoholic trouble in Chicago"...that's a bit exaggerated. Herman and I somehow wound up having lunch and possibly one or two drinks, if that many, at some kind of restaurant when we were spotted by some gentleman, who having noticed our uniforms, enthusiastically identified himself as someone who "manufactured tanks", adding ... "the sort of material you guys will be called upon to fight with!" Next thing, he ordered all sorts of food and drink for our table, all the while extolling us as proverbial saviours of the world. Spotting a nice-looking girl in private conversation with a male companion in civilian clothes at another table, he boldly went up to the man and told him to leave the restaurant, whilst simply more or less ordering the girl to go seat herself at our table and "to take care of the boys!" Whatever the stature and apparent influence of the alleged 'tank manufacturer', both the girl and her friend complied instantly with his commands."

I rest my case.

From Chicago our Union Pacific Railroad train was called 'The Challenger', for which the blurb announced that we would be taking "the strategic middle route" (pronounced "raut") from Chicago via Omaha,

Cheyenne and Ogden to San Francisco. Crossing a continent in four days by train is an experience which befalls very few people nowadays. We slept in the type of sleeping cars peculiar to the USA and which played an important part in movies like Marilyn Monroe's 1959 comedy, "Some Like It Hot." Unlike the *wagon-lits* of Europe, you undressed in a small dressing room and then, in nightie or pyjamas and robe, proceeded to your numbered *couchette* in the carriage which had double rows of curtained-off sleeping berths on both sides of a central corridor. I cannot remember much of this experience, which repeated itself four times, but I do know that we did not have robes on like Marilyn or Tony Curtis, nor regretfully any Marilyn clones rushing about. Jim, our Lothario, however, still recalls a pretty girl called Janet (I think) who made this journey such a pleasant one for him.

I found the extent of support of the American people for military personnel during the war nowhere else, as we would again experience on this trans-continental train journey. Wherever our train stopped during daylight hours, even at day-break, the townspeople, like those in Ogden, Utah had lined up trestle tables with coffee, milk, sandwiches, cakes, candy, cigarettes and magazines "for the boys". Kind, mostly middle-aged and elderly ladies would be waiting to serve us "poor, brave boys going to war".

After leaving Ogden and crossing the Great Salt Lake, and the desert of the same name, the train reached the Rocky Mountains, where we enjoyed the spectacular scenery as the train drove over the winding track through valleys and steep-sided gorges. Regretfully, a great part of the Rockies was negotiated in darkness.

It was on the 12th day of August that 'The Challenger' descended to the lowlands, through which the Sacramento and San Joaquin Rivers flow to the Pacific Ocean. Soon thereafter our trans-continental trip ended in 'the gateway to the Orient', the city famous for the 'Golden Gate Bridge' and remembered for the 1906 earthquake.

The very next day a 'V-girl' picked us up at a Servicemen's Centre and drove us in her own automobile around San Francisco to show us the sights. Afterwards we had a very civilized cup of tea at her parents' home. These V-for-Victory young ladies were vetted and selected to make sure that they would 'properly' give servicemen a pleasant time in their city.

One day we attended a double feature at one of the many cinemas where one movie featured Frank Sinatra, who only a year ago was an unknown singer, and were astonished when teenage girls started screaming as soon as Frankie started crooning. Somebody later told me that his clever manager, in the very early days of Frankie's career, placed a group of young females at a table nearest the stage and, as soon as Frankie finished wailing, they would jump up and rush to the stage screaming in adoration. This soon got out of hand when 'bobby soxers' started screaming hysterically as soon as he exercised his vocal cords. I have never forgotten that first manifestation of young female ecstasy.

26. Across the Pacific

On the 19th of August we boarded the MV "Lurline" a well-known pre-war Matson Line luxury passenger ship built in 1932 for the San Francisco-Honolulu run. It had been converted into a troopship. Cafeteria-style meals, collected on metal trays divided in sections, were served twice a day in the ship's original dining room. Two meals a day had also been the rule on the RMS 'Queen Mary', albeit that we were now not served by a steward but had to line up with our trays and find a seat at the long tables with fixed benches. The troops would, as on the 'Queen Mary', sleep on so-called standees—fixed metal frames the size of a narrow single bed, covered with canvas, of which two, three or four were connected to a heavy metal support. They were vastly superior to the hammocks used on troopships like the SS 'Orduña'.

The next day, on my mother's birthday, the 'Lurline' departed from San Francisco bound for the Southern Hemisphere. The decks swarmed with soldiers, women from the WAC (Women's Auxiliary Corps), US Medical Corps Nurses and seven Dutch girls of the NAWC who stood pressed together waving their farewells to well-wishers seeing them off to a war in the Pacific. The ship sailed away unescorted under the Golden Gate Bridge into the Pacific Ocean.

In the United States of America, the coast of which slowly disappeared behind the wake of the MV 'Lurline', war was unimaginable.

Our accommodations on the 'Lurline', while not comparable to those on the 'Queen Mary, was certainly not as miserable as in the hold of the SS 'Orduña'. We were assigned a small four-berth cabin situated at the very stern on the lowest deck and literally above one of the propellers, where, after a while, we got used to the constant turning noise of the shaft and the turbulence of the sea churned by the propeller. A porthole thankfully provided us with fresh sea air.

On crossing the International Date Line we received, like passengers before in peacetime, a certificate from the MV 'Lurline', printed by The Matson Line and signed by the Captain, Frank Jenkins. It was a reminder of peacetime while at war.

On the 5th of September, the 'Lurline' dropped anchor in the Huon Gulf off New Guinea where shipwrecks and denuded palm trees attested to the fighting that had not long ago taken place. By September 1944 the crisis of 1942, culminating in the Battle of the Coral Sea, was well past. Japan was no longer a threat to Australia and New Guinea. The largest island on earth was now back in Allied hands except for some small pockets of Japanese troops starving in the jungle. Apart from the US Army personnel, some nurses were taken ashore and the ship turned east again along the New Guinea Coast to Oro Bay, near Buna, where we anchored the next day. There the rest of the nurses and all the girls of the WAC left the ship and were transported to shore in DUCKS (amphibious landing craft). On reaching the jetty, they were greeted with cheers, shouts and whistles by the GI's who had been starved of female company for so many months.

Henk, Jim and Herman decided to hitch a ride to shore in a DUCK while I stayed on board to finish off pen sketches of the wooded shoreline at Oro Bay and of ships at the wharf loading tanks. Standing under palm trees again for the first time since his youth in Java, an irresistible urge overcame Jim and, when the others dared him to do so, he promptly clambered up a large coconut tree. Short of reaching the coconuts he was so exhausted that he did not have the strength left to climb down and sliding down was out of the question as some large nails had been driven into the lower part of the trunk. Herman found it at first a most amusing situation and, ignoring Jim's pleas for help, encouraged passers-by to look "at the big ape" up there in the coconut tree. But Henk and the American soldiers, realizing Jim's dangerous predicament, went into action. An American soldier, equipped with spike shoes and a belt secured around the trunk, climbed the tree and reached Jim, but found it impossible to get down again while supporting most of Jim's weight. He called for a truck equipped with a hoist which, in the ensuing panic, was quickly located in a nearby US camp. Hanging on the hook of the crane, our coconut palm climber was thus safely lowered to earth to everybody's relief.

After Oro Bay, the 'Lurline' sailed down the north coast of New Guinea and through the straits between New Guinea and the heavily-wooded d'Entrecasteau Islands. I clearly remember seeing a few, very dark-skinned, natives standing under coconut palms near their thatched huts, looking at us. We were so near, and at one point perhaps not even a hundred yards separated us—yet two worlds apart.

It was off the far eastern tip of New Guinea that I had a nightmare to end all nightmares and my three comrades had to restrain me from crawling (literally) out of the porthole. They told me that I was shouting that a man with a knife was chasing me, but I could not remember at all what had caused the nightmare. Apparently I already had an arm and my head through the porthole when my three friends pulled me back. Recurring nightmares are a legacy of war-time experiences for many.

Soon after leaving San Francisco we were issued with Atabrin tablets and subjected to a rigid anti-malaria discipline which had been instituted by the American and Australian Militaries in 1944. Malaria mosquitoes had, before the drug's introduction, caused mounting sick lists which had seriously affected the campaigns in New Guinea. For every war casualty there were six men put out of action by malaria. The prevention of dysentery, so easily contracted in the tropics, was however another matter and so was 'jungle rot', as the soldiers called tropical ulcers, eczemas and other skin diseases as well as intestinal infestations.

27. The Continent Called Australia

On the 10th September we steamed across Moreton Bay and up the Brisbane River. After disembarkation, a KNIL Army truck drove the nine of us, three KNIL troops from Surinam, and seven Dutch girls who had also come aboard in San Francisco, to Camp Columbia, the large Dutch base at Wacol, near Ipswich, and not far west of Brisbane. Camp Columbia was one of those excellently-designed camps the Americans built all over Australia, New Guinea and other Pacific Islands, as they re-conquered the Pacific Islands on their way to Japan.

My first impression of Brisbane was that of a hick town, a view that did not change on many subsequent visits during the War years. The *cuisine* in particular was poor certainly by European standards, even at their premier Lennon's Hotel. For lunch and dinner I would therefore, on subsequent visits to Camp Columbia, patronize the Dutch Club and the American (Officers') Club when in Brisbane. If one city in Australia has changed beyond recognition in the past half century then it surely must be Brisbane.

In September of 1944, Camp Columbia housed the Dutch Minister for the Colonies, Lt. Governor General H. J. van Mook, and the Netherlands East Indies Government-in-Exile, as well as the KNIT headquarters and the counter-intelligence unit called NEFIS (Netherlands Indies Intelligence Service). The KNIL-ML (Air Force) headquarters was still situated at St Kilda Road in Melbourne. After only a few days ensconced in a comfortable two-bedroom wooden hut at Camp Columbia, we received our 'Movement Order' instructing us to proceed to Melbourne on the 15th of September.

It was here at Camp Columbia that my destiny would take a new turn because of a chance meeting with a friend of my father, a senior official whose name I recalled because he had been a regular visitor to my parents' homes. This visit occurred when we lived on the van Heutz Boulevard and Madioenweg No 1 in Batavia between 1929 and 1934. Mr. van Hoogstraten remarked: *"So you are the son of Piet Zeeman,"* when I was introduced to him. Learning that I was an air cadet on my way to fighter pilot training with the RAAF, he opined that with my schooling, language skills and knowledge of the Netherlands East Indies, I should join the NIGEO (Netherlands East Indies Government Import Export Organisation). Besides, he added: *"your future career will most likely be in commerce in 'Indie'* (as we called the NEI) *and I am sure your father would agree."*

When Mr. van Hoogstraten suggested that he would arrange for the necessary papers for the transfer from the Air Force to NIGEO, I did not dare to object but I had, at that time, no wish to sign up and give up the chance of getting my pilot wings. The glamour of wings pinned on my uniform and piloting a fighter plane was far too great.

It was only some time later, during my first five months in Australia, that I learned that after the surrender of Singapore at the beginning of April 1942, and just before the fall of Java, that it had been decided by the NEI Government in Batavia to send selected members of the NEI Colonial Administration and business community, headed by Lt. Governor General H. J. van Mook, to Australia. Among the van Mook party of some two dozen who were flown out of Java were Mr. Crena de Jong, a friend of my father, and Mr. Raden Loekman Djajadiningrat, at whose home his nephew and my friend Didi lived, and whom I had met many a time when playing in his large garden in Laan Raden Saleh in the early 1930s. Some others had left by ship and amongst these was Dr. (of Economics) J. E. van Hoogstraten who was Director of Economics of the NEI Government in Batavia.

On the two-days (and nights) train journey from Brisbane to Melbourne there were no sleepers. It was not a particularly comfortable trip, and the scenery during the daytime did not particularly enchant me. Sydney, from our train compartment window, appeared to be a true metropolis. This vastly improved our opinion of Australia. We were most surprised at having to change trains at Albury-Wodonga because of the different rail gauges at that time between the states of NSW and Victoria.

In Melbourne we felt immediately at home. It was, and still is, the most European city in Australia. After reporting to Lt. Col. B. F. Fiedeldij of the KNIL-ML (Air Force) at HQ in St Kilda Road, we were housed in a KNIL hostel in Coburg called 'Weston Court'. It was only a short tram ride from where the action was and, therefore, the Dutch Club and several good Italian restaurants such as 'The Latin', 'Florentino's', 'Molino's' and 'The Italian Society'.

After about a week we were directed to the RAAF eye-testing facility. After the examination, we were informed that we would be told of the results through "your HQ," Since we had passed the RAF tests, we expected to get our clearance to join the RAAF Training Scheme. So we enjoyed ourselves as much as we could afford on our limited KNIL cadet pay. If my memory does not fail me, we were given an additional 'off-barracks' allowance since only breakfast was provided at the hostel in Coburg.

Hanging around in Melbourne, while waiting for the results of our eye tests, was no punishment. One day, on Wednesday the 26th of September to be exact, Jim and Herman insisted that I join them for a visit to 'The Dug Out' in Swanston Street. They had just discovered its existence and described it as something like a cross between the Pepsi Cola Center and the Stage Door Canteen in New York.

The Dug Out was the brainchild of Mr. Sidney Myer of the Myer Department Store chain. It consisted of a large hall with amenities in a basement of a commercial building and was used as a "home away from home" and entertainment area for service men. Female employees from several large banking and insurance companies were asked to make themselves available one evening a week from 6 p.m. until 10 p.m. to serve food and soft drinks, at a very low cost, to sew on buttons, shine shoes and make small clothing repairs. There was always a jazz band playing and the girls would, of course, be free to dance with the boys, but leaving The Dug Out with service men was strictly forbidden, as was making dates, but that was, of course, very difficult to police.

That September day the three of us walked into The Dug Out. As clearly as the day it happened, I can still see a slim dark-haired girl dressed in a white top and light blue skirt standing across the hall. That was the moment a young woman succeeded, where the Germans had failed, to capture me. But, like so many men, I did not know yet that I was no longer master of my own destiny. I did not fall in love with her on the spot, those notions are recalled when, later on, love blooms.

Wednesday was the evening for the Colonial Mutual Insurance Company, where Berna worked, and had I come on another evening, we would not have met. I was told later that she, her friend Valerie and others had wondered who those three chaps in American uniforms were for they were obviously not Yanks. Our shoulder patches brought the required answer and when we produced American cigarettes our popularity soared. In fact, Berna's friends made sure that she kept me on a string to ensure further offerings of Chesterfield and Camel cigarettes. Little did these girls realise that it had not been necessary at all to kick Berna in the shins to get her attention and charm me for their nefarious reasons.

During my first visit to Berna's family, her mother, at the first opportunity, made it known that Berna was engaged to an American Marine. I soon realised that an American was, to her parents, less of a foreigner than I. Since Berna was not married and still had the undeniable right to change her mind, I saw no reason to not, using the old-fashioned word, court her.

In early September it had been made known to the passengers of the 'Lurline' that the Allies had liberated Brussels on the 3rd of September and then, on arrival in Melbourne, the newspapers had reported that Maastricht, on the far southern tip of the Netherlands, had been captured on the 14th by the US Army. This news raised our hopes that our families in the provinces of North and South Holland would soon be liberated, but it would take another eight months after the 'market-garden debacle' at Arnhem and a terrible 'hunger winter', in which more than 30,000 people died, before the Netherlands north of the Rhine and Meuse Rivers would be liberated on the 5th of May 1945.

The results of our eye tests, administered by far more stringent RAAF rules in 1944, were most disappointing and I was turned down for pilot training but passed for observer-navigator. Apparently I had a miniscule deviation at the point of convergence when locking my eyes on an object. This deficiency has only manifested itself some 50 years later when playing snooker at the Launceston Club. I have always wondered whether it would have affected my ability to fly a plane. I think not. Henk, however, did qualify for pilot training, while Herman and Jaap failed the test and both decided against an administrative appointment or becoming air gunners for, as Jim said: *"I did not walk over the Pyrenees to fight the enemy from behind a desk"*.

It was at this junction that Herman and Jim parted company with Henk and me because we were despatched by train to Canberra in the Australian Capital Territory to temporarily join the KNIL-ML party attached to 534 RAAF Squadron at Fairbairn Airbase. Years later I learned that Herman joined the Engineers and then, as a Sergeant, somehow ended up in Camp Columbia while Jim had joined the NEFIS and had been promoted to Sub-Lt., the equivalent of Ensign in the Navy.

Canberra in 1944 was no doubt the most unusual capital city in the world with acres of empty spaces between big government buildings, few houses completed in areas planned for houses, and only a few completely built-up streets. There were a few cinemas and, if I remember correctly, one or two modern hotels—that is to say that they were not of the pub-type kind which in 'Down Under' graced cities, towns and villages. However, in the nearby town of Queenbeyan in New South Wales, outside the Capital Territory, there were two more hotels where most officers were put up. At one true-blue Aussie pub the publican explained to me that the tiled walls and cement floors made cleaning easier after the daily '6 o'clock swill'! The ban on serving alcoholic drinks after 6 p.m., as incomprehensively stupid to us Europeans as Prohibition was in the United States, often resulted in loathsome scenes of men drinking themselves into a stupor between when they left work and 6 o'clock approached. Pub food in those days was generally terrible and when at Fairbairn, if we went to see a movie, we would invariably go to the cafe of George the Greek for a tasty steak and eggs.

At Fairbairn, Henk and I were joined by a Dutchman from Brazil, Dimmie Vermeulen, a few chaps from Surinam of Indonesian descent and, as well, a number of African origin. Except for Dimmie, all the others were to be trained as air gunners and ground crew. The coloured boys did not have an easy time in a country where coloureds at that time were generally looked down on as "black fellahs". In today's multi-cultural Australia, it is difficult to understand that the presence of non-Europeans and mixed-race Dutch nationals from the NEI and the West

Indian Colonies marred the relationship between the Curtin and Chifley (Australian Labor Party) Governments and the NEI Government-in-Exile. We newcomers to Australia were ignorant of the then White Australia Policy until we were posted to Canberra where I noticed that brown and black-skinned KNIL soldiers from Surinam, while not discriminated against, were only accepted on sufferance. Having spent many years of my youth in the NEI, Malaya, Japan and India, as well as some time in Shanghai, I had no racially superior feelings toward Asians and mixed-race people. In fact, amongst my closest friends in the 1930s had been Bernhard Yo Heng Kam, the son of the Kapitein (Head) of the Chinese community, and the aforementioned Didi Djajadiningrat, while many other mixed-race Dutch and Chinese became good friends of mine then and later in life.

At Canberra's Fairbairn Airbase we were lectured on navigation and air combat while Sgt. Dimmie Vermeulen instructed us on military drill which in the Dutch Army is different from the KNIL and different again from that of the RAAF and AIF (Australian Imperial Forces). It was rather confusing and, in the short time at Fairbairn and RAAF Sommers, I was not sufficiently trained in the KNIL drill to be confident enough to command a platoon let alone a KNIL battalion. It would nearly lead to a possible 'face-losing' moment when I had to take command of a battalion of KNIL prisoners of war from the Japanese on Flores Island.

It was at Fairbairn that most of us, including myself, had our first ever aeroplane flight in a B-24 Mitchell Bomber on a target practice run which necessitated steep dives, evasive action and steep climbing. Several of us rookies got violently air-sick and I had to use my forage cap not to soil the interior of the bombardier's compartment in the nose of the fuselage. Since I am not easily prone to sea-sickness, I thereafter had no air-sickness problems after this rather violent introduction to flying in an aeroplane, despite the turbulence one nearly always encounters flying over Australia's land mass. In those days, when aeroplanes could not fly at today's 'stratospheric' heights, my memory of flying a Tiger Moth was that of yo-yoing along in the turbulence and air pockets over inland Australia. The landings were sometimes hair-raising.

Every second Friday, in the late afternoon, bystanders at Melbourne's Essendon Airport would look with disbelief at the large number of uniformed men exiting from a Dutch B-24 Bomber to start their off-duty weekend. The unlucky ones would have to sit in the bomb-bay, but nobody cared since it meant escaping from the boredom in Canberra to the fun of big city life in Melbourne.

We had just returned from a most pleasant Christmas in Melbourne where I had spent most of the time with Berna at her friends, the Floyds, family residence in the suburb of Ormond when Dimmie, Henk and I were directed to report at the RAAF Camp at Sommers. On the 29th December we reported to the commanding officer of the near-deserted camp situated on the east coast of the Mornington Peninsular, opposite Philip Island, and learned that the RAAF Aussie trainees would not arrive until after the New Year. We considered ourselves to be victims of a case of SNAFU (situation normal all f---ed up) and a bleak turn of the year was spent by the three of us consoled by a few bottles of BOLS gin.

The camp's kitchen at Sommers must have been manned by chaps who had been anything but cooks in civilian life and, finding the 'tea' (as dinner was then called by most 'dinky di' Aussies) uneatable, I existed mainly on bread, butter and sugar or jam. Every late Friday afternoon, on arrival at Flinders Street Station in Melbourne, the first thing I would do was to go to 'Mindy's' for a huge portion of steak and eggs before meeting Berna.

At the end of January, a throat infection put me into Heidelberg Military Hospital to have my tonsils removed and where, only a few days after the operation, a few Aussies and I would abscond after 'tea' by crawling under the mesh fence and make for the lights of Melbourne. If our absence was detected then the nurses never reported us, lovely and understanding humans that they usually are.

28. Ordered to Camp Columbia

I had hardly returned to Sommers when, at the end of February, I was called into the office of the commanding officer who informed me that I had been claimed (or words to that effect) by the NEI Government's Department of Commerce and Industry and was to report for duty at Camp Columbia, Wacol.

For the life of me, I cannot recall ever having signed a request for this transfer. Mr. van Hoogstraten must have arranged it for me. Although I would have liked to have earned my observer-navigator wings, and partake in bombing the 'Nips', it did not have the same appeal as that of piloting a fighter plane. I also could see the logic behind Mr. van Hoogstraten's reasoning of joining an outfit like the NIGEO for a future career in business.

On one of the last days of February 1944, on arrival at Camp Columbia, I was informed of my duties in the NIGEO and that I was to fly to Hollandia within a few days to join a NICA detachment. Without further ado, I was sworn in as a Vaandrig (Sub Lt.) and issued with my officer's rank's insignia and, a few days later, I boarded a C-47 Dakota of the KNIL Air Force Transport Squadron at Brisbane Airport.

The NICA (Netherlands Indies Civil Administration) was brought into being to restore Dutch administration in the NEI if and when areas were re-occupied by the Allies. The NICA was out of necessity militarised and thus a hybrid of NEI civil administration and military.

Its task was to bring relief and rehabilitation to the liberated areas as soon as the area was cleared of enemy troops. However, these relatively small detachments were also expected to defend the local population from Japanese counter-attacks. To many of us, particularly those with military experience, this task seemed fanciful without substantial KNIL troop assistance—which was simply not available. History would luckily not call on the NICA to perform that task without US Army assistance, although NICA detachments had, in the first month or so after the Japanese surrender, some unpleasant run-ins with Indonesian revolutionaries on some of the islands, mainly on Java and Sumatra.

After crossing over Torres Strait and the lowlands of New Guinea, the clouds started to build up at the foothills of the high mountain ridge, which forms the spine of New Guinea. It reaches 5030 metres at its snow-capped highest point. To the east is a 4750-metre high mountain which the Dutch called Wilhelmina Peak. These snow-capped mountains were beyond the flight ceiling of a Dakota, certainly a fully-loaded one. Even further to the east, careful navigation was required to fly over and through them especially during the monsoon when the hot and very humid air from the hundreds of square kilometres of lowlands which lie between the Arafura Sea/Torres Strait and the New Guinea mountains forms huge clouds. These clouds produced heavy rainfall that fed the rivers and the swamplands of this largest island on Earth. The heavy concomitant clouds often created dangerous flying conditions. The story was told that parts of cargoes, including Japanese POWs, were jettisoned in bad weather to safely secure passage across this true wilderness.

After crossing the mountains, sometimes flying between high peaks, we crossed a carpet of endless evergreen tropical forests to land at Sentani Airport.

General MacArthur's island-hopping strategy had resulted in American amphibious landings at Humboldt Bay and Tanah Merah Bay on the 22nd of April, 1944. Five days later, the Americans had secured the airstrip near Hollandia—the capital of Dutch New Guinea, situated on Lake Sentani which, at a guess, is about 200 metres above sea level. Here, in a very short time, they created the largest base in the Pacific where at one time some 150,000 men occupied the area and a whole fleet of ships could anchor at Humboldt Bay.

I recall the endless barracks, workshops and rows upon rows of warehouses and marshalling yards of trucks, bulldozers, jeeps, DUCKS and mountains of new tyres. Once, when invited to dinner on a US Navy ship, my host pointed out a complete US Navy repair base for small ships, up to destroyer size, as well as a large oil terminal at Tanah Merah Bay for refuelling ships The NICA detachment at Hollandia, Dutch New Guinea, to which I was assigned, occupied a former US camp bordering on beautiful Lake Sentani and was under the command of Lt. Colonel Radon Abdulkadir Widjojoatmodjo—a highly civilised, pleasant and capable Javanese aristocrat. There I joined 10 or 11 other officers and a number of other ranks.

I was billeted in a two-berth hut with a concrete floor and tin roof, where I slept on a camp-bed covered by a *klamboe* (mosquito net). The hut stood only some 10 metres or so from the lake, under and surrounded by coconut trees and a large-leaved tropical tree, the species of which is unknown to me. It was an ideal bedroom for the tropics since it allowed the air to freely flow through the partially-enclosed sides of the hut.

My commanding officer one day instructed me to perform what was considered to be a duty not without danger. I had to take charge of a small detail and collect a truckload of cases of Dutch gin at a warehouse in Humboldt Bay and ride shotgun back to our NICA mess on Lake Sentani. Seated next to the Ambonese KNIL soldier, with a loaded rifle across my knee, and a corporal sitting on top of the load of cases marked 'BOLS-Jenever', we drove with some apprehension up the winding Queen Wilhelmina Highway, climbing 25 kilometres past many a US camp and depot, followed by a steep rise and over a hump, signposted "The Devil's Elbow" by our American friends, to reach the NICA camp without incident. I have always believed that the markings 'BOLS-Jenever' had no meaning for the GIs and that I would not have returned with all the cases if they had been marked beer, whisky or gin.

In the evenings we could go to the aptly named 'Blue Sky Cinema' where a 'to-nite' sign announced the movie to be shown. It was also here in another clearing and surrounded by the jungles of New Guinea that I, seated on a simple wooden bench, saw the hit musical 'Oklahoma'. The explosion of joy at the end of the war in Europe on 9th of May, and the earlier capitulation of the German Forces in Holland at Wageningen on the 5th May, passed me by. Our small NICA community was very happy of course, but it was a subdued celebration in our small officers' mess, the more so since many of us were still in the dark about relatives in Holland.

The road from the two bays to Lake Sentani was named the Queen Wilhelmina Highway and it had been sparsely signposted as such. Between the sea and Lake Sentani, passing kilometres of military stores and barracks, was a winding stretch through tropical forests where, at a road junction, I once spotted a little market run incongruously by American soldiers dressed in their deep green US Army fatigues. A few curious Papuans were looking on from across the dusty crossroads. Most of the goods displayed on upturned cardboard boxes were obviously purchased from so-called PX Stores (US Army shops) or pilfered somewhere along the line from a wharf in the USA to New Guinea. Some items were undoubtedly presents from relatives and friends, which the recipient was now flogging for cash, perhaps to pay off his gambling debts.

I asked one chap, who spoke with a strange dialect I had not heard before, where he came from and was told 'Arkensaw'. *"Where is that town?"* I queried. *"It ain't a town mister, it's a state"* he replied. A bystander explained in proper American-English that it was spelled Arkansas but pronounced 'Arkensaw', and grinned. He then asked me what nationality I was since I was obviously not an American. I was by then wised-up enough to say that I was a *Hollander,* since to most Americans, up to that time at least, the mainly German settlers in Pennsylvania were called 'the Pennsylvania Dutch'. Someone from the Netherlands was called a *Hollander* in America.

Sometime in June I fell ill and was admitted to the 77th US Army General Hospital, where I was subjected to a great number of medical tests over a period of some three weeks. The physicians concluded that I had contracted amoebic dysentery and also mentioned some other interesting, difficult to pronounce and to remember, Latin names of diseases which had infested my guts. This diagnosis did not surprise me, having spent most of my youth in tropical countries and recalling that, after a short year in Calcutta in 1924/25, the whole family came down with amoebic and bacillar dysentery forcing us to go on early home-leave back to The Hague. The US Army doctors prescribed medicines and, to my delight, three weeks' sick leave in a cool climate.

It was while in the hospital in Hollandia that I received a letter dated the 28th of May 1945 from Lt. H. A. van Oort of the RN Army's Princess Irene Brigade as well as a telegram of the 6th of June 1945, despatched by the NHM Bank in London, from my father, telling me that my family had survived the "hunger winter" of 1944-45. His letter and my father's telegram, with the same short message, had been the first good news received from Holland since the surrender of the German Army on the 5th of May 1945.

The medical treatment at the US Army Hospital impressed me greatly and the nurses were marvellous, as nurses all over the world tend to be. In my hospital ward I became friends with three Americans, Capt. Jim Spurrier, Lt. George Ryan and Capt. Thomas Richey (of the 11th Cavalry Regiment). It was here at the 77th General Hospital that a nurse typed out, on Red Cross paper, the first account of my escape from Occupied Europe.

In 1961 my wife and I visited the USA and we spent a delightful evening at the Ryan's large house in the San Fernando Valley. We also met up with Tom Richey and his wife Barbara, who would give my wife and me a fabulous time in Washington, DC, and at their home in Newport, Virginia, where Tom, who had rejoined the US Army after a stint in civilian life, was posted. Cherry blossoms were in full bloom. We visited all the sights in the United States capital, including the Pentagon, had lunch at the Capitol with a Congressman from the State of Texas and saw the old colonial capital, Williamsburg, as well as the battlefields of Yorktown and Gettysburg.

In 1987, 26 years later, they were once again our marvellous hosts in Sierra Vista, Arizona where Barbara and Tom, by then a retired Colonel, had organised a memorable party in an authentic saloon in legendary Tombstone. In its cemetery, called "Boot Hill", the tombstones carry marvellous epitaphs. One which I still remember was:

HERE LIES
LESTER MOORE
FOUR SLUGS
FROM A .44
NO LESS
NO MORE

When we were at dinner in the old Dance Hall, there was suddenly a great commotion and a young woman, in period dress and a feather boa around her neck, rushed in and accused me of not having paid her for her services! I was promptly arrested by the Sheriff and his posse who escorted me to the stage where, in a hastily assembled court of justice, I was found guilty and sentenced to hang. With the noose already around my neck, reprieve came at the last minute when the real culprit was dragged into the saloon by two Deputy Sheriffs. It was the most unforgettable party I ever had. Tom and Barbara since then have left the deserts of Arizona for the northern climate of the State of Wisconsin where, in the winter, knee-deep snowfalls are a regular feature. We still exchange letters to this day.

After parting with backslaps from my American friends at the hospital and after exchanging addresses, I spent one last night in my hut on Lake Sentani and took leave from my CO, Colonel Widjojoatmodjo, who would, quite likely, have been one of the important people of post-War NEI if the Dutch had not been forced by the USA and others, like Australia, to hand over the reigns of Government to Sukarno's Nationalists.

In Sukarno's *Repoeblik* Indonesia, there was no place for the Colonel, only retirement. In 1949 he would come to live across from us, at No 47 Soerabajaweg, in Batavia when the Indonesian Republic became a sovereign state and the street name and city became Jalan Surabaya, Djakarta.

Arriving early in the morning at Sentani Airfield I was requested by a senior officer to assist a fellow officer, in escorting a colleague suffering from a mental breakdown on the long flight to Brisbane. It proved to be a rather harrowing trip in more ways than one. I was introduced to Lt. L. M., who looked tense but otherwise in control of his senses. But as soon as my colleague (whose name escapes me) mentioned that the C-47 Dakota was to leave in a few minutes, L. M. got agitated and shouted that he had changed his mind and would not leave because our plane would crash. *"I know it will"* he added *"for I am Jesus Christ."* Our arguing that God would never allow his Son, Jesus, to be killed in an aeroplane crash and that WE would feel completely safe having him on the Dakota, made him change his mind again.

After flying for a while over verdant tropical forests and unsuccessfully trying to get a glimpse of the snow-covered tops to starboard, I noted that the clouds had increased. By the time we negotiated the highest part of the chain of mountains, the plane was quite suddenly enveloped by dense clouds. It was a situation not without danger. It caused all aboard some anxiety except for L. M. who, at one point, exclaimed *"We are now nearer to God!"* And he continued with a discourse on religion and his role as Jesus before he quite suddenly went quiet and seemed to go into a trance.

Flying across the spine of New Guinea was, in those days, never without some risk for, apart from the weather conditions, there were many parts of the New Guinea mountain area still not mapped. One important valley was actually discovered by a Dutch Air Force pilot during the Pacific War. Expeditions to the valley after the War found, to the delight of anthropologists, the secluded valley inhabited by a stone-age Melanesian tribe that had had no contact with the outside world since time immemorial.

After a short refuelling stopover at Cairns, the weather deteriorated rapidly across the Torres Strait and over the North Australian mainland. Before long the plane bucketed along in a quite frightening, violent electrical storm. L. M., not surprisingly, now became very agitated and Lt. A. N. and I, sitting on either side of him, had to physically restrain poor L. M. when his fear turned into panic. Trying to calm him down, we kept talking, arguing that for whatever reason, God had unleashed this terrible lightening and thunder storm. It surely must be for the sinners and not for his Son, Jesus. Even if we had a sinner aboard then, without doubt, God would not cause the storm to destroy the plane since he, Jesus, was on it. For short periods, it had the desired result and calmed him down, but it seemed an interminable time that we sat there talking and restraining him during recurring bouts of panic before our plane flew out of the storm into calmer air. An exhausted L. M. eventually fell asleep and we could let go of him and stretch our legs. It was with relief that we handed him over to waiting medical personnel at Archerfield.

After reporting my arrival at Camp Columbia I caught an ANA flight to Melbourne where my three weeks' sick-leave passed far too quickly.

Australians are, generally speaking, not comfortable with overt shows of patriotism and, while the Dutch are perhaps more so inclined, both view the American display of the "God Bless America" type somewhat "over the top".

We fully understood the resentment of Australian soldiers, returning from the Middle East, boiling over against "the bloody Yanks", who were so popular with the Australian girls while they were away fighting a war in

North Africa. By now I had been long enough among Australians of all walks of life to note similarities between the Aussies and the Dutch. Neither is inclined to immediately accept or do what the Government tells them. We like to make up our own minds. I was however taken aback learning of the ferocity of the fighting and the "kill 'em" cries heard at 'the battle of Brisbane' in November 1942. It must be said though that, on the whole, the Aussies during those war years did not have the finesse of the Americans in romancing the girls. I can still see US soldiers with a box of sweets and a bunch of flowers meeting their dates! And the girls loved it.

Berna and her friends told me that a few weeks after the Brisbane riot there was a serious, but smaller, clash near Flinders Street Station in Melbourne in February of 1943 which induced the authorities to put out a warning to parents over the radio to keep their daughters at home. A fight also broke out outside a Sydney hotel in the beach suburb of Bondi ("where the good girls are good and the bad girls are good—oh"). By the end of 1943, most American military had departed from the East Coast of Australia, except for Townsville and further north. The fights were soon forgotten and a thing of the past.

Another trip by civilian aircraft returned me to Brisbane's Airport, where I reported to the NIGEO's head office in Camp Columbia. The atmosphere at Camp Columbia and the general attitude was not that of the stiffly formal goings-on in London. This was not surprising for, in pre-war days, Dutchmen who had lived in the Indies, whether West or East, would speak of the stiff and stuffy Hollanders in the old country on the North Sea.

In London, our *Engelandvaarders* Club, 'Oranjehaven', was the conduit of news, rumours and scandals, but in the close community of Camp Columbia at Wacol we underlings literally lived amongst the makers and shakers of Government. It was quite generally known that there was disagreement between the Dutch PM Gerbrandy in London and Dr. H. J. van Mook, the Lt. Governor of NEI and now Minister for the Colonies, regarding the future of the Indies. Dr. van Mook, born in the NEI and with an intimate knowledge of the country and its many tribes and nations, had a far superior understanding of the culture, wishes and demands of the population than the London Dutch or for that fact, most Dutchmen. Dr. van Mook was strongly supported by Dr. van der Plas, the ex-Governor of West Java, who had been one of those evacuated in April of 1942. Dr. van der Plas, a controversial figure, had converted to Islam and it was rumoured that, as a Muslim, he expected to play a starring role in the post-War Indies.

29. Back to New Guinea

A few days after my return to duty from sick-leave, on or about the 10th of August, I boarded a KNIL transport plane bound for Merauke with instructions to assist the resident NIGEO Officer, Dolf Mantel, with the closing down of the NIGEO office and the handover of the stores to the KNIL military.

The trip, seated on the hard benches of the C-47 Dakota was, as usual when flying over the Australian Continent, bumpy while Cloncurry Airport was hot and dry, in stark contrast to the tropical heat and extreme humidity at Merauke.

Merauke was of great symbolic value to the Dutch since it was the only significant regional territory still in Dutch hands. After 1942, it became important to the Allied war effort as well and a small KNIL force was soon joined by Australians and a fighter squadron.

Dolf Mantel was, like me, an *Engelandvaarder* and also born in the Indies of Dutch parents. We got on well from the start. We shared a hut, the walls of which, as at Lake Sentani, consisted of mainly mosquito mesh allowing whatever air movement there was to circulate and give some relief from the moist tropical heat.

Merauke, an insignificant colonial outpost in pre-War days, lies on a small river west of the Papua New Guinea border, opposite Australia's Gulf of Carpentaria and on the south coast of Dutch New Guinea. It is surrounded by a flooded plain which stretches some 300 kilometres across and at its deepest some 200 kilometres northwards to the foothills of New Guinea's massive east-west mountain range. At low tide, ugly grey mud stretches out into the Arafura Sea for hundreds of metres. I pitied the

Government servants posted to this most unattractive settlement in this unpleasant environment, often for many years at a time.

By the time I arrived in Merauke the Dutch No 120 Squadron of Kittyhawk Fighters of the KNIL-ML had left and were based on Biak Island off the north coast of Dutch New Guinea. A Dutch Mitchell B-25 Bomber of the squadron to be stationed at Jacquinot Bay landed on the 15th of August, the day before the Pacific War ended, allowing the crew the doubtful pleasure of joining the celebrations on the 16th in the humid, stifling heat of these Godforsaken lowlands.

I felt doubly cheated by the course of the war to miss both the celebrations of V. E. and V. J. Days in Australia, a feeling I know most others in Hollandia and Merauke shared with me. At the end of the war in Europe, I had at least been near a beautiful lake in a lonely, but beautiful, part of an outpost of Empire, but now on the day Japan capitulated I was in the boondocks of the Indies.

The atom bombs and Emperor Hirohito's decision to surrender not only prevented an estimated well over 1 million Allied casualties but also, by not having to invade Japan's home islands, spared the lives of thousands of seriously ill POWs and internees and prevented a massacre amongst the civilian internees and POWs.

It irks me time and again to hear or read someone condemning the dropping of the atom bombs on Hiroshima and Nagasaki as inhumane acts of terror, as if the bombing of Warsaw and Rotterdam, the London Blitz and the bombing of Darwin and firebombing of Tokyo were not intended to terrorise the population. Rational thought is foreign to many,

After dinner at the mess in Merauke, on the evening of the 30th of August, the day before our return to Brisbane, Dolf and I, on a last inspection of the office, found a telegram on his desk. He opened and read it, then without a word handed it over to me. It came from NIGEO-HQ at Camp Columbia ordering us to postpone our return until further orders. Since the NIGEO affairs had been wound up and there was nothing more left for us to do, we had no intention of hanging around in Merauke of all places until the authorities at Camp Columbia made up their minds. Besides we were booked on the transport plane for early the next day and would arrive just in time for the Queen's birthday party on the 31st of August. Dolf, who had been separated from his wife, Alison, for quite some time, said to me with a straight face: *"We never received a telegram, did we? No, otherwise it would have been handed to one of us to be signed for receipt."* I replied, *"Quite so, I'll just leave it on the desk."* He folded it neatly and put it back where we had found it.

In the morning 'our' Jeep was loaded up with our baggage and Frederik, our *'mandoer'* (the head of local personnel, a Malay), took a rear seat. We made sure that we did not show up too soon and parked the Jeep out of sight beside some bushes near the airstrip just in case the Wireless Officer, who knew about the telegram, was around and would spot us. This was a necessary precaution since the arrival and departure of a C-47 Dakota was a popular event.

About 10 minutes before the transport plane's scheduled departure, we quickly drove to the wide-open cargo door, gave our names to the Cargo Officer, who checked them off on the manifest. We threw our bags into the plane, shook hands with Frederik, the *mandoer,* wished him *"selamate tingal"* and quickly climbed into the plane. A grinning Frederik took the steering wheel of the Jeep, gave us a last wave and shot away.

I can still see the surprise on the face of our Commanding Officer at HQ when Dolf and I walked into the large function room at Camp Columbia where Queen Wilhelmina's birthday party was already in full swing. His first words were: *"I sent you a telegram yesterday with new instructions! You were to remain in Merauke."* (Or words to this effect.) Dolf and I looked at each other questioningly and then with studied surprise Dolf remarked: *"A telegram? When did you send it, Major?"* And I observed: *"No telegram was handed to us* (the truth!) *before our departure, Major."*

I believe the Major realised he was faced with a *fait accompli* and perhaps it really did not matter much whether we were in Merauke or Wacol. Anyhow, suppressing a smile, the Major ordered us to report the next day and wished us a pleasant evening.

Alison, the young secretary at the British Embassy in Madrid whom Dolf had married, nearly fell off her chair from surprise at seeing Dolf to whom, at that moment, she was typing a letter seated at her desk in the NIGEO head office. It was she herself who, as the Major's secretary, had typed the telegram in question.

After debriefing, I idled the days away at Camp Columbia and, in a hire car, made a. trip with Alison and Dolf to the now famous Gold Coast, where we found a superb sandy beach but only a very mediocre two-story Lennon's Hotel amongst the long rows of bungalows lining the

Pacific Coast. When, on the off chance, I asked for and was promptly granted three weeks leave, it was quite clear that we would have languished in Merauke's heat, twiddling our thumbs in utter boredom if we had not ignored the instructions in the telegram. Taking risks sometimes not only pays off, but sometimes offers dividends.

I took the first possible ANA (Australian National Airlines) flight to Melbourne after phoning Berna at the CML (Colonial Mutual Life) Insurance Company to tell her that I had unexpectedly been granted three weeks' leave.

Like all military who had to serve in the Pacific theatre of war, my skin had turned yellowish from the Atebrin tablets we had to swallow as a prevention against contracting malaria.

The house on 43 Bethel Street, Ormond, where I was always received with open arms, belonged to Mrs. Grietje Floyd and Mrs. Kin Binnington, twin sisters and daughters of the Reverend Beukers, a Dutch immigrant. The tragically widowed Kin, who was serving in the Australian Army, was Berna's good friend and Valerie's mother. Although young Beverley Floyd and father Bob also lived there permanently, there was always a bed in the small 'sleep out' off the back verandah for son Bernard Floyd, i.e. 'Harpus' of the RAF who came from Peterborough, or for me, when we were on leave in Melbourne. Countless Aussie and Allied soldiers and sailors have found an open house at Bethel Street. There was always a stew or tea and toast available, although we knew that the heads of the two families were not well off.

In March of 1942, food rationing had been introduced in Australia for tea, sugar and butter but I, in 1944 and thereafter, did not notice any shortages. The quality of the tobacco in cigarettes was, however, well below that from America and I would always arrive from 'the islands' with an extra kitbag full of cartons of American cigarettes for Berna and my dear friends in Ormond.

It was at the Dutch Club on Elizabeth Street that Berna. was introduced to *Hondenportie* (literally meaning 'dogs-portion') that is, white rice, steak and the butter sauce in which it is fried, as well as two fried eggs, sliced cucumber and a half spoonful of curry powder on the side of the plate. She would learn to make it expertly herself to my great pleasure. Apart from the Dutch Club, we did not neglect the Italian restaurants, the bills paid with money saved from when I was in New Guinea and Camp Columbia.

Berna managed a week's leave from the CML and we decided to spend it on the island of Tasmania. It was on the ANA DC-3, on the 22nd of September, that I made one of my fateful decisions and popped the question. What made me choose that moment flying high above the snow-covered Central Highlands of Tasmania? It certainly was a most unusual and, in fact, perhaps unique, venue, most certainly in 1945, to ask a girl to become your wife. I can however in all honesty say that I had not intended to propose while up there high in the sky. It was pure intuition, on the spur of the moment, that made me say those famous words that have been said trillions of times. It had been intuition that had saved my life in Paris. It was intuition that would further determine the path my life would take.

At Hobart Airport we noticed, to my surprise, I may add, a B-25 Bomber with US markings parked on the tarmac and I soon found out it belonged to an USAF Major General. It surely must have been a very long side trip from the General's US base all the way to Hobart just for a weekend at The Wrest Point Hotel. Berna and I had booked two single bedrooms for six nights, since in those years it was frowned upon to share a bedroom with a girl who was not your wife. In fact, you could simply not get a booking in most hotels or decent boarding houses, while trying to circumvent the rules. This would mean expulsion. However, to share a room with a man, never raised an eyebrow. How times have changed.

Tasmania was discovered in the 17th century by the Dutch navigator, Abel Tasman. Berna and I found its beauty a revelation and, on a motoring trip to the top of Mount Wellington, Berna stood in ankle-deep snow for the first time in her life. The Tasmanian landscape is much more like Europe and particularly parts of England. Ever since the early 1800s, the early settlers planted many kinds of European trees, shrubs and plants and succeeded in creating a feeling of 'ye olde England'.

When we flew out of Hobart to return to Melbourne, we could never have guessed that 41 years later we would settle permanently in the Northern Tasmanian city of Launceston and that it would be the best move we ever made.

The modest engagement ring, for I could not afford a more expensive one, cost Australian £35, a lot of money for a 2nd Lieutenant. It was after all the equivalent of perhaps Aus. $5000 in early 21st century money.

I half expected that Mr. Mortimer, Berna's father, would not give his blessing and was therefore not surprised when he told me he would never consent to the marriage. Later in life I came to comprehend his feelings as a father and I realised that I, myself, would consider no man worthy of my daughter and most certainly not a foreigner who would take her away to faraway lands where I would perhaps never, or hardly ever, see her again.

Anyhow, Berna and I realised that we would have to wait until she turned 21 years of age and, besides, I had to return to duty to serve somewhere in the NEI for a still unknown length of time. It never entered our minds to consider the consequences and practicalities of marriage in a war-ravaged world. Having taken risks and succeeded in overcoming obstacles, most of my generation lived for the moment and expected the future to take care of itself. I certainly was of that mind.

It was at Florentino's in Collins Street that Berna and I had our last dinner together before my return to Camp Columbia. At Flinders Street Station I put her on one of the last trains to Carrum, the suburb on Port Philip Bay where her parental home was situated and only a 'brassie' distance, in old Scottish golfing terms, from the beach. We did not know what the future held for us except to believe—using a dinkie-di Australian expression—that *"She'll be right."*

30. News from My Family in Holland

The first letter from my parents, written on the 5th of May 1945 after the surrender of the German Army in the northern part of the Netherlands did not reach me until the second half of July when I was on sick-leave in Melbourne. It had been sent via the National Provincial Bank in London to the Netherlands Trading Society on Clements Lane. Mr. van de Stadt had sent it on to Camp Columbia, from where it was forwarded to Hollandia, back to Brisbane and finally to me in Melbourne!

My father had started his letter on the 7th of May with:

> *Although I do not know yet to which address I must send this letter from our liberated Netherlands, I want to write a few lines to have it ready to mail as soon as I know where you now are.*

To my surprise, they knew about the Paris escape through visits from Albert Starink when in Holland on escape-line business.

Before the Normandy invasion, in a letter written by a Mr. de Heer to my father's close friend Mr. Michielsen in The Hague (and mailed in a neutral country which had passed the German censors), very carefully-worded news had reached them about his sons Erik and Ady (as Karel Jr. was nicknamed in his younger years) as well as about me. It was my mother who drew the correct conclusion, from de Heer's vague descriptions, that I had joined the air force.

Together with my postcards from Lerida and a telegram from Madrid their minds were put at ease. This was no small comfort to both families in the darkest days of the war, living in what would remain the German-occupied part of the Netherlands after the failed attack at Arnhem. Letters

they wrote to me, addressed to my hotel in Madrid and which Albert
Starink posted in Paris, were returned from Spain as being undeliverable.
After the Normandy landing of the 6th of June, 1944, no more mail via
neutral countries was received. When electricity was cut off in that terrible
"hunger winter", they were bereft of any news from the outside world.
About that terrible 1944-45 winter which has gone down as "the hunger
winter", my father wrote and I translate:

> *That we here in Holland have gone through a time of great misery, a time of
> cold, darkness and hunger, you of course already know. We long
> for electricity, gas, heating and all other things which we have had to do
> without for so very long a time. We have, thank God, managed to keep our
> heads above water, but you have no idea and you will never be able to envisage
> how much your mother has done for us all in these past years, assisted by
> your sisters, Mary and Anita.*

Both had lost a lot of weight; my mother scaled at 55 kilograms and
my father, who was exactly my size (except for a smaller head
compensated for by better brains), weighed only 60 kilograms, both with
their clothes on. I weighed 89 kilograms at his age.

For many months during that winter and until well after the liberation
in May, my family, like most, camped in the kitchen, the only room in the
house with some heat derived from the cooking stove. Lighting in the
long, northern, winter months came from a few oil lamps until they
managed to get a carbide lamp. Candles were also used until electricity
was restored.

With the food ration being reduced in the end to, for instance, one
half-loaf of terrible quality bread per person per week, on which one
could not stay alive, the black market flourished and not only for
foodstuffs but also for fuel to cook and provide some warmth around the
kitchen stove. Prices became exorbitant, trees were cut down and
the brick-size wooden blocks used between the extensive tramline system
were broken up and stolen since they were a perfect size for a cooking
stove or heater. There was nothing left of the street pavement in 'our' De
Lairessestraat where my family lived.

The shops ran out of what little food there was and the farmers
would only accept payment in kind. To survive, my parents, like countless

others, sold their valuables for foodstuffs. Thirty-thousand people died from under-nourishment or lack of medicines to treat their diseases. Tradesmen were forced to ask for payment in foodstuffs and goods since money had become worthless. Soon the black-market insisted on payment in gold.

My father wrote:

The Moffen (Huns) had, of course, enough of everything and the Gestapo *terror got worse. Mass executions took place in the Apollolaan and the Weteringplantsoen, but since 5th May we are a free people again. The NBS* [Netherlands Binnenlandse Strijdkrachten—organised Resistance] *are already taking over and the Huns must be astonished to see all those motorbikes with sidecars and automobiles in which they drive through Amsterdam brandishing modern weapons and to cap it all, running on petrol. The Grüne Polizei and* Gestapo *must have chafed inwardly seeing how well-organised these boys are and that they have been unable to arrest them despite the terror and round-ups of the past years.*

My father finished his 14-page letter on the 8th of May telling me about the events of the first few days in a liberated Holland. He described the indiscriminate shooting by German soldiers of people on the Dam Plein, the celebrations there on the day before the liberation, the triumphant entry of the Canadians into Amsterdam, the parachuting of food by British and American planes, how they often had nothing else to eat but tulip bulbs, that the first slice of 'real' bread tasted like cake, and the jubilation when the first ships carrying food for the starving population had docked in the port of Rotterdam.

He expressed the hope to soon hear from my brother Tommy and me and that there was a possibility that he would have to visit the NEI on the bank's business as soon as the Japs were defeated.

Together with my father's long letter of the 7th and 8th of May, I received his of the 30th of May, telling me that they had been pleasantly surprised to receive a postcard from my friend Octave Redele in Eindhoven. In Hollandia, I had written to Octave, who had extended hospitality to me at his home in the south of the Netherlands whenever there was reason to make myself scarce in Amsterdam. Octave gave them my current Brisbane address and my latest news while, at the same time, my good friend Zdenek Kôkes, in RAF uniform, had called on them.

The good news had been overshadowed by, as he wrote, 'our' Erik Michielsen having lost his life in a plane accident This news totally devastated his parents as well as mine, for Erik had been treated as one of the family.

The situation for the 4.5 million people in occupied Holland after "the hunger winter" of 1944-45 had become desperate by April of 1945.

By April the daily ration had been reduced to 230 calories and by the 27th of April, the bread ration was 200 grams a week and after the 4th of May virtually no food could be obtained on food ration coupons.

The German surrender in Holland on the 5th of May came just in time and avoided an unmitigated disaster for the Netherlands. The failure of "Operation Market Garden", for which Cornelius Ryan chose the brilliant title *A Bridge Too Far* for his book, was to cause a near catastrophe for the Dutch Provinces north of the great rivers and west of the re-inundated Grebbe Line in Central Netherlands. The disaster at the Battle of Arnhem could have been avoided if Field Marshall Montgomery (full of himself) and his staff had not disregarded the Dutch Underground's reports of recent German troop movements which included two SS Panzer Divisions being re-equipped not far from Arnhem.

The situation in the Netherlands deteriorated quickly after Arnhem when, in retaliation for the September 1944 railway strike to aid the Allies at Arnhem, the Nazis banned food transport on canals, rivers and lakes. The severe winter of 1944-45, with temperatures dropping way below zero, which was complicated by a very severe shortage of coal caused more misery. In The Hague and Amsterdam half of all the trees were chopped down for firewood. The wooden blocks between the tramlines disappeared and the woodwork in unoccupied houses was removed and used as firewood, as was wooden furniture.

At the end of February the distribution of white bread made from pure wheat flour and yeast not seen or tasted for years, and margarine donated by the Swedes and Swiss, had brought some relief. The white bread tasted like cake, one of my sisters wrote me.

However, by April, food supplies were exhausted and the Supreme Allied Command decided to parachute or drop food over the still German-occupied western part of Holland. The drop was sanctioned by the Germans, who by then were well aware that Hitler's Third Reich had lost the war.

"Operation Manna" started on the 29th of April, when some 300 low-flying, four-engined Lancasters dropped food parcels over allotted zones. The air crew engaged in these drops will never forget the exultation of the people waving with hands, flags, orange pennants, bed sheets and tablecloths, people who had existed for months on beet pulp, nettles and tulip bulbs.

It had however taken quite a few days before all the 4000-tons of parcels dropped by parachute had been distributed. By then the Germans in "Fortress Holland" had capitulated, but the psychological effect had been great.

While "Operation Manna" saved many lives, it had come too late for those with advanced cases of malnutrition. They would join the unfortunates who had died earlier in hospitals and in temporary primitive 'hospitals', or had literally fallen dead in the streets (as had happened in the Russian City of Leningrad).

More than three weeks after the liberation, in Amsterdam, and no doubt in many parts of the Netherlands, there was still no gas or electricity, no trains running, and transport was still wanting. However food supplies had improved and butter, sugar and even chocolate were again available, albeit in small rations. *"Thousands however still suffer from famine oedema"* wrote my father, *"but the long, cold and desperate hunger winter is now behind us."*

Thanks to a radio and battery, which my younger sister Ann had borrowed from a Canadian officer friend, they could listen again to the BBC and radio stations in the South of the Netherlands and Belgium.

Because of the chaotic situation in Europe at that time and the resultant irregular postal service between Europe and Australia, plus my own moving from Australia to New Guinea and back to Brisbane and Melbourne, I would not receive any of their letters, written between June and August 1945, until early October when at Camp Columbia.

31. To Koepang on West Timor

When Berna and I were still at the Wrest Point Hotel in Hobart, the newspapers had reported on the 24th of September 1945 that the Communist-controlled Waterside Worker's Union and the Seaman's Union had the day before blacklisted Dutch shipping in support of the Indonesian Revolutionaries who were seeking self-determination and an end to colonial rule. It was, of course, principally to assist their comrades in gaining political power in the future Indonesia.

These were the same wharfies who had gone on strike and refused to load work ships with supplies for Australian troops fighting a desperate battle in New Guinea to keep the Japanese from the shores of Australia. My friend, Pete Beveridge, serving at that time in the jungles of that island, still spoke, 30 years later in the 1970s, with bitterness about "those bastards" who held up vital supplies for the fighting men of their own country.

By the time I boarded the Dutch 19th Transport Squadron's C-47 Dakota at Archerfield for Koepang on the 5th of March, loading teams of albeit unskilled personnel from all the Dutch Military and civilians had been organised. They, after a while and during the next year, managed to considerably increase the loading rate of the 'professionals' of the unions. Among these temporary wharfies was Jim Jongeneel. He wrote to me in the Dutch language, which I translate:

> *In the spring of the Southern Hemisphere, the KNIL Headquarters*
> *was transferred from Camp Columbia to Batavia and everything was to*
> *be transported on the Dutch troopship SS Van Heutz. Aided by an anti-*
> *Imperialist press campaign, the Communist-oriented Wharf Labourers'*

Union blacklisted Dutch ships and we were forced to load the ship ourselves.
As far as I remember none of us had ever operated cranes and other
loading equipment and not surprisingly things were occasionally dropped onto
the quay and decks or into the water, and regretfully someone was killed.
We Imperialists however completed loading and sailed down the
river accompanied by loud cheers of countless Australians standing on the
shores who had been alerted by the publicity in the media.

During my short stay before departure for Koepang, I learned that
NIGEO had come into existence shortly before we had arrived by the
MV 'Lurline' in September 1944. The urgency of rehabilitating the
liberated population of the NEI required a body that could concentrate
on supply matters from procurement and storage to distribution, as well
as the export of produce. The first problem was to recruit the necessary
staff capable of running the show and this meant that they had to be
found amongst the existing NICA and KNIL personnel. It partially
explained why Dr. J. E. van Hoogstraten, the Director of the Department
of Economic Affairs, considered my future would be best served
by joining the NIGEO.

Having nothing to do during the few days before my departure for
Koepang and being in poor financial straits after the purchase of the
engagement ring for Berna, I would not venture into Brisbane but wander
around this attractively laid-out camp. It had served as the United States
6th Army HQ and was offered by the Australian Government to the
NEI Government-in-Exile in June of 1944. The Dutch further upgraded
the already comparatively lavish facilities.

The best features, as far as I was concerned, were the
accommodations in small, well-spaced huts, with individual showers and
toilets, as well as the high standard of food served in the several messes.
No doubt this was to be attributed to the excellent cooks wisely recruited
from Dutch merchant ships. There was also a hospital and barracks,
to which the Dutch had added more office buildings, a club with a large
function room and a laundry block. Situated across the road from Wacol
Station on the Ipswich rail-line, Camp Columbia gave us good access to
the City of Brisbane.

Camp Columbia had such a large semi-permanent and transient
population that I regrettably did not run into Albert Starink, the man who

had been instrumental in my successfully reaching Spain. Unknowingly, we were both in the camp during those first days of October. He would also pass through Koepang just when I boarded HMAS 'Katoomba' for Soemba on the 4th of November. We were destined not to meet again until September of 1977.

On my return from Melbourne I received my 2nd Lieutenant's commission and soon thereafter Movement Order No 2095, dated the 3rd of October 1945, to proceed to Koepang on the 5th of September (sic!). Early on the 5th, the C-47 Dakota left Archerfield and we made a re-fuelling stop at Cloncurry, where the 49°C heat greeting us on opening the cargo doors was so intense that it felt like a thick curtain of hot air pushing us back into the plane. Staying overnight at Truscott, the old base of the 18th Squadron's B-25 Bombers, I found the water in the open-air showers at sunset too hot to take a shower. It is one of those unimportant things you remember all your life, just as I recall shivering from the cold standing under the open-air shower at Camp Columbia after our arrival in July 1944. That was in the midst of the Australian winter when even in Queensland it can be cool.

The next day, on arrival at Koepang, I reported to Major Schermers, the Commanding Officer of the NICA Unit, which had accompanied the AIF troop assigned to taking the surrender of the Nips and to re-occupy Dutch West Timor.

To my disbelief I learned from Captain Dobbenga that, at the surrender ceremony on the 11th of September, Brigadier L. G. H. Dyke, the AIF Commander, had not only denied him and Major Schermers to go ashore and co-sign the surrender document, but that also the Dutch flag was not allowed to be raised over the (then) Dutch Sovereign Territory. Most likely this affront had been directed, perhaps through General Blarney, the AIF Senior Officer, by the Australian Labour Government's Foreign Minister, Dr. Herbert Evatt, whose anti-Dutch sentiments and designs on parts of post-War NEI were to be made public after the War.

Not long after my arrival in Koepang, 2nd Lt. Westerbeek and I were directed to join the military detachment under the command of Major John M. Baillieu (AIF), which was to take the surrender of the Japanese forces on the islands of Soemba, Soembawa and Flores. Lt. Westerbeek, a university graduate in NEI Civil Administration, was fluent in High Malay as well as Passar Malay. I could speak the latter, which is the *lingua franca* in commerce and in the *passars* (markets). At college I had acquired some knowledge of High Malay, as spoken by the educated elite. Having had military training, I was to represent the KNIL. We boarded the corvette HMAS 'Gladstone' on the 10th of October and were welcomed by Major Baillieu and by the Captain of the corvette.

As mentioned earlier, I lost my notebook with notes on Timor that also contained the names of the corvette's officers and those of the AIF of Major Baillieu's unit, as well as which corvette carried the AIF Force and which one took the Dutch Officers to Soemba afterwards. Luckily, when I was peeling off the photo of Major Baillieu's unit from a page in a 60-year old album, I noted on the reverse side that the name of the corvette was HMAS 'Gladstone'. I still have the Japanese ten-guilder banknote signed by all, but I cannot decipher all the signatures, except those of Captain J. Stevenson (AIF), our interpreter, the Japanese-American Sergeant Paul T. Bannai, Clive Ham, Bruce Dooland (AIF), H. Allan, Johnstone (AIF), Captain Crilley (AIF) and Squadron Leader Rex Cormie (RAAF). I cannot put rank or face to the others. The AIF war photographer in our party was Keith Davis. For the names of Schemers and Dobbinga, I must thank Jack Ford for mentioning them in his excellent book, *Allies in a Bind*.

In the obituary of John Madden Baillieu in "The Australian" of the 20th of August 1999, it was stated that his AIF unit had to take the surrender and to disarm the Japanese forces. This is not correct. The Japanese were to keep their arms to enable them to uphold law and order until Allied Forces could take over at a later time. While RAN officers were part of the detachment, the Captain of the HMAS 'Gladstone' was the Major's Deputy.

On the small corvette there was not enough sleeping accommodation for the whole Baillieu party and, for Westerbeek and me, folding canvas-covered campbeds were placed and secured under the two life-boats and between the davits. He and I therefore slept in the much-cooler tropical night air, enhanced by sea breezes, to the envy of those billeted in the cramped quarters inside the corvette. This ship was not designed for service in the tropics where it would become unpleasantly hot. Keeping in mind my susceptibility to nightmares and fearing a repeat of the 'Lurline' escapade, I tied a thin rope to one wrist and secured the other end to the davits. After all, there was only a waist-high railing to prevent me from falling overboard.

Immediately upon the capitulation of Japan on the 17th of August 1945, Dr. Achmad Soekarno declared the independence of the *Repoeblik* of Indonesia and by September it had become clear that the sudden capitulation of Japan required a rethink of strategy by the Allies. They lacked the necessary manpower to quickly move into Japanese-occupied Southeast Asia to disarm the Japanese. It was actually not until late-September that a beginning could be made with the re-occupation of the major islands by South East Asian Command Forces under Lord Louis Mountbatten.

Meanwhile in the NEI, principally on Java, more than 200,000 internees and prisoners of war were caught up in the Indonesian Revolution and the chaos created by the Japanese surrender, often with tragic consequences. After suffering terribly under the ruthless, generally inhumane and denigrating, treatment by the Japanese, many Europeans and Indo-Europeans, even inside internment camps, and Chinese beyond the protection of the Japanese military, would fall victim to young revolutionary hotheads.

These *pemoedas*, as they were called, would, like mobs throughout history, find it necessary to murder innocents and mutilate their victims in a whipped-up frenzy of hate. The Indonesian Nationalist officials tried unsuccessfully to control these mostly uneducated young men infused with hate by rebel-rousers. It is the same type of mentality the world is faced with in the 21st century with Islamic terrorists. It was ironic that these unfortunate, half-starved, POWs and internees were now to be protected by the same Japanese military which had incarcerated and mistreated them since early 1942.

By early October 1944, news had filtered through about trucks full of women and children, many suffering from malnutrition and tropical diseases, being ambushed and shot at and the trucks set on fire. Hundreds of women and children after years in those terrible internment camps were slaughtered by the *pemoedas* at the moment of their liberation. I could not then, as I cannot now in the 21st century, understand or accept the necessity of murdering innocent people, particularly women and children, for whatever cause or reason.

The KNIL military, upon release from the Japanese POW camps, finding their women and children had been murdered, would in revenge take it out on the nationalists, in particular the *Pelopors,* during the so-called Police Actions when the NEI Government tried to regain full control. We therefore knew about the dangerous state of affairs on Java, but had little information about the islands east of Java except that the Japanese Army was still in control.

In the afternoon, after weighing anchor, Major Baillieu called us to a meeting on the rear deck to explain, with the aid of a large map of the Lesser Soenda Islands, the route we would follow and where the Japanese surrenders were to take place.

32. Accepting the Surrender of Japanese Forces

I awoke early the second morning at sea in a thin equatorial dawn on the 'Gladstone' cruising over a calm sea and within distant sight of the island of Soemba. By the time we reached the small pier sticking out into the sea, the Japanese reception party was awaiting us. Japanese faces never betray much emotion. To me they seem to be more inscrutable than other oriental races. We were received with smiles by the mostly friendly, local population and a bevy of chiefs dressed in colourful (and much sought-after) Soemba-kains, who had arrived on horseback from outlying districts.

Here at Waingapoe on Soemba I had for the first time come face-to-face with soldiers of the Japanese Imperial Army in their ill-fitting trousers, loose tunics and the yellow star on their droopy, peaked, soft cloth caps. The putties were wrapped, often untidily, around their generally bandy and short legs. The officers' uniforms were of better fit and most wore polished high brown leather boots.

It was also for the first time since my family disembarked from the MV 'Shanghai Maru' of the KSK Line at the port of Shanghai that I had last been in contact with Japanese. That was in 1928 in the years of the International Settlements in Shanghai. The sight of a long row of grey painted warships lying for anchor in the broad yellow-brown Huangpu all the way to the famous Bund had made an everlasting impression on an eight-year-old boy gifted with a strong visual memory.

It was also in Shanghai at the Majestic Hotel that I would befriend an English boy by the name of George Mayne with whom I would resume our friendship in Hong Kong 27 years later.

We had lived in Kobe from 1926 to 1928, where we had arrived three years after the great Kanto earthquake of 1923 which had devastated

Tokyo and killed 145,000 people. The deaths resulted from the fires that had raged through the typical Japanese houses made of timber and paper. An earthquake within a year of our arrival in Kobe caused a general panic and I recall us scrambling down the stairs of our two-storey house and running through the garden to a street called Kitanocho-something,

The Japanese were always kind to children. It was perfectly safe for my sisters and me to play in the park-like grounds of the nearby Tor Hotel. I also remember, during a weekend stay at a European-style hotel, being allowed to roam on my own through the ancient town of Nara with its magnificent temples, gardens and deer park.

My opinion of the Japanese people had undergone a quantum change when, as a teenager, I started reading newspapers and, at my high school history lessons, learned about the Rape of Nanking and other atrocities committed by the Japanese Imperial Army in China.

Yet now, dealing with these polite and correct Japanese Military, it was hard to believe that they were part of the Japanese Imperial Army accused of inflicting inhuman treatment on civilians and POWs.

The surrender document was signed inside a bamboo and thatched-roofed open-sided hut, to shield the participants from the sun on the town square. It had been one of many such surrender ceremonies that took place in South East Asia and on the Western Pacific Islands. For the Japanese Colonel, having to hand over his sword to a lower-ranking Australian Officer must have been the ultimate loss of face.

Soon after the officer commanding the Japanese troops on Soemba had handed over his sword to Major Baillieu and the surrender documents had been signed, we boarded the corvette and sailed in gathering darkness along Soemba's north coast to Bima on the island of Soembawa.

The Lesser Soenda Islands, from Bali to Timor, span an area of about 650 miles wide. The farther east one goes the drier the climate becomes, which is not surprising since it is situated just north of the dry continent of Australia.

In the morning, the 'Gladstone's' Captain navigated his ship through the straits between Soembawa and the barren Komodo Islands, where extraordinary currents, engendered by the prevailing tide, caused the sea to form a rip up to 100 metres wide that made the small warship slew from one side to the other. In 1993 my wife and I made the voyage from Sumba (as it was then written) to Komodo Island, where I saw the famous dragons at close quarters. We travelled in the P & O's 44-passenger 'Island Explorer', but we approached Komodo's main island on the eastern side and over a smooth sea. Komodo has hardly changed since dinosaurs roamed on this Earth and has perhaps the most unusual national park in the world. Komodo is the habitat for the largest lizards in the world, each up to three metres in length and weighing 100 kilograms. Their principal pastimes are eating and sleeping. These 'Komodo Dragons', as they are called, will swallow a whole goat, including hair, hooves, teeth and bones which are dissolved by the saliva excreted from their tongues. In the 1970s a Swiss gentleman, not heeding the warnings of the guides, wandered off and only his camera and glasses were ever recovered.

Soembawa, to the east of Lombok, is a fairly large island, not as parched as Timor, but nearly as dry as Soemba and is quite mountainous.

Upon arrival in Bima, the capital of the Sultanate of East Soembawa, most of the AIF and RAN Officers, accompanied by our interpreter, US Army Sergeant Paul Bannai, inspected the Japanese Military facilities and scrutinized the surrender documents. Major Baillieu, Westerbeek and I made a courtesy call on the Sultan, the ruler of the Eastern part of Soembawa, at his palace. After ascending a broad, tiled staircase we were received by the tiny Sultan on the huge, covered, front verandah. We had noted a distant attitude amongst the locals. There were no smiles as in Waingapoe on Soemba and a general avoidance of eye contact. The tiny Sultan seemed nervous and ill at ease but not unfriendly and, since the Sultan spoke only a little English, a polite conversation was conducted in Malay and Dutch. This was translated for the benefit of the Major. After the required cup of tea which had been ceremoniously presented with due regard to the Sultan and his guests' social standing. Major Baillieu left early to attend the Japanese surrender ceremony.

At the local police station and jail, Westerbeek and I were received correctly in accordance with our officers' rank and late in the afternoon we sailed for our next destination. It was in the waters near Soembawa that we at long last saw the typical Boeginese ubiquitous *pinisi* (sailing vessels) of Celebes (now Sulawesi) Island, which nowadays are nearly all equipped with engines. It was only then that I realised how very few fishing *prahoes* with their square sails we had come across since leaving Timor.

On Soemba I had noted the absence of the typical black cap worn by male Moslems in Indie and Malaya. In Bima nearly all wore such a *kopiah*, while quite a few women covered their heads in the Islamic head-dress, the *hiyab*, but I did not see anything as extreme as the *burkah*.

Back on board our corvette, an RAN Officer told us that the Japanese cruiser 'Isuzu', damaged in an air attack, was torpedoed by American submarines and sunk in Bima Bay, but when we sailed into and out of the bay we found no trace of the ship. Many years later I read that the 'Isuzu' was damaged by attacking Dutch B-25 bombers of the 18th Squadron based at Batchelor in the Northern Territories of Australia.

Off Soembawa's north coast, soon after the sun dipped into the sea, we passed the volcano Tambora, or rather what is left of the once over 4000-metre high cone-shaped mountain which literally blew its top on the 10th of April, 1815 and produced the most powerful and destructive natural explosion in recorded history. It actually lost some 1400 metres off its top and is now a flat-topped volcano of some 2000 metres height. Picture a monumental volcano cone which had been half-decapitated.

From my camp-bed on port-side, I watched its massive, dark outline on a brilliant starlit night and wondered why the eruption of Krakatau in 1883 had always been portrayed at high school, and by my grandmother, Sophie Portengen, as the most devastating eruption in history. As the young wife of a KNIL medical doctor, my grandmother had arrived at Tandjong Priok, the Port of Batavia (now Jakarta) in 1885 and had met people who were in Batavia and elsewhere on Java on that fateful August of 1883. They had not only been frightened out of their wits but had suffered its terrible after-effects which lasted well into 1885.

My grandmother's stories of the experiences of people who had been on Java fascinated me, the more so since I had not only experienced an earthquake and tremors when in Japan, but also as a child on Java.

Her friends in Batavia and further east on Java recollected that the day before Krakatau exploded they had heard repeated rumblings in the course of the morning. At first, they thought that the noise was caused by distant thunder. But towards the late afternoon, the thundering was at intervals accompanied by dull detonations. These could not have come from a light thunderstorm passing over the cities of Batavia and Buitenzorg (now Bogor). After 7 o'clock that evening, continuous detonations could be heard and it was realised that the volcano Krakatau, which had already had a minor eruption a few weeks earlier, was building up to a major explosion. By midnight people were aroused in their sleep by ever-increasing loud rumblings, so strong that while there was no earthquake yet, the doors, windows and cupboards rattled. Shortly before one a.m. they heard a tremendous bang which was far louder than anything anybody had ever heard before and which caused the whole house to tremble. *"It sounded like a cannon being fired next to one of our open windows"*. Throughout the night continuous explosions and rumblings were heard and not long after 10 a.m., a greyish brown and lead-coloured cloud mass moved in from the west. The already hazy sun now disappeared completely and it became frighteningly dark. The temperature dropped sharply and after a few strange strong wind gusts from the east it became dead calm in Batavia and further east on that 27th of August in 1883.

Near noon a light streak, like daybreak, appeared on the eastern horizon. The cocks started crowing and the birds resumed fluttering. Krakatau's eruption had seemingly thrown nature out of gear. That night flames could clearly be seen in the western night sky and not only in Batavia but even more than 250 kilometres away.

Grandma Sophia told me more, but for those who want to learn more about Krakatau and the subject of volcanoes, I highly recommend Simon Winchester's book, *Krakatoa,* which, with its wealth of detail, brought my grandmother's simple stories to life. The book also made me remember that distant weekend in 1931 when my parents took the family to a government guesthouse situated near the beach on Java's side of the Soenda Strait and opposite a small island called Anak Krakatau (the child of Krakatoa). There, in that idyllic place, I had first learned about the loudest volcanic explosion ever and how ships were carried far inland by, what is now called, a tsunami. In 1953 I came within about 1500 yards of one of those ships when inspecting the black pepper crop in the Lampongs district; it was miles inland from Telolc Betong on the south Sumatra coast, and overgrown by the jungle. My party was not tempted to make a detour to the historic ship since, apart from having to hack a path through the undergrowth to reach the vessel, we were also in tiger country. Thus the reason why a tiger hunter accompanied us traders—Indonesian, Chinese and me—on our inspection trip.

Having, myself, in 1934 and in 1951 seen the enormous Lake Toba created in North Sumatra by the eruption of the volcano Toba at some time in the pre-historic distant past, I believe that eruption must have been the biggest bang ever heard, frightening all living creatures on Earth.

33. Soembawa Besar and "Merdeka"

The 'Gladstone' had reduced speed during the night in order that we would arrive after dawn at the bay leading to the harbour of the town of Soembawa Besar. It dropped anchor out of sight of the town which was obscured by a small hilly peninsula.

The Major, Paul Bannai (the Japanese-American interpreter), Westerbeek and I climbed down a rope ladder into the small motorised boat steered by a coxswain. It was too small to carry more than six people. There was only room left for a RAN leading seaman to assist, with his boat-hook, in the mooring of the small craft.

The moment we rounded a neck of land we sighted a fairly large crowd standing near a wooden jetty. The crowd was surrounding the reception party of four Japanese officers. As soon as they spotted the small boat, a roar went up. It was not a welcoming sound. At the same instant we noted a few red and white flags of the Indonesian Nationalists, the colours of the new *Repoeblik* of Dr. Soekarno who, by the way, when he needed a ready, large supply of flags obtained them by simply removing the (third) blue panel from the Dutch flag. We were sharply aware that we were in a potentially explosive situation and, quite ironically, grateful that we could count on the protection of the Japanese soldiers, whose surrender we were to accept.

Turning back was out of the question. *"Just ignore them!"* Major Baillieu ordered and a few minutes later we reached the jetty, clambered up the steps and, ignoring the crowd, returned the salute of the Japanese Officers. A small group of mostly young men formed a wall around us shouting *"merdeka"* (freedom) and taunting us with some choice epithets. All four of us studiously ignored them. They made way when the senior Japanese officer led us through the throng to the waiting automobiles. Obviously respect for the ruthless Japanese occupier had not (yet) left the demonstrators but we could sense that, if we did not leave the jetty soon, the situation could become unpleasant. It made us realise that the political situation in Soembawa Besar was delicate and prepared us for a possible confrontation with hostile or unfriendly republican sympathisers.

We four were most correctly received by the Sultan of Soembawa Besar on the large covered front verandah of his palace, which was not as imposing as the palace at Bima. It was quite apparent that the Sultan and his retinue were in a highly nervous state. His tea cup rattled on its saucer when his trembling hands lifted it from the table.

After taking our leave and respectfully saluting the Sultan, the Major and Sgt. Bannai left in one of the motorcars to attend the signing of the surrender document while Westerbeek and I decided that he would call on the officials at the jail while I would inspect the police station.

Arriving at the main police station in a motorcar driven by a Japanese soldier, and walking up the path of the palm-fringed grounds, I saw a sentry dressed in the old colonial style uniform and brown wide-rimmed straw hat stand to attention when seeing my KNIL black triangle and Lieutenant's star on my epaulettes. But, to my surprise, he did not salute but raised his arm into a fist and shouted *"Merdeka"*. I had the presence of mind to ignore this provocation and unexpected greeting and entered the building. There at the front desk another policeman got up and shouted *"Merdeka"*. Ignoring the man, I went for the Sergeant's desk and, before the Police Sergeant had fully risen from his chair, I greeted him with a friendly: *"Selamat ketemu, apa khabar, Sergeant"* (nice to meet you, how do you do).

My friendly and for him totally unexpected informal greeting by a KNIL officer must have floored him and he could not but reply in the same friendly tone: *"Ada balk Luit, selamat datang"* (I am well Lieutenant, welcome).

To say *"Luit"* instead of *Luitenant* was common in the Dutch Army, KNIL and Police when a friendly rapport had been established. The Sergeant was an older man and had most likely served many years in this post under a Dutch Police Lieutenant before the Japanese invasion.

I invited him to sit down and politely asked his *"permissi"* before lowering myself into the visitor's chair in front of his desk. After exchanging pleasantries and asking him and his staff about their families and explaining that I was an *anak Soerabaja* (born in Soerabaja), the initially tense atmosphere had become quite friendly. I had, meanwhile, noted Nationalist and Communist pamphlets displayed on one desk and, pointing to them, I remarked that *polisi* and *tentara* (military) should remain above politics and such pamphlets should not be displayed inside a police station. Furthermore, while in uniform, *kita* (which means we, including the persons addressed) men in uniform should avoid politics and act impartially.

I got up, wished them *"selamat tingal"* (goodbye to someone staying), gathered the pamphlets, saluted and was in turn, this time correctly, saluted also by the sentry outside, and drove off with my Japanese driver, quite relieved that no young hotheads, like those at the jetty, had been around. We carried side-arms but a pistol is not much use against an excited mob.

The coxswain and a sailor were waiting for us in their small boat at the jetty, which was now deserted but for a Japanese sentry. On the way back to the 'Gladstone', Westerbeek translated the contents of the pamphlets I had impounded. It was rebel-rousing language, particularly from the Communists who were agitating for a 'red revolution'.

After we had weighed anchor we were treated to one of those glorious sunsets for which Indonesia is famous but which are particularly outstanding on Lombok/Bali and in West Java on the Soenda Straits.

On the next, and relaxing, day at sea, Major Baillieu and I discovered our mutual passion for the ancient game of golf and I became once again aware of the easy-going manner between high and lower-ranking officers and the relaxed discipline maintained between officers and other ranks amongst the Australians. No stiff-necked pomposity here as is so often found amongst British and Dutch Officers.

Early in the morning of the 16th of October, the 'Gladstone' called at Larantuka on the northern coast of Flores (which means flowers in Portuguese). My wife and I would visit Maumere, some miles further along the coast, in 1993 not long after a tsunami had virtually wiped out the town and had even damaged the strong concrete landing pier. The volcanoes on Flores fit neatly into the Pacific Rim of Fire. In fact,

Gunung (Mount) Egon came to life four times in 2004, sparking panic amongst the thousands living on its slopes.

A Japanese Officer, with car and chauffeur assigned to take me to two POW camps, was already waiting for me. Driving through the town I noted a difference in appearance between the inhabitants of Soembawa who, like those on Soemba and further west were of Malay stock, and those on Flores. Some mixing with Melanesians was quite evident. Driving for about an hour through lovely mountainous country, we arrived at the first POW camp. A battalion of Ambonese KNIL soldiers and some Japanese military had already been called to attention on a command in Japanese.

A buzz went up from the POWs, who were already assembled on the parade ground, when the car with my Japanese Captain and I came to a halt just outside the barbed-wire enclosed camp. When we stepped out of the open army car, the KNIL prisoners were ordered in Japanese to stand to attention. I could feel a rising emotion of joy and expectation when the Ambonese (for I recognised them as such) saw the KNIL insignia on the, for them, foreign khaki-coloured uniform, the old KNIL one being green.

The Ambonese in the KNIL were the equivalent of the Ghurkas in the British Army and were the most loyal and respected colonial troops the Dutch ever had. Their loyalty and aspirations would be shamefully betrayed under pressure of international post WWII politics.

After they had been ordered to stand at ease, I asked them to come forward and make a semi-circle around me. I spoke to them in a mixture of Dutch and Malay. Senior Ambonese NCOs nearly all spoke at least passable Dutch but I was not so sure about the other ranks. I told them that it would regretfully take a few more weeks before the Dutch administration would take over and they could be repatriated to their home islands. I stressed that, meanwhile, the Allies held the Japanese responsible for their welfare and safety and instructed them to make careful note in writing of the names of any Japanese who had mistreated them and of any act perpetrated in contravention of the Geneva Convention (even though the Japanese were not signatories to the Treaty).

After exchanging some banter and sexually rude remarks about the Nips, one of them asked my permission, which I of course readily granted, that since they were no longer POWs they could form up as a

KNIL unit. I asked for the Senior NCOs to come forward. There were three 'adjutants' (Warrant Officers) and marvellous types they were. I introduced the most senior adjutant and his two deputies to the Japanese Camp Commandant and my Japanese Officer escort. It was a poignant moment when the ex-POWs, on my taking leave, shouted: *"leve de Koniging, leve Churchill, leve Roosevelt!"* They had not yet heard that President Roosevelt had died in April that year. Stalin was not mentioned but Queen Wilhelmina was.

As friendly and enthusiastic as the Ambonese POWs' reception had been, as distant and luke-warm was I received in another camp by some one hundred or so KNIL soldiers from Java. I therefore restricted my address to informing them of their new status but with the Japanese remaining in overall charge and responsible for their well-being. They had already chosen the person who would take charge of their group, obviously not the senior NCO and likely, I surmised, a political activist.

It was on that tour of the POW camps that my escort, the Japanese Captain, became upset by something and shouted at a sentry who promptly ran up the incline, holding his rifle in his left hand. When he reached the Captain, one boot slipped on the cobble-stone surface and he came crashing down. With disgust, his superior watched him get back on his feet, come to attention and salute. The Captain addressed him harshly, which does not need much effort in the Japanese language, and then, to my astonishment, slapped the man left and right across the face. It made Prussian discipline pale in comparison to that of their Samurai allies.

On Flores we also encountered a pitiful group of Romushas (native forced-labourers), the equivalent of the forced labourers of the Nazis in Europe. Not far out of one of the towns we passed a 'comfort station', which is not what it sounds but a Japanese Army brothel. We made one more call along the coast of Flores a day later, to Endeh if I remember correctly, and noted that there was still a substantial Japanese Army presence on Flores.

After dinner in the ship's wardroom, on the day we sailed from Flores, we gathered for a last drink at the stern of the corvette and that night from my camp-bed on deck, covered by a light woollen blanket against the night chill, my wrist tied to my 'nightmare' rope, I watched the constellations until I fell asleep,

When I woke up at dawn, on the 29th of October, the low silhouette of Western Timor lifted over the eastern horizon against the glow of the rising sun. Soon the HMAS 'Gladstone's' engines stopped pounding and the island was now so close that I could pick out single trees on the shore of Timor, an island, at least the western part of which, I do not find particularly scenic.

34. Tragic News Awaits Me in Koepang

At HQ in Koepang, a heap of letters awaited me from my father from home and from Berna in Australia as well as an unexpected telegram and a movement order for a posting to Waingapoe on Soemba.

The telegram had been sent from Amsterdam on the 23rd of September to APO 926, SONICA 2, US Army Brisbane (my mailing address since Hollandia, New Guinea) and forwarded from US Army, Victoria Park to CTO Brisbane on the 2nd of October. It must have arrived at Camp Columbia Post Office the day I departed for Koepang. It read:

> *"Received unofficial news Tommy murdered by Japs find out truth."*
> *Eugenie Zeeman*

It was devastating news and my being thousands of miles from strife-torn Sumatra and in no position to make any direct enquiries made matters worse.

Among my mail I found a letter written by my father from Colombo from which I learned that he had left Amsterdam by plane the day before my mother telegraphed me. My mother had therefore been on her own when she received the worst news a mother can receive about her child.

When in Colombo my father had received the news that a Mr. Ebbink had reported the death of my brother and that a report would follow. A few weeks later in Waingapoe, I received my father's letter of the 9th of November, written from Batavia, which also enclosed Lt. Ebbink's and Captain van de Lande's reports. These reports left no doubt that my brother had been killed by the Japs at Tiga Roenggoe in North East Sumatra on the 14th of March 1942.

The typed reports of (Res) Lt. Ebbink, dated the 29th of October, 1945, and of (Res) Captain J. J. A. van de Lando, dated the 27th of October 1945, stated that after a clash with the invading Japanese troops they retreated to the *kampang* (village) of Tiga Roenggoe, about 50 kilometres from Pematang Siantar in Northeast Sumatra. Captain van de Lando was the CO of the Regional Homeguard to which Sgt. T. S. Zeeman belonged. On the road to Kaban Djahe, not far from Lake Toba, they ran into a Japanese ambush and in the ensuing firefight several men were killed or wounded. Capt. van de Lande, Lt. de Boer and Sgt. Been managed to escape into the bush, but Tom and others, including Lt. Ebbink, were captured. The latter was put on top of a Japanese tank, as a hostage and shield, and driven towards the Dutch defence lines. It was at that moment, sitting high on the top of the tank, that he saw Tommy and others with their hands tied behind their backs being marched into a trench. That night Ebbink, having survived the tank's attack and returned to Tiga Roenggoe, heard shots fired at about 9 p.m. The next day, after having been transported to Kaban Djahe, he was reunited with Lt. Suthof, also captured at Tiga Roenggoe. Lt. Suthof told him that the Japs had executed all 22 Europeans, including Tom Zeeman. It was believed that the cause for this atrocity was the *Stadswacht* (Homeguard) insignia which all had worn. The Japanese CO had asked what *"Stadswacht"* meant and when it was translated literally as "town guard" he flew into a rage saying: *"Oh, you must guard the town but here is not the town"*. This, it was believed, must have been the reason why he ordered the execution. Ebbink and Suthof had not worn the badge and thus were spared the same fate, although some other captured officers had been decapitated.

At the direction of the Japanese, the executed men had been buried by the local Battak population in the trench where they had been executed. When exhumed after the war, they were found with their hands still tied behind their backs.

My sister-in-law Hetty and her little daughter Patricia had survived and been liberated from Aek Pamienke Internment Camp in the Asahan District just south of Pematang Siantar. When a dangerous situation similar to that on Java developed, they were evacuated from Medan to Singapore.

Early news of the shocking conditions in the camps had been reported in Australian newspapers on the 19th of September but it had taken another two months to receive news about my sister-in-law Hetty, and her descriptions of the terrible conditions prevailing in the camps for women and small children as well as the separate camps for men and boys. She also spoke of bad sanitation conditions and small food rations, which were usually of dubious quality.

The racism of the men from Nippon, who had proclaimed "The Greater East Asia Co-Prosperity Sphere", was blatant and required not only the European and Chinese, but also the native population, to bow to the Japanese.

Disrespect shown in the personal view of individual Japanese would result in beatings of both men and women, some so severe that bones were broken. The situation in Batavia three months after the Allies had arrived was still chaotic, my father wrote. The native population—not always on their own volition—were boycotting the *Belandas* (Europeans). Anybody in a khaki uniform was considered belonging to the NICA and the NICA was the *bete noir* of the *Repoeblik*.

He had found lodgings with the nice Indische family de Kooning in Kebon Sirih and was pleased to have acquired a bicycle since transport was a great problem. On reading this I had to smile. My father, who had been chauffeured around Batavia in a black Packard limousine in the 1930s when he was the *Tuan Besar'* of the NHM Bank, was now pedalling in his Colonel's uniform on a bike through the streets of Batavia.

Somehow the incongruity of my courtly father on a bike in Batavia made me recall a hilarious situation involving my brother Tommy during his compulsory six months of military service in Batavia in 1930. He had, as had some others, received permission from his CO to spend the evenings and nights at home; thus, every morning, just before roll-call at 6 a.m., Tom would park his silver and blue Auburn-Cord sports car with compressor (comparable to today's Chevrolet Corvette) at the gate of the barracks. After a day of soldiering, the lowly conscript soldier would drive off applauded by the admiring crowd of *katjongs* (street brats) while the junior officers of his unit would walk or bicycle home. (That was just after the crash of 1929 and the Great Depression soon forced him to sell the Cord with its chrome exhaust pipes, and get himself a second-hand car.)

My father ended his letter expressing his deep worry about political developments and, luckily, he would return to Holland before the terrorism of the so-called '*Bersiap*' period made life in Batavia most unpleasant and dangerous.

That evening after dinner, sitting in a rattan easy-chair on the verandah of the officers' mess, I re-read the letters and telegram and unavoidably my thoughts turned to recollections of my murdered brother. I remembered, and still remember, with great clarity that in 1934 my mother, sisters and I had visited and stayed with Tom at the Bah Biroeng Oeloe tea plantation in the highlands near Pematang Siantar, a small town south of the city of Medan. His house was situated on a minor hilltop, framed by tallish trees and stood out against a background of undulating rows of tea bushes which gave the impression of a huge ribbed green carpet.

One day Tom drove us to the magnificent large and unique Lake Toba and the next day to a lonely tea-planters house, at the highest part of the area's tea estates, where he had himself once lived for a year. Around midday, standing on its terrace above the expanse of green tea bushes interspersed with shade trees, we could clearly see the coastline of Sumatra and the greenish-blue Straits of Malacca melting into the slightly darker outline of the coast of Malaya. This was a truly tremendous panorama which, even in those pollution-free days, would only present itself for a few days a year.

It was in this beautiful part of Sumatra that Tom was executed by the Japanese and was one of the many victims of Japanese atrocities committed before and during World War II. The ancient Bushido Code, in which the interpretation and importance of one's honour is paramount, made the Japanese despise their enemies for surrendering instead of fighting to the death. Prisoners were therefore treated with unusual savagery and it was quite common for recaptured escapees to be beheaded or bayoneted to death in public. However, the degree of sadism displayed by the shooting of shipwrecked uniformed nurses or their summary execution in their hospitals' forecourts, and the numerous stories of cruelty against POWs and civilians cannot be explained away only by the Bushido Code.

In 1950, when posted to Medan by Internatio, the international trading company I worked for, Berna and I visited the War cemetery where Tom had been buried. Arriving at the entrance the supervisor was not in his small office but conducting other visitors and I decided to find the grave myself. For no explicable reason I chose a wide path to the left of the entrance, which divided rows of crosses, and after Berna and I had walked up the slight hill and passed several rows of graves I turned left again and, as if directed by a sixth sense, found the white cross with the inscription:

"T. S. Zeeman, Stadsw. Sgt. KNIL, 5-8-10/15-3-42."

In 1989, when our cruise ship visited Jakarta and docked in Tandjong Priok, Berna and I went to the military cemetery at Ancol, where my brother had been re-buried. I do not believe in Divine guidance nor in supernatural powers but I have no logical explanation for my again, without having received directions from the supervisor, walking straight to the row of graves where a cross marked Tommy's grave.

35.   Posted to the Island of Soemba

On the 4th of November, in light winds and fairly calm seas, the corvette HMAS 'Katoomba' set course towards Soemba Island which would be my home for the next seven months. Early in the morning of the 5th, we, the five officers assigned to administer the island, were met by four poker-faced Japanese and a crowd of smiling locals who had gathered at the harbour to watch our arrival.

Among the welcoming committee on the wharf, apart from a number of colourfully-dressed Soembanese chieftains, was a Chinese gentleman who introduced himself as "Pauw, Captain of the Chinese community". The head of Chinese communities all over the Indies were always called *"Kapitein der Chinezen"*. Pauw and his charming Indo wife became part of our small social circle.

The Chinese, as in other parts of the Indies and Malaya—Singapore was and is predominantly inhabited by Chinese from many provinces of China—invariably make up the commercial element of communities larger than hamlets.

We drove the short distance from the little harbour to the old Colonial-style villas on the *aloeng-aloeng* (Municipal square) which, in the years before 1942, had been the homes of the *Controleur* (the Government official in charge of a sub-district) and another Government official. During the Japanese Occupation it had been the residence of the Japanese Commanding Officer and his staff.

From these two high-ceilinged old Colonial homes situated on and overlooking the grassy square we could see the Timor Sea and part of the Northwest coast of the island. The *Controleur*, veterinary surgeon and I moved into the larger of the two villas and the KNIL and Police Lieutenants into the other, also sparsely furnished, villa.

The *Controleur* of the NEI Government for the sub-district Soemba, with the rank of Captain, was our senior officer. He was an Indischman and, as all NEI Government Officers, a graduate in Indology of Utrecht University.

Direct governing by the NEI Government's servants was avoided as much as possible. That was done by the native rulers of all ranks from the Sultans and *Radjahs* down to the village chiefs who had ruled before the 17th-century Dutch arrived.

The Governor-General, Governor, Resident, Assistant Resident down to the *Controleurs* made sure, however, that nothing happened against the economic interests of the Netherlands. This was the least oppressive, easiest and cheapest way to run the colony but it resulted in a medieval government structure remaining in force longer than was good for the country and its native population at large.

Our *Controleur* would, as all *controleurs* had done before him, regularly visit the *dessas* (villages) and *kampongs* (suburbs) often mounted on a *kuda* (horse). Our veterinary surgeon and Police Inspector would do the same.

The KNIL commander was also an Indischman, a descendant of several generations of KNIL Officers. Life on Soemba had quickly returned to the peace and quiet of pre-war days and the KNIL Officer and his squad, after a month or two of extensive patrolling of the island, returned to Koepang.

Three centuries of colonisation had, and could not but, lead to a large Indo-European population in the East Indies. In the 17th and 18th centuries, in particular, few Dutch women went to the far-away colonies and mixed marriages were the norm. Their offspring, in contrast to the Anglo-Indians in British Colonial society, could be found in all strata of Dutch society. It was particularly true that in the Army and Civil Service, the "Indischman" would rise to the highest positions. Also in the KNIL, foreigners, as in the French Foreign Legion, could be found in all ranks, especially before the 20th century.

There was a subtle distinction between an 'Indischman' and 'Indo', often because of a lighter skin colour but more so because of their social position.

The Lt. of Police, called de Jong, was the oldest of us five and not far from retiring age which, in the Tropics, was 55. The veterinary surgeon was the only *baroe* or *totok* amongst us. A *'totok'* or a *'baroe'* was a person who has not earlier been in the Indies. *Totok* had a disparaging connotation and, depending on the emphasis, could have a derisory meaning,

Our light blond white-skinned vet and a *baroe* was also a different *putih* (white man) from the rest of us who had lived or served 'in the islands', since he had not yet acquired a yellowish skin from the Atabrine tablets which had to be taken against malaria.

My dual function of looking after the military and the civilian population was not uncommon in those very early years after the war. The Dutch East Indies Government's available manpower, at the time when the B-29 Bomber called 'Enola Gay' dropped the first atom bomb on Hiroshima, was less than 10,000 in the KNIL, RNN, NICA and NEFIS (NEI Intelligence Service) combined. As a result, KNIL personnel, who had suffered years in Japanese POW camps, were asked, if physically capable, to put on (new) uniforms to assist in the protection, repatriation and the keeping of order in the areas under SEA Command and those of the NEI Government.

A large camphorwood trunk crammed with Japanese Guilders, which had replaced the currency of the NEI, was discovered in the former HQ of the Japanese in Waingapoe. Although the exchange rate for one Japanese Guilder had been pegged to one NICA cent, the contents of the trunk were still worth a lot of money. The *Controleur* had the trunk sealed and despatched to Macassar, the capital of the island of Celebes (now Sulawesi), the administrative centre of the Soenda Islands.

On the island of Java, after introducing the NICA Guilder, it soon became necessary to reintroduce the Japanese Guilder (luckily not yet destroyed but stored in secure warehouses). This was necessary because the *Pelopors,* as the members of the militia and criminal gangs were called, considered any Indonesian or Chinese to be a traitor if they possessed NICA money and these unfortunates were promptly shot or *tjintjankt* (cut to pieces) with a *klewang* (sabre) or killed in other unpleasant ways. The *Pelopors,* like the militias 60 years later in East Timor, were generally nasty types backed by but not under the effective control of the TRI, the Indonesian Republican Army.

During the Japanese occupation, when all imports ceased, the people of Soemba had an even more basic lifestyle than before. It was therefore true to say that from the moment that I, as supply officer in charge of imports, set foot on the island, I became an important person since all goods were imported through the NIGEO.

Lack of shipping was a major problem and hampered the re-supply of the 12,000 or so islands spread out over some 3,300 miles of the old NEI. Many ships of the KPM, the Dutch inter-island steamship line, were sunk during the Japanese invasion of 1942; about 30 ships managed to escape and reach Australia, where Townsville, in Queensland, became their temporary home port from which many trips were made. In the most critical phase of the New Guinea campaign in 1942-43, these KPM ships transported 100,000 soldiers and supplies. Their contribution was hailed thus in an American report:

Thank God for the Dutch ships. Their officers and crew cooperated with us as much as possible, if need be even 24 hours in a row. Without them we would have been nowhere". (And in those desperate days the Aussie wharfies went on strike!).

The available KPM ships were now, after the Japanese surrender, mainly employed in the shipment of goods to the major islands like Java, Celebes and Sumatra.

Soemba, as with most small islands, was provisioned by fairly small, mostly wooden boats which would call about every second or third week. Their arrival was always an event and the mailbag was invariably the first item to be unloaded onto the small jetty near the NIGEO *goedang* (warehouse) at the end of Waingapoe's jetty. Berna and I took to numbering the envelopes of our letters so that we knew which one to open first.

The Macassars of Celebes (now called Sulawesi) have through the ages been seamen and navigators of great skill and in the Indonesian Archipelago they fulfilled, and still do, a similar task as the Hansa League once performed in Northern Europe. A *pemissi* from Celebes, chartered by the NIGEO with a Macassan crew, would occasionally land supplies at our small port.

Other than by ship, our only other mode of contact with the outside world was by radio telegraph. The repair of a damaged airfield was therefore one of my priorities. Gangs of prisoners from the jail were set to work on clearing debris and mowing the knee-high *alang-alang* (grass) with *parangs* (broad, long knives).

By early December when the grass had been cut and the landing strip's perimeters marked with small whitish stones pounded into the ground, we immediately telegraphed Kupang and Macassar on the island of Celebes (under which all the Lesser Soenda Islands resorted) that the airfield was serviceable.

To everybody's great disappointment no plane had landed by Christmas and by the end of January the *Controleur* decided that the convict gangs could be better employed elsewhere. Within weeks the grass had grown knee-high and we became resigned to remaining an isolated outpost.

The supervision of the motor pool also fell to me. Thanks to the chief mechanic, a charming Chinese called Mea, and his mechanics, we had within weeks several more trucks and two additional 1930-1940 model Chevrolets as well as a Pontiac added to our motor pool. By the time I left Soemba towards to the end of May 1945, the motor pool had however run out of cannibalised spare parts and, apart from tyres and petrol, had received few of the parts on order.

Apart from the American-made motor cars and trucks we had inherited from the Japanese, there was also a circa 1936 Nissan Cabriolet. It was a near but roughly-made copy of a 1929-1930 American sedan, yet Japanese industry could, at that point in time, manufacture the world beating "ZERO" fighter plane.

The day after our arrival on the island the *Controleur*, the Police Inspector and I inspected a Japanese Comfort Station just outside Waingapoe proper. The establishment consisted of some 30 small one-room wooden huts each occupied by a youngish woman. Most of the girls originated from Java and had previously been in the sex trade or had been forced through economic necessity to make a living in these brothels run by the Japanese Imperial Army. The compound was well-kept, the women were well-dressed and, in addition to their, shelter had received proper food rations and good medical care and medical supplies, like quinine, all of which were lacking in the internment, POW and Romusha camps. The establishment was fenced off and the visiting soldiers had to buy an 'entertainment' ticket at the entrance. Repatriation of these women to their home towns or island was not completed for several months, also because of the chaotic situation on Java.

Within a day or two of our landing at Waingapoe Jetty, the *Controleur* received news that a Japanese soldier had reported to the village chief of the town of Melolo to the south-east of Waingapoe. Instructions were given to take the man on foot, accompanied by a horseman, to Waingapoe. Two days later a dead-tired, typical bullet-headed Japanese peasant-type going by the name of Ishii arrived at our mess on the *aloeng-aloeng*. He was told he had to work for his keep and given a bed in the go-down of the house. Within a few days Ishii became our indispensable factotum. This simple, kind Japanese farm boy, who had gone AWOL to avoid leaving with his unit, did more to restore our belief that surely not all Japanese were Bushido-mad, cruel bastards. To his and our regret Ishii had to be repatriated to Japan a few months later.

Besides our factotum Ishii, we had, like all families in the East who could afford them, employed women from the local population, one to do the cooking, another to do the laundry and a male *kebon* to look after the gardens. The latter, while lowly-paid, did not have an onerous job and many a day his only activity was sitting on his haunches smoking a cigarette or leisurely sweeping the, usually quite clean, drive and paths with a *sapoe*.

On Sundays our cook, a Malay, would prepare for us a simple edition of the Rijsttafel made famous by the Hotel des Indes in Batavia where as many as a dozen *djongos* (waiters) would each offer two or more different dishes to accompany the rice.

On the island of Soemba there were no large commercially-run plantations and the main export before the War had been that of the ubiquitous small Soemba horse, the Indonesian equivalent of the Mongolian horse which had carried Genghis Khan and his successors and their hordes from the Steppes of Asia into the centre of Medieval Europe.

At times I would accompany the *Controleur* visiting local chieftains and we were always welcomed with friendliness and, in accordance with their custom, offered betelnuts to chew, which, in order not to offend, we would never refuse but gracefully accept. Luckily one was not obliged to consume the precious gift on the spot. Many of the older Soembanese had blackened teeth by chewing betelnuts and the juice would colour their mouth and lips red.

The main import, apart from foodstuff and consumer goods, was Catholic and Protestant missionaries. They succeeded to some small degree in converting the mostly Animist population to their particular brand of salvation. However, by 1946 they had most certainly not succeeded in covering up the female population who, except in Waingapoe, still went about their business and pleasure bare to the waist and in the shape in which it has pleased their creator to fashion them. This generally quite pleasant sight is familiar to those who admire the paintings of Balinese women by artists like Hofker and le Mayeur de Merpres who painted his beautiful Balinese wife Ni Polok.

Every six weeks or so I would usually go by truck, as the dirt road for most of the year was too rough for passenger cars, to Waikaboebak in the centre of western Soemba and some 80 kilometres from Waingapoe. The Protestant Missionaries had their church there while the Catholic Mission was some 30 kilometres further west at Waikelo on the coast.

I would, for preference, always stay overnight with the three priests, who I made sure were always well stocked with mission wine. In the evening I would be the fourth man at the bridge table and produce a bottle of Dutch Gin to ward off the bugs. In the Indies it was the generally-accepted wisdom (and excuse) that there was no better precaution against illnesses of all kinds than a strong alcoholic beverage like brandy or whisky but particularly Dutch Gin. It was for me a new experience to play cards in a room lit by kerosene lamps and it struck me that it must have been a daily experience for those who lived in the Colonies before the advent of hurricane lamps and electricity.

On Soemba, like most of the eastern islands of Indonesia, there are no verdant tropical forests like those on Sumatra, Borneo, West Java or in the wet highlands of New Guinea. The soil in the Lesser Sunda Islands east of Bali and Lombok is also much poorer and dusty in the dry season but Soemba has not as dry a climate as Timor.

36. A "Pasola" and a B-25

The Soembanese living in the outer districts had little previous experience with meeting foreigners and the *Controleur* and I must have sometimes been apparitions from another world, especially for the inquisitive smiling children. One day we were invited to attend the *Pasola,* a horse festival. The local chief was our host and before the spectacle a big meal was served inside his wood and bamboo and palm-thatched roofed house. We were seated in a circle on mats on the earthen floor opposite the *Radjah* (chief), the men dressed in their best Soemba-kains and colourful headcloths. The *Radjah's* wife, pretty daughter and other women sitting behind the men were dressed according to local custom, which enlivened the otherwise dull and most boring affair. The conversation was very limited since our hosts spoke far worse Malay than I, and the *Controleur* had not yet acquired sufficient knowledge of the local tongue. The *karbouw* (ox) meat served was very tough and the sago-palm 'wine' tasted soapy. On many other occasions during my stay on Soemba I was forced to imbibe sizeable quantities of this liquid they called 'Soppi' in order not to offend my hosts.

The *Pasola,* which was held after the feast at the *Radjah's* house, is an ancient war-game held in the western part of the island. The two opposing parties of horsemen run in a gallop towards each other and then, when at spear-throwing distance, release their sharp spears. Casualties, some deadly, were not unknown but were no deterrent to the holding of this exciting but dangerous event.

The riders are dressed in the colourful *'ikats'* for which Soemba was famous. These genuine handmade and dyed Soemba-kains now fetch very high prices. Although in 1945 it was already more a ceremonial than a war game, the Indonesian Government, to minimise serious injuries and the occasional deadly accident, nowadays only permits the use of blunt spears.

To the Animists, and perhaps to most of the Soembanese, the blood thus spilled placates the evil spirits and squaring off against each other on horseback ensures the community's good health.

Not much ever happened in Colonial outposts and it was no different in Waingapoe. We led a placid and uneventful life with a simple routine which was interrupted one day in early April by the sound of aeroplane engines. To the great excitement of everybody it was a B-25 Mitchell bomber with the Dutch flag painted on its fuselage and wings.

While the B-25 made several passes of the township, I raced in 'my' Pontiac to the airfield situated just outside the town proper, cursing the decision not to keep the *alang-alang* (a certain type of high-growing grass) short and the strip in good repair.

After several slow passes to clear the airstrip of grazing horses, the B-25 had landed by the time I reached the river alongside the airstrip and crossed it in a small boat. To our mutual surprise the co-pilot was Lt. Morrie Groen with whom I had made the voyage from London to Australia in July-September of 1944. The crew had been instructed to inspect Waingapoe airfield from the air but, with two of the most daring KNIL pilots aboard, they had decided to land. Within an hour they took off again promising to report that our airstrip was serviceable. It did not occur to me to ask the crew whether any planes of the 18th Squadron had been shot down near Soemba because, soon after our arrival, we had been told that, in 1943, an Allied Airman had been captured by the Japanese and held for many days in the Japanese military prison at Waingapoe. His nationality and rank were unknown. Had I done so I would have learned that the prisoner was the ONLY crew member of the whole 18th Squadron who, after their planes had been shot down, survived the war.

There is something of a fine irony that 50 years later, in Australia, it would be the telegraphist-gunner of this B-25, Hans van Beuge, who would tell me that the Captain of the B-25 was none other than Frits Pelder who had piloted the only plane to escape from Japanese-occupied Java. Hans also told me the story of the airman Jan van Burg who was captured by the Nips and held in Waingapoe for ten days in 1943. Hans gave me a photocopy of Jan van Burg's official report, a shortened version of which follows.

The B-25 Mitchell N5-136 of the 18th Dutch Squadron, operating under the direction of 79th RAAF Wing at Batchelor in the Northern Territories, on reconnaissance on 7th of September 1943, spotted a ship in the harbour of Waingapoe and promptly attacked. Having dropped their bombs on their target at only 100 meters height they were set upon by ZERO fighters. In the ensuing fight they shot down two ZEROs and damaged a third, which trailing smoke, broke off the attack, but by then their very badly damaged burning B-25, with every one of the crew wounded, was finished off by the fourth ZERO. Full of holes, the hydraulic system failing and the guns now inoperable, van Burg, who was the wireless operator, sent a distress signal before the plane ditched off the east coast of Soemba. Only part of his distress signal was received in Darwin. The pilot, Sgt. Visser, was killed when the nose of the B-25 hit the water and the rest of the crew took to a half-inflated rubber dinghy. The observer, Lt. Zeydel, died of his wounds that night and was put overboard. Drifting for another day, lashed by thunder storms, the dinghy capsized and they lost their precious water container. After four more days and nights, becoming weaker and literally starting to die of thirst, they sighted land on the 12th of October. The mechanic, Sgt. Hoogtij, by now delirious, jumped into the shark-infested sea and was not seen again. The three remaining wounded crew, with assistance from the wind, paddled slowly towards the shore and were thrown by the heavy surf onto the beach where they collapsed. The next day they were spotted by a native who must have reported them to the Japanese for soon a lone Japanese soldier appeared who, before the exhausted and wounded men could rise to surrender, promptly shot the air-gunner, Corporal Gerards. The next shot killed Sgt. de Hoog, the co-pilot. A third bullet missed van Burg, as did the fourth, whereupon the soldier walked up to him and hit his badly injured arm with his rifle butt. The Nip then ordered van Burg to undress and tied him naked to a tree. Just as the soldier was about to bayonet him, a Japanese officer on horseback arrived and timely intervened. Refused water he was marched naked to an army post 30 minutes away where he was finally given water and food. Before putting him on a truck, the Japs gave him an old green KNIL uniform. Half an hour later and after transfer to a passenger car, he was escorted by two Japanese officers to the Japanese HQ in Waingapoe. A Japanese Lieutenant, through an interpreter, interrogated him at length and seemed pleased with the response consisting of pure lies and misinformation which however filled pages and pages with Japanese script. This seemed to particularly please the representative from the 'land of the rising sun'.

One morning, ten days later, van Burg, blindfolded, was driven to and pushed into a plane and flown via Bali to Soerabaja. After more interrogations and transfers to other over-crowded jails, one meal a day and regular beatings—among others with a baseball bat for the amusement of one jailor—he reached Japan via Celebes, Manila (where he was for a change well-treated and fed on orders of the Japanese Navy's CO) and Formosa (Taiwan). In February 1944 he left the Otuna Camp, about 10 miles from Tokyo, where selected POWs from all nationalities were closely interrogated, to end up in a camp near the industrial town of Ashio where he joined about 250 under-fed and neglected Dutch POWs and, despite his crippled arm, was put to hard work in the copper mines.

For many, V. J. Day came too late but Jan van Burg was liberated and flown to Manila. He was awarded the Bronze Cross and after World War II settled in the USA where he, according to my latest information, lived in Vista, California.

Talking about military decorations, the Dutch are not awarded campaign medals (apart from medals for bravery) but only a war medal and a clasp for serving in more than one war zone. It is to me typical of the parsimonious mentality of the Netherlanders.

I once or twice visited the North Coast of Soemba to the east of Waingapoe and was particularly taken by the village of Melolo (one of the villages to which van Burg, after his capture, must have been taken). It was a pretty village with a small Balinese-type temple and thatched-roof houses, fenced in with bamboo to keep the externally pecking chickens and lean black pigs scurrying around inside the yard. In the villages and in the countryside the inevitable *karbouw* (buffalo) could often be seen tethered to a pole or tree. Pigs one can find on many of the islands but I cannot recall ever having seen them on predominantly Moslem Java, although they must have been kept there before ending up in a Chinese or European kitchen.

On the coast near, and further east from, Melolo, coconut groves adjoined the narrow beach, a sight one always associates with islands in the Pacific. It had been from somewhere east of Melolo that our Japanese factotum, Ishii, had walked the 50 kilometres or so to Waingapoe.

Soon after arriving in Waingapoe, a locally-born telegraph master and radio operator had been put in charge of our post office's sole communications with the outside world. An experienced Dutch male 'medic', well versed in tropical diseases, who treated me once for a mild bout of malaria, joined us a few weeks later.

It was and has always been a lonely life in the outer provinces and islands and it was no different for us six Europeans in 1945/46. In the evenings we would adopt the old Indische custom, still practised in remote parts of the archipelago, to dress in pyjamas after a splash bath in the *kamar mandi* and sit in our *krossi males* (easy chairs) on our covered terrace and enjoy a cool breeze wafting in from the Timor Sea. It always made me feel so much a part of the old Indie of my grandparents and my *Controleur* Uncle, Jan Zeeman.

We had a tennis court but only old 'bald' tennis balls and poorly strung racquets. The sand beaches were too far away from Waingapoe and there were only very few books brought along by us five officers. There were no newspapers, only the short news bulletins received through our wireless station but we could read Time Magazine, for which Ata Ceurvorst had taken out a subscription for me. They were a few weeks old by the time I received them. We had no radio receiver or gramophones and were starved for music, unlike in Hollandia and Merauke. Letters delivered about every fortnight or sometimes every three weeks by the small cargo ships were therefore looked forward to with great anticipation. The postal service remained erratic and mail often took a long time to reach me, taking anywhere from two weeks from Melbourne to more than a month from Holland.

Apart from scores of personal correspondence in numbered envelopes from Berna, my parents and sisters, I now also received letters from friends, the Editor of the Dutch Motoring magazine, Motor, and from the Rector of my old high school, the Amsterdam Lyceum. Piet Nortier, the editor of Motor and one of the well-known sports personalities in the Netherlands, wrote me a most cordial two-page reply to a letter of mine written soon after my arrival on Soemba. He said he would be pleased if I would continue to be a contributor and outlined his plans for the post-war Motor magazine. Rationing of paper would however seriously affect the number of pages of the magazine for some years. It was only on my return to Holland that I heard that Nortier's wartime resistance exploits had landed him in a Gestapo jail.

Dr. C. P. Gunning, my high school Principal, wrote how very pleased he was to receive so many letters from former students from a great number of foreign countries which *"all show that they have not forgotten their old school."* It was however not only the excellence of the education we had received, but the part our Rector personally had played that accounted for the great esteem in which he was held by us all.

Dr. Gunning also mentioned the names of the teachers who had lost their lives during the German Occupation. One lost her life in an extermination camp, two died in a concentration camp in Germany, and another took his own life in a Gestapo jail. All four had lectured me in various subjects. Dr. Gunning did not tell me that he, a prominent person in Dutch society had been taken hostage and had therefore lived in fear of being executed in reprisal for attacks made by the Dutch Resistance.

My father wrote about a Dutch Officer *(Engelandvaarder* Lt. Hazelhoff Roelfsema) who, a day or so after the 5th of May, on behalf of Queen Wilhelmina, had placed a wreath on the spot where only very shortly before the end of the War, the Germans had executed 20 Resistance fighters. He also related that a few Resistance men had been shot by firing squad on the Apollolaan, a few hundred yards from our home, while the public had been forced to watch the execution.

Most of the bridges in the Netherlands north of the Great Rivers had been blown up and the only way to cross over the Maas (Meuse) River was at the bridge at Nijmegen, and over the other parallel-running major rivers only by pontoon bridge at Arnhem. It had taken some time before the Allied Command had declared the lands above Nijmegen safe for the return of our impatient Queen Wilhelmina who received a rapturous reception from the crowds in the streets festooned with the Dutch flag and Orange pennants.

My mother wrote of the grey misery of the 'hunger winter' of 1944/45, of the many months of no heating, of no electricity and hardly any food and how she, by the light of a carbide lamp purchased on the black market, had cooked tulip bulbs, thistles and, if lucky, sugar beets in the cold kitchen on an ingeniously-improvised small coal-fired 'stove' filled with small pieces of coal which my sisters had laboriously chiselled from very large chunks also purchased on the black market. The coal-fired furnace for the central heating of the apartment building had been out of commission since October of 1944 and the only room not freezing cold was the kitchen where they stayed until bedtime. The Christmas of 1944 had been the most dreadful mother had ever had, a sentiment no doubt shared by all of the population. Since there was no electricity they had also been without news from the outside world for many months.

My youngest sister, Anita, wrote how in the dying days of Hitler's War, she had stood at a window overlooking the intersection of de Lairesse and Cornelis Schuyt streets when a teenage boy, living opposite, arrived on his bicycle at the front door of his parents' flat. It was perhaps two minutes, if that, after the 6 p.m. curfew imposed by the Germans. An SS soldier patrolling the intersection at that very moment unhesitatingly raised his rifle and killed the young man as he was about to enter his home.

She also told me how one day she and my elder sister Mary were surprised by the sound of very low flying planes. They rushed to the second-floor corner window overlooking the two aforementioned streets and, looking in the direction of the bridge across the canal towards the Apollolaan, saw more RAF Mosquitos passing thunderously low over the roof of the flat building, and dropping bombs on the Gestapo HQ at the former girls' high school situated some 300 metres away in Euterpe Street. Little did they know at that moment that they were watching one of the famous RAF air strikes of World War II. The object of the raid was to destroy the Gestapo archives and try to free political prisoners in their cells (in the basement I believe) and kill Gestapo agents. They succeeded spectacularly but it had a downside since some prisoners were killed as well as people living nearby when their apartment buildings were destroyed by stray bombs. One of Anita's close friends and her parents were among those killed.

My sisters had witnessed an historic air strike, one that compares with the similar attack on the Gestapo HQ in Copenhagen and, in July of 1943, on the jail of Amiens, where the Gestapo also held arrested leaders of the *Maquis*. Air compression bombs toppled the walls and surviving prisoners escaped. Hence the codename Jericho was given to this attack to tumble down the walls of the prison.

My sister Mary wrote to tell me the good news that my old friend Bobby Nikkels, hiding from the Nazis, had survived the war, and had joined a British Royal Engineers' unit as an interpreter. He had taken several officers to my parents' home and unknowingly had played cupid, for Anita would marry Richard Saunders, a RE Captain, and Mary would meet and marry a RN Lieutenant and "Swordfish" Pilot called Rory Connor.

My good friend Jan Doornik was liberated by Canadian and French troops shortly before the German surrender of *Festung Holland,* the occupied part of the Netherlands, on the 5th of May 1945 at the *Hotel de Nieuwe Wereld* in Wageningen.

Sometime early in May I received a telegram from KNIL-HQ in Batavia ordering me to proceed to Batavia and informing me that volunteers having served the required two years in uniform were eligible for demobilisation. It was quite unexpected in view of the still serious lack of manpower in the KNIL and NICA.

On my last night in Waingapoe, lying on my camp-bed in the front room of the house which in the 'old days' must have been the study, and wondering what the near future held for me, I could hear the chirping of the crickets and dogs barking in the part of the town further inland from the coast. Dogs are smart, they cope with the tropical heat of the day by sleeping through it and you find them always stretched out somewhere in the shade. They seem to do their barking only in the evenings.

37. Java Brings Memories of Three Generations

I do not remember anything at all about the 6th of June, the day of my departure for Batavia, but I, no doubt as always, first headed for the bathroom and had a bath. This in those days invariably meant splashing water from a fairly large, often tiled, cement tub over oneself with a small bucket, called a *gajong*. It has a handle across the open side which the bather grips and dumps into the tub to fill with water which can feel quite cold. Not forewarned, and to the amusement of old hands, many a *totok*, having just arrived in India, when confronted with a typical Indische type bathroom for the first time, would in their innocence crawl into the tub. Shame and ridicule would then await them.

I must also have had a last look over the *aloeng-aloeng* in front of the house to the glistening blue Timor Sea and said my goodbyes at the wharf before boarding the small ship taking me to Koepang.

Humphrey McQueen wrote in a book review in "The Australian" of Steven Rose's *The Making of Memory*:

> *"Researchers claim that after four weeks we forget 85 percent of our experiences unless prompted by a diary. Yet with the appropriate stimulus, we can provide detailed accounts of events from decades back."*

It is my experience that memory is selective, only the highlights remain as recollections of the mind. In Batavia, on my return flight to Australia, this stimulus was particularly strong, for the island of Java has featured in the lives of three expatriate generations of my family. I cannot, however, remember at all how I travelled from Waingapoe to Batavia except for overflying the island of Lombok. We could clearly see Rindjani, the 3720-metre high volcano which dominates the northern half of the island of Lombok. It had been on Lombok in 1894 that my grandfather, Senior Officer of the Medical Corps, Dr. J. W. Portengen had won the Dutch VC, the MWO *(Militaire Willems Orde)* for bravery under enemy fire.

The Sasaks, the original inhabitants of Lombok had asked the Dutch Colonial Government in Batavia to free them from the oppression of their Balinese overlords who had conquered most of Lombok in the years from 1740 to 1805 and to suppress the original Sasak population. The NBI Government in Batavia was often still referred to as the 'Compagnie', although early in the 19th century the Dutch Government had taken over the governing of the Indies from the VOC (Vereenigde Oostindische Compagnie, i.e. United East India Company) which had ruled from the 17th to the end of the 19th century. It had until then not shown much interest in Lombok and left the governance to the Balinese overlords. The Dutch were, after all, still fighting an insurgency in Atjeh (like the Indonesian Government in Jakarta would have to more than a century later!). My grandfather had incidentally also served in a military hospital in Atjeh (Aceh) in the late 1880s and early 1890s during the long, drawn-out guerrilla war with the predominantly fundamentalist Islamic population.

On the 5th and 6th of July 1894, Dutch warships and coastal steamers arrived at Ampenan carrying the expeditionary force. The terms of an ultimatum given to the proud Balinese were quite unacceptable but nevertheless meetings were held at Mataram by the Commander, General Vetter, and Major General van Ham with the Balinese Princes. From the lengthy account given by W. Cool in his book, *De Lombok Expeditie,* published in 1896, it is clear that General Vetter should have asked for further instructions from the Government in Batavia but instead and in spite of having received warnings that an ambush of his forces was being planned, he chose to instruct General van Ham to advance to the town of Tjakranegara. Here, van Ham's column was ambushed in the streets by the Balinese ensconced behind the high walls of the *puris* (walled compounds of building and temples). The KNIL columns were in the most vulnerable situation and were massacred in the crossfire of an enemy protected by the high walls. My grandfather managed to retreat with his field hospital, together with a platoon of soldiers, to a partly walled-off area which adjoined a little river and, having clear fresh water, was ideal for treating the wounded. The position soon came under Balinese attacks and became untenable and grandfather, now attending to the wounded under enemy fire, instructed the bugler to sound the alarm for urgent assistance. When the bugler was shot, grandfather picked up the bugle and sounded the alarm until help arrived. For his bravery he was awarded the MWO. My grandmother told me that when grandfather returned to Batavia from Lombok, his blond hair had greyed at the temples.

The 'Dewa Puri' is still there and little changed from that fateful 25th day of August 1894. General van Ham's grave, which the Indonesian officials maintain in perfect order, can be found in a corner of the *puri* of the Dewa Temple.

A second Expeditionary Force subsequently overwhelmed the Balinese and the Sasaks would then continue to govern themselves under the 'supervision' of a Dutch Resident and a few *Controleurs*.

When my wife and I travelled to this area in 1993, my travel agency had advised the local authorities of the reasons for my interest in visiting Mataram and Cakranegara (today's spelling). Two Indonesian city officials assigned to show us around had researched the events of 1894 and had found my grandfather's name in the archives. They took us to the spot on the Kali Ancar where my grandfather must have blown the bugle nearly a hundred years ago.

The little unspoiled River Antjar of 1894 was no more. The once clear shaded brook had been converted into a concreted, dirty canal, while the green countryside had given way to housing. Our Indonesian friends shared my disappointment at the hideous transformation. When parting, at the port of Ampenan, they asked me with typical Oriental good manners whether the doctor had enjoyed a long life. I had to reply in the negative for Grandfather Portengen died in 1915 of an, at that time, untreatable illness, most likely hepatitis (his skin had turned yellowish), when on the verge of joining the French Army's Medical Corps on the Western Front. I could however tell them that my musical grandfather had composed the Tjakranegara March in memory of the Lombok Expedition, a well-worn copy of which is still in my possession.

On a humid and hot afternoon, the KNIL Transport Squadron Dakota touched down on Kemajoran Airport, inaugurated in 1938, and the existence of which I had not been aware of, or it had escaped my mind. I had expected and had been looking forward to seeing Batavia's Tjililitan Airport again for it was there that I, before the Douglas DC-

2 all-metal aeroplanes had come into service with the KLM in 1934, had as a spectator watched the KLM-Fokker Type XII called the 'Postduif' arrive after a record-breaking four-day special flight from Amsterdam's Schiphol Airport to deliver the Christmas mail. Previously the three-engined Fokkers had taken ten days for the flight from Schiphol to Tjililitan. The earliest flights had taken no less than 40 days.

Soon after landing I was billeted in a requisitioned villa in the Laan Holle area of Batavia where I shared a stiflingly-hot go-down room with three other officers. For ventilation there was only one about 20 x 120 centimetre window (actually an opening covered with gauze) situated just below the ceiling. In spite of leaving the door open, I spent the hottest and most uncomfortable night since Merauke in the humid swampy low lands of New Guinea.

The next day I was driven from the once-genteel suburb of Weltevreden (it means "well contented"), where the well-to-do lived, to the Benedenstad (down-town) of Batavia, which is situated seven kilometres to the north and where Governor General J. P. Coen of the VOC had established its first fort, go-downs and dwellings in 1619.

Exiting Laan Holle, the vehicle turned left; it was at this part of Koningsplein that the 'Pasar Gambir' was always held. It was a "fun fair" which was one of the highlights of the year, especially for children. At this pasar malem, as the indigenous population called such fairs, my main interest, as a pre-teen, was in the electric dodgems marquee. I and my friend Bobby Nikkels, would spend most of the time at the wheel of a dodgem on the oval pitch while my parents and sisters visited other attractions.

Turning right at that same junction of Koningsplein one would soon pass the large house with the two guest pavilions of the Michielsen family where, after Indonesia's Independence, the Vice-President, Dr. M. Hata, would reside, while the Governor General's Palace on Koningsplein North would, after 1949, house the Presidents of Indonesia. After sighting the Harmonie, in pre-War days a social club, and the well-known Hotel des Indes, we drove along the somewhat infamous Molenvliet Canal which, with people separated by only a few yards, washing clothes, bathing and defecating, seemed not to have changed at all from the old days.

At the KNIL Administrative HQ, I was informed that I had completed my two years of military service as a volunteer and would be returned to Holland for demobilisation. This was the last thing I wanted since I realised full well that if I did not succeed in first returning to Melbourne, Berna and I would remain separated for years and with every chance that we would never see each other again.

I had to 'find' a reason for the military authorities to agree to my first being sent to Australia before demobilisation and remembering my observations of the mentally disturbed LM—with whom I had travelled from Hollandia to Brisbane in a C-47 Dakota—I decided there and then to feign being emotionally 'fragile' as a result of my wartime experiences, compounded by now not being allowed to go back to Australia first to marry the girl to whom I was engaged. I must have made an at least half-convincing case for I was told to report to a doctor at the military hospital for a medical examination in two days' time.

Later that morning I called at the very modern offices (for that time) of the NHM Bank situated on the Binnen Nieuwpoortstraat opposite the Stationsplein and next to the Javasche Bank in the business district, and just north of the Chinese quarter called Glodok and its Chinese restaurants. I noted on the commemorative plaque unveiled, on the day the building was inaugurated, my father's name as one of the three directors.

I have ever since wondered whether that plaque is still there. If so then in Jakarta one can find my father's name on a bank building, my brother's on a cross at the War Cemetery, and my name on the Champions Board of the then Jakarta Golf Club where, in 1950, I had the great good fortune in that the two best players had 'off' days when playing against me.

To my surprise it was a Mr. K. F. Zeeman (no relation) who now occupied my father's old office and by whom I was most cordially received. Learning about my terrible accommodation he immediately arranged for me to stay at the employees' mess of the bank. *"Connections! Connections!"*

That same late afternoon, after advising the KNIL of my change of abode, I moved into an airy clean room of the large modern villa where Dutch employees of the bank were housed. Apart from making new lifelong friends, with whom paths would cross more than once, like Rijn de Wilde and the *Engelandvaarder* Chris van Oosterzee, I also ran into Jaap Oost-Lievense who in London every Friday had paid out the £7 loan of Mr. van de Stadt. They and my new bank employee friends—nearly all of whom, curiously, had been accepted into the NHM Bank after final interviews by my father—upon hearing of my demobilisation problems provided me with dubious advice and outrageous suggestions to secure the desired outcome.

Their plying me with large quantities of alcohol and inducing me to smoke many large cigars caused me to arrive the next day at the military hospital's consulting rooms with a serious hangover. This must, no doubt, have had a profound effect on my blood pressure and pulse apart from causing a slight tremble of my hands and resulted in a 'so-so' fitness report and I was directed to see a neuro-surgeon (nowadays it would be a psychiatrist) two days later.

The neuro-surgeon—hearing about my (true) recurring nightmares and disturbed sleeping pattern, and after listening to my faked nervous and emotional replies to his questions and my pleas to be first allowed to return to Australia—decided that it was highly desirable for me to be sent to Australia for rest and recuperation before demobilisation in Holland.

That evening at the NHM Mess I celebrated the happy outcome appropriately with alcoholic beverages and ignored my friends' facetious suggestions to become an actor and go to Hollywood.

In spite of the 19th (Transport) Squadron having been enlarged considerably with Dakota aircraft by April of 1946, all flights to Australia were fully booked, allowing me a few more days to explore Batavia and try to gain a better insight into the military and political situation as well as to visit the homes where I had lived as a boy. The RAPWI (Repatriation of Allied POWs and Internees) could not receive all the military assistance needed because the SEAC (South East Asia Command) had not been able to quickly send an adequate occupation force to the NEI. This had contributed to the chaos following the Merdeka Revolution of the 17th of August and had resulted in the atrocities committed against defenceless civilian internees.

A most disagreeable consequence was also the need to give the hated Japanese, who had inhumanely treated the same internees, the task of acting as proxy for the Allies to protect and keep the internees, sometimes for many months, in the camps. Japanese aircraft and pilots, under the command of a KNJL-ML Captain, were also mobilised for the delivery of food and medicines to towns marooned in a hostile TRI (Indonesian Republican Army) *Pemoedas* and roving, bandit-controlled hinterland of Java. The sick and wounded internees, many still staying in their old internment camps under the protection of Japanese soldiers, would be evacuated on the return flights.

One-fifth of the half-starved Dutch Internees and POWs did not survive the cruel and barbaric conditions they had to endure in the Japanese camps, where they were executed, killed (murdered), died of dysentery, malaria, cholera, hook worms, jaundice, leg ulcers, various foot infections and other illnesses, as well as malnutrition.

The policy of the then Schermerhorn-Drees Dutch Government to refuse direct contact with the Nationalist leaders Soekarno and Hatta had contributed to the chaos and the Bersiap (be prepared/ready) period of terrorism by various armed gangs, who became known as *Pelopors*. A KNIL infantry officer described them to me as terrorists and bandits rather than freedom fighters since they would also terrorise the local population. (Sounds familiar to us in the 21st century, doesn't it?)

The end of the war had not meant liberation for a great many internees, on Java especially, and they remained, not without cause, living in fear in the internment camps. Many inmates of a men and boys camp were beaten to death and otherwise killed by the *Javanese Pemoedas* or *Pelopors*.

When the internment camps in Batavia were opened, many women, not aware of the chaotic situation in town, had left their camp and had fallen into the hands of *pemoedas* who, armed with knives and sharpened bamboo sticks, knew no mercy.

The generally prospering *Tjiong Hoa* (as the ethnic Chinese were known), ever since they settled there had been subjected to repeated flare-ups of hate, resulting in killing and looting by the natives of southeast Asia. Yet, in spite of setbacks, they continued to prosper. It was no different in the revolutionary days of 1945 and 1946 or later in Indonesia. Even the *Peranakans,* the Chinese-born who were raised in the islands of the Indies, some with native blood in their veins, were not spared during the outburst of hate or disaffection with something or another.

War and revolution always bring out the worst in people and it was in Asia no different from Europe where the SS (Auschwitz, etc.), Soviets (Katyn, etc.) as well as others, committed heinous crimes.

During my short stay in Batavia I heard more details of the experiences of the tens of thousands of men, women and children during the War, and of the dramatic weeks immediately after the 15th of August. A mother of two young sons who had been interned in a camp for men near Soerabaja—after she had been allowed to leave her camp—had gone to the nearby camp for men where she learned from her younger 12-year-old son that his 15-year old brother had died "from a heart attack." The boy couldn't tell his mother the ghastly truth that his brother had been forced to drink water to excess and stand to attention on pain of being severely beaten, and that he died of a ruptured bladder. It is documented that other boys were beaten with sticks on full bellies until they died. When the distraught crying woman returned to her women's camp, a Jap guard asked her why she cried. She told him that she had heard that her son had died. When he demanded to know who had told her, she refused to answer since the women were strictly forbidden to go to the camps for men and boys and to speak with them. She was thereupon punished and beaten until she lost consciousness.

I was told of a mother of three children who was beaten to death. A girl of 13 was raped and killed while women, including nuns, were forced into prostitution in Japanese 'comfort stations'. I know personally of a woman threatened with harm to her baby if she did not submit. Yet these same Japanese people, capable of unspeakable acts of cruelty, perform an utterly serene tea ceremony and created magnificent temples and fascinating feudal castles set in exquisite gardens. In WWII atrocities were, of course, also committed in the European theatre of war and the history of the world is laced with killing, looting and raping by so-called human beings.

At that time, in June 1946, reports had also reached us about the large scale and repeated raping of German women by the victorious Soviet troops and similar assaults by French Moroccan troops in the Stuttgart area of Bavaria. We also knew about incidents involving American GIs in Dutch Limburg.

Most of us also know about Katyn Forrest, Lidice and Oradour-sur-Glan, not to mention Auschwitz, Bergen-Belsen and other infamous concentration camps.

The veneer of civilisation is indeed very thin for the greater part of humanity, who are basically still savages, and of which we are reminded daily in our newspapers and on TV.

Bushido—the Japanese code of honour—and the education of boys in Japan, where boys were segregated from girls at school at the age of 10 and given a Spartan education, is perhaps partly an explanation of their heartless treatment of POWs and internees. Ironically it was that same Bushido code of honour and the near-religious veneration of the Emperor as a living god that brought about an immediate and total acceptance by the Japanese military of the Emperor's decision to lay down their arms and implicitly follow orders they received from the Allies.

It was not until January 1946 that the NICA had taken over the civil affairs administration from AMACAB (Allied Military Administration Civil Affairs Branch), which was under British Command. During that period, from September 1945 to mid-1946, the *Pelopors* and *Pemoedas* had infiltrated and terrorised Batavia. It had taken some months to fully restore order with a small force of 20,000 men of which many were brave ex-KNIL prisoners of war who had spent three terrible years in Japanese POW camps.

By June 1946 there was no longer a feeling of vague hostility in the air, as my father had experienced in September the year before, and the tension during the so-called Bersiap period, but unease or perhaps a sense of insecurity remained.

Henk Brinkman (the present Editor of the *Engelandvaarder* Association's periodical, De Schakel) had been in Batavia during that unpleasant time but the *Pelopors* had not prevented him from taking a *betjak* to, and enjoying lunch at, the Hotel des Indes or the Hotel der Nederlanden where, in October/November, some women and children who rescued from going to the besieged internment camps, were still awaiting repatriation to Holland.

After peace had returned, *'passar atom'* (atom market), a legacy of the *Pelopors*, remained. Here goods of dubious provenance, most likely looted by the *Pelopors* and stolen by common thieves, continued to be offered for sale.

Stories of those who had made forays into the countryside spoke of neglected *sawahs* (rice fields) and overgrown plantations. The *orang-tanis* (farmers) saw no sense in working their fields when the harvest was promptly requisitioned by the Japanese and, after Merdeka (i.e. after the 17th of August of 1945), by the TRI, or 'confiscated' by the *Pelopors*.

38. Nostalgic Visits in Batavia and Indonesian Independence

Having returned to Batavia in 1946 after a 12-year absence and with a couple of days on my hands, I decided to try to make a nostalgic visit to the homes I had lived in from 1929 to July of 1934.

The evocation of memories of times spent on the island of Java, on this first visit since 1934, was powerful. Foremost was the pungent smell of *roko kretek* (cigarettes made with cloves) and the delightful aroma of charcoal-roasted *sate*. We used to buy satays from the itinerant *toekang sate* (roast meat vendor) carrying his burning charcoal stove and supplies on a bamboo or wooden stick over a shoulder while intermittently crying out *"Sate! Sate!"*

Without motor transport I had no opportunity to roam around extensively but since it was now fairly safe and since the homes we lived in were not far from the NHM Mess, I could make use of a *betjak* (bicycle taxi).

The *betjak*, or *betja*, had not yet appeared on the streets of Batavia when my family sailed for Holland on the SMN passenger liner MV "Marnix van St Aldegonde' in July 1934. The *betjak* was invented in old 'Betawie', by whom it is not known. The first models offered passengers hair-raising rides including tipping over, for the early models were unstable, or even ending up in one of the city's canals. The 1945 improved model still required the passengers to face the traffic totally unprotected, seated in the oilcloth-covered *fauteuil* while the *betjak* driver pedalled furiously and continuously rang his bicycle bell while tacking about in the notorious traffic surrounded by trains, horn-blowing motorcars, trucks, mopeds and *opelettes,* as well as *sado-sados* (two-wheeled carriages pulled by a small horse) and bicycles. The passengers must at times have had their hearts in their mouths during a perilous trip from Pasar Baroe to Glodok via the Harmonieplein and Molenvliet since *betjak* drivers, like bicycle riders all over the world, are the foremost offenders of traffic rules. The number of passengers carried and, indeed, cargo could vary greatly from one large or fat European or Chinese to two smaller adults plus two small children, to a cargo of many baskets of cackling chickens, mangoes, doerians, ramboutans or other fruit. Legend has it that young men would get into the *betjak* and half an hour later step out grey-haired old men. Premature births would occur by the jolting and scare the daylights out of pregnant female passengers.

The *betjaks* of Batavia/Jakarta are invariably painted in bright reds, yellows and greens and are garishly festooned with plumes, small flags and the like. The *toekang betjak* is very simply dressed in a singlet, tank top or short-sleeved shirt while wearing an assortment of headgear. I have seen one with a bowler hat but straw hats, *kopiahs* and baseball caps are more common.

'My' *betjak's* driver had a large military straw hat which, at one time, must have graced the bead of a *'spandrie'* (soldier 1st class) of the KNIL, and he was dressed in a *pendek* (shorts) and singlet. The *betjak* had a girl's name, 'Salina', painted on the wheel covers over the two bicycle wheels on either side of the seat. After some haggling, we settled the fare for the trip to the two homes I had lived in.

It was on a particularly hot, sticky and windless day that I seated myself on the red plastic seat of the garishly-festooned *betjak* and soon arrived on the van Heutsz Boulevard where the gardens, as elsewhere, looked rather neglected. Some resembled a jungle from which the large Raintrees rose high into the sky. The asphalt, as elsewhere in Batavia, was also here broken up, causing the *betjak* driver to take evasive action. It was noticeably quiet on this divided tree-lined boulevard, which Indonesians would understandably and ironically rename Jalan Tuku Umar after the leader of the Achenese who had been defeated by General (and later Governor General) van Heutsz in the 1890s.

I had already seen enough on my trips in army transport to note that it was no longer the prosperous Batavia of yore. 'Our' home on the van Heutsz Boulevard, with a pavilion for guests where my brother Tom had his room, and steps in the centre of the main building leading to a covered wide entrance and hall, looked run-down. Indeed, most of the other homes of my boyhood friends also looked run-down, e.g. the homes of the three Smits brothers, who lived opposite and next to Rob Meyer Ranneft and Paul van Geelgildemeester with whom, in the 1930s, I would usually bicycle to our school, the CAS (Carpentier Alting Stichting) on Koningsplein East.

The gardens and indeed the houses appeared smaller than I remembered. This was quite logical for I had grown another 25 centimetres or so in height since 1934. My next-door neighbour and friend was known as Krikie Ariens even though Krikie was not his proper name but only his nickname, a very common practice in the Indies. I recall nicknames like Ketjil (small), the recipient of which could be either a small or a big lad, Tikoes (mouse) for whatever reason, and Tjalie (resembling a *tali* (string)) by being very thin. These nicknames originated in the Indische/Indo communities, who speaking about someone else often used the preface *"Sie"*. The one I shall never forget is a schoolmate at the CAS Primary, Sie Beentjes (Bones), because he was a skinny, gangling chap and tall for his age.

After crossing the bridge over a narrow drainage canal at the Grisseeweg, the *betjak* driver took me up the incline at the Burgemeester Bisschop Square with the Mason's Lodge and Nassau Church, and crossed the Oranje Boulevard (now Jalan Imam Bonyol) to the right and Jalan Dipo Negoro to the left of the crossing. We soon reached our second home, built in modern Indische style. It was a white-stuccoed house with a red-tiled roof and with lawns all around and hedged by flowers and shrubs where we lived before we left for Amsterdam in 1934. It was situated on the Madioenweg No 1. The property would be fenced in to a height of some seven feet and capped with razor wire when it became the Saudi Arabian Embassy some time after 1940.

After the war, housing in Batavia/Jakarta would remain very tight for a very long time. Henk Brinkman, who had been charged with the registration of houses, told me that by October 1945 all available and liveable dwellings had been registered and allocated by the Housing Authority because the city had become the haven of refuge from the chaos and lawlessness generally prevailing in West Java.

After 1945, housing would remain in short supply. In 1948, Berna and I, after a spell in one room of a house in Laan de Riemer which we shared with two other couples and my old friend Philip Altes (from my Amsterdam Hockey Club days), were allocated a dwelling situated in the back garden of a house at 47 Soerabajaweg. This consisted of the original kitchen while the adjacent garage and go-downs had been converted into a living room, bedroom and small en-suite bathroom. In 1950, within half an hour of it becoming known among the 100-plus European employees of Internatio, where I was employed, that I had been transferred to Medan, three men had called on the company's housing officer and applied for our most desirable converted garage!

Housing remained tight and, at the end of 1952, having been re-posted to Djakarta after home leave, we regressed to two rooms, en-suite and kitchenette in a flat building in tropical Djakarta. Here we stayed until I was transferred to the Holland China Trading Company. We sailed in May of 1955 with the "Tjiluwah" of the Java China Japan Line from Tandjong Priok to Hong Kong where we were to spend five marvellous years.

Ever since the 17th-century young Dutchmen had pursued expatriate careers in the Indies, some in the West Indies but most in the East Indies, and spent long years in the tropics. My father had started his career with the NHM with a stint of six years in Burma and on Java before going on eight months home leave. In the early days, a six to eight-year first stint was a usual tour of duty. Even in my time, four years followed by six months leave in Europe was the norm.

Java in particular has been a constant in my family. My grandparents and six of their children, three from each side, made a career and/or married in the NEI and Far East. Four would end their lives there. My Uncle Jan Zeeman, the *Controleur*, is buried near Medan; Uncle Bob Zeeman, a Bank Officer, died of illness in Shanghai; Uncle Wim Portengen's grave is in Madioen; and my brother Tom's last resting place is in a war cemetery near Batavia.

Before the War it had been accepted without being mentioned, that I, like my father, grandfathers, uncles and brother, would make my career in Indict and/or the Far East.

The NEI had fallen into ruin from the once prosperous colony it had been and the political situation was volatile. The future of the NEI was not surprisingly a major topic of discussion at the 'factory' mess and with the military with whom I came into contact.

The Second World War changed the world and there was no longer a place in that world for colonial powers like the Netherlands in the Indies, the French in Indo-China, or the British in India and Malaya. Some politicians with an intimate knowledge of the NEI—or having lived as expatriates in Indie before WWII—had already realised, as early as the 1920s, that fundamental changes in the governance of the NEI had to be made and some form of autonomy ought to be granted to the peoples of Indie.

It was therefore that we, who had ourselves experienced occupation by a foreign power, understood the position of the Indonesian peoples wanting independence. But the Dutch Government would not, or perhaps could not, accept that it was the twilight of the more than 300-year-old Dutch Empire.

In June of 1946 the future of the old NEI was still in the 'hands of the gods' and in view of the many uncertainties I decided to try to find employment in the old country, preferably in shipping. I foresaw many years of unrest even if, at best, an autonomous Indonesia as part of a Netherlands Commonwealth would arise from the chaos of revolution.

However, as time would tell, finding a suitable employment at adequate pay in war-ravaged Netherlands was not easy. Many an *Engelandvaarder* would also find some employers not inclined to offer employment to chaps who had shown independence of mind and action and would perhaps not readily accept authority. Their own 'sitting on the fence' attitude or perhaps collaboration with the German Occupier for personal or their firm's financial advantage may have also been a reason to avoid employing an *Engelandvaarder* or Resistance members.

Companies with overseas branches were, however, not adverse to employing men with an adventurous spirit, a good grasp of the English language and particularly if they had an intimate knowledge of the Indies and/or the Far East.

I have digressed, back to the upheaval in the NEI. After WWI, the victorious European Powers had set up new states (of which Iraq is a prime example) with little consideration for ethnic, cultural, religious or tribal affiliations. In the aftermath of WWII, the USA, Australia and India were similarly at fault in ignoring the ethnic make-up of the NEI which encompassed an area wider than the USA or from the western shores of Europe to nearly the Caucasus Mountains. This archipelago of over 13,677 islands, was and is, peopled by many nations and untold tribes with a great variety of cultures and some 250 different languages. The major islands and greater part of the archipelago are populated by different peoples, albeit of the Malay race, with brown skin and straight black hair. In the eastern part however, are racially different peoples with tightly curled black hair and a much darker skin. If they knew more than one language it was Behasa Malajoe (Malay), the language of the traders and of some 3 million Malays who had settled on the coasts of Java and many of the other islands where trade flourished. The highly-cultured Javanese made up far more than half of the total population and it was feared that they would completely dominate the archipelago without certain checks and balances.

The argument that the Javanese and Sumatran Empires once held sway over the whole archipelago holds no water, since their power did not extend much beyond the two major islands of Java and Sumatra. It was the VOC and later the Dutch East Indies governments which united this vast area into one entity.

The abrupt end of World War II after the atom bombs on Hiroshima and Nagasaki had given the Nationalists of Dr. Soekarno time to take advantage of the situation and establish footholds long enough to ultimately prevail with the open, and covert, assistance of America, Australia and India. The Dutch had no choice after the USA threatened to withdraw Marshall Plan aid but to grant Indonesia its Independence. History has since told us about the dictatorships of Presidents Soekarno (a nearly Communist one) and General Soeharto and Javanese domination of the Indonesian Republic as the Dutch had feared.

It was no surprise to those in the know when the Moluccas revolted on 24th of April 1950 and declared the Independence of the "Repoeblik Maluku Selatan" (RMS or Republic of South Moluccas). In spite of the International Court of Justice in The Hague declaring the RMS Independence valid under the Constitution of the Indonesian Republic, the UN and its Security Council Members, for reasons of their own political aims and advantage, ignored the plight of the Ambonese, as did the World Press.

In 1961, the Papuas of New Guinea would be sacrificed to the interests of the US and Australia in particular, and the Netherlands Government was forced to hand over sovereignty to President Soekarno's Indonesia. It would be to the chagrin of our close and good American friends that the same Soekarno created "Nasakom", a form of national communism, which was introduced in the 1960s. It still riles me when some maintain, or doubt, that the failed 1965 coup, which resulted in General Soeharto getting into power, was not backed by the Communists.

Those of us born in the NEI felt a great attachment to Indië. It was truly our motherland. For many of mixed race the attachment was even stronger since for many it was also their permanent home.

The dictators Soekarno and Soeharto have passed into history and we can only hope that Indonesia in the 21st century will at last become a true democracy under President Susilo Bambang Youdouyono.

I am no apologist for and do not intend to defend the colonial system for it had its negative sides. But the Dutch did not act like barbarians, although the penny-pinching VOC administrators could be ruthless towards their own Dutch personnel. Besides, colonial powers more often than not had replaced harsh peasant cultures under autocratic potentates.

It should also be remembered that it was through those Dutch 'barbarians' that the Indonesian intellectuals leading the independence movement had nearly all studied and graduated at universities in Holland and at the expense of the Netherlands Government.

39. A Memorable Flight Over Java

In the latitudes near the Equator, evening darkness and morning light arrive quickly. By the time I had left the *kamar mandi*, where I found the water had cooled off considerably during the night, it was broad daylight.

Quite soon after, having taken leave from my friends at the Bank's mess on their departure for the office, an army truck picked me up and took me to Kemajoran Airport to embark on a Dakota. Soon after taxiing onto the runway the tail came up and we were airborne. Little did I then suspect that one and a half years later I would again step from a KLM DC-4 onto the soil of Java at this same airport.

On a glorious day, after take-off from the island that is home to 17 active volcanoes, the C-47 Dakota circled slowly over Batavia while it climbed to only, as the captain had promised before departure, about 1500 metres. It was therefore lower than the tops of the major volcanoes. This allowed us to enjoy the unique sight of Java on an exceptionally clear day, a very rare occurrence even in the dry season and in pre-pollution days.

Through 'my' window I could see the brown Kali Tjiliwoeng wind its way through the countryside from the mountains to the south towards and through the city itself, to the blue-green calm sea which turned dark blue towards the horizon. Beyond the harbour of Tandjong Priok, the first of the so-called 1000 islands, standing out in the gleam of many shades of blue in the Java Sea, came into sight as the Dakota continued turning eastward. Flying parallel to the coast, I was provided with a direct view of the large mass of mountains to the south, starting with the nearly 3000-metre high Goenoeng (Mount) Pangrango which is joined to its twin, the slightly lower Goenoeng Gedeh with its lop-sided large crater rim. On its slopes I had spent many a weekend with my family at Megamedoeng and on the Poentjak pass in a rented *pondok* (holiday bungalow) in the beautiful area of Java beyond, known as the Preanger.

The Tangkoebangprauw (upside-down boat, because of its shape) Volcano, with the holiday resort Lembang on its slope, came into sight before the C-47 reached Tjiribon. And there they were: a row of perfectly cone-shaped volcanoes, the names of which we had to learn by heart at the geography lessons in the CAS Primary School in Batavia. The pilot now hugged the coast and from my high vantage point a virtually cloudless Java looked like a perfectly-made huge model with rows of volcanoes rising from the plains where, as we passed over the mouth of a river, the yellow-brown river water would blend gradually with the blue water of the Java Sea.

Only a short time after passing the typical volcano-shaped Goenoeng Tjirema and the (about) 3400-metre high Goenoeng Slamat (two of the 17 active volcanoes on Java), we flew over the port, Semarang River, and the city of Semarang. Here, as is shown by photos in my parents' family album, I had been looked after at the tender age of about one year, and carried in a *selendang* (usually a batik cloth the size of a sarong that is worn over one shoulder to carry babies, small children or parcels). My *baboe* (nursemaid) Inem was a young woman with a soft and pleasant Malay face. It was from her that I heard the first few words of the Malay language spoken, and thereafter could speak Malay with the intonation of those born to the language.

The world is small, as the saying goes, for some 30 years later, during our years in Batavia/Jakarta, we engaged a Malay *kokki* (cook) by the name of Djoe who one day excitedly told Berna that she had, in a photo album of ours, seen her cousin Inem carrying a baby in her *selendang* and was that perhaps the *tuan*? It was.

Even before we flew over Semarang we sighted Java's most active and classically-shaped volcano, Goenoeng Merapi, which showed a plume of smoke rising from its crater above the plains of one of the most fertile lands on earth. Behind and to Merapi's east in the heartland of Java are the Sultanates of Djokjakarta (now Yogyakarta) and Soerakarta (Surakarta).

My parents and grandparents Portengen, when living in Solo, experienced an eruption of the Goenoeng Merapi which was strong enough to make the ground vibrate audibly, the glassware rattle and red glowing lava to glide down a slope from its smoking crater.

Occasional trembling of the earth had become part of life due to earthquakes and erupting volcanoes on Java, Sumatra and Japan. It was part of the reality of living in countries on the Pacific Rim. After the 1927 earthquake on Japan's Honshu Island, we kids would no longer panic as we did when living in Kobe in 1927. In the capital of Soerakarta Sultanate, of the same name but usually called Solo, my parents met and were married in 1913. I could just see the northern loop of the Solo River near which the Dutch doctor, Eugene Dubois, in 1891 discovered a tooth and part of a cranium believed to be a direct human ancestor and which he named "Java Man"; this was years later recognised to be a Homo Erectus, only one of our many ancestors.

To the east of Solo, an hour or so by motor car past G Lawoe, is the town of Madioen, where my uncle, Wim Portengen, had a mineral water and lemonade factory called "Kracht" (Strength). At every evening meal, when having guests, Uncle Wim would hold up one of his factory's bottles and loudly ask the servant: *"Apa inni?"* (what's this?), and he or she would have to answer, *"Tjap Kracht! Yang paling baik!"* (Kracht brand and the very best).

Near Madioen, at the sugar factory, Poerwodadi, I spent what was for an 11-year-old boy a most marvellous one-month holiday with a school friend called Paul van Geelgildemeester, the son of the factory manager. It was here, on the estate's private roads, that I learned to drive a 1906 Opel. It had a huge round brass tank behind the two seats at the back and brass gear shift handles and an outside hand brake.

The annexe to the *administrateur's woning,* as the home of the plantation manager was called, stood near a steep incline to a river where the women of nearby villages would do their laundry and bathe. Paul and I, both aged 11 and subjected to early stirrings in the loins, would climb onto the roof of the annexe to observe the women at the river in the, alas seldom fulfilled, hope of seeing some at least partially-disrobed females.

The sound of Gamelan music, which is mainly performed, and based, on percussion instruments and sometimes accompanied by a *suling* flute and two-stringed instrument held vertically, will forever be connected to my memories of *Indië* and Java in particular. Among the clearest of recollections are the tropical evenings at Poerwodadi, before falling asleep in bed under the *klamboe* (mosquito netting), listening to Gamelan music emanating from the distant *dessas* (villages). Sounds carry, particularly at night in the tropics. Gamelan music, like Ravel's Bolero, is somewhat repetitive but it is, to me, an appealing texture of sound that evokes remembrances. I can recall with great clarity the last time I listened to Gamelan music played by a trio of Javanese musicians at a hotel on Sanur Beach in Bali in 1993.

By the time we had passed over Semarang, the tropical sun, known by the old colonials as *De Koperen Ploert* (the brass scoundrel), had caused a heat haze over the *djatti* (teak) plantations and paddy fields below us.

One could not be but enraptured and continue looking through the small window of the Dakota as the Goenoengs Liman, Welirang and, to its south, the Goenoeng Butak, also higher than 2500 metres, as they came into sight. In the valley to the east of Mount Butak is the town of Malang, famous in the old days for its madhouse. *"You should be sent to Malang"* was a way of telling someone they behaved like an idiot.

Not long thereafter, the Dakota reached and overflew Soerabaja, well away from Morokrembangan Airport with its two X-marked landing strips, and crossed the yellow-brown River Kalimas sneaking through the spread of the city where I was born in a modest white stucco bungalow at No 3 Niasweg. That quiet street is now a bustling major thoroughfare. My family returned to Soerabaja from Japan in early 1928 and I remember how, from our house on the Palmenlaan, my sister Mary and I would go to school in a two-wheeled buggy pulled by a small horse called a *sado-sado* (derived from the French *dos-a-dos*). On Sundays we would swim in the seawater pool at Tandjong Perak, the harbour of Soerabaja or, in the canvas-topped Hudson motorcar, drive up to the cooler mountain resort of Tretes and take a dip in the cool mountain water of the swimming pool.

It was also here in Soerabaja. that I would meet the sisters Hetty and Ata (Mary) Potjer at the latter's birthday party, where my sisters and I were treated to ice cream, the greatest treat for children living in the tropics.

It was the first time that I saw ice cream being made in a wooden tub, the size of a standard bucket, by the family's *djongos*. Commercially-produced ice cream was at that time unknown, in Southeast Asia at least.

Hetty would become my best, platonic, female friend and I, her trusted male friend to turn to. She was also a most accomplished dancer with a superb feel for rhythm. Eleven years after that first meeting she would become my sister-in-law.

Proceeding on its easterly course, our plane passed the volcanoes Semeroe (3676 metres high), G Bromo and G Raung. The beauty and unique spectacle of the silhouettes of a continuous row of volcano after volcano against the light blue cloudless sky on this glorious day was unforgettable, and one I can still visualise clearly. On many a volcano one could also discern those scarred parts of the slopes where the lava had slipped down leaving a bare strip on the steep slopes near the cones.

The pilot now guided the Dakota slowly around the second volcano on Java called G Merapi, which looms high just north of the small port of Banjoewangi on the far-east coast, to take a bearing to the WSW for Den Passar Airport on Bali. On this air trip we saw 14 of the 17 active volcanoes on Java, one of the most densely populated areas of the world with, at that time, some 70 million inhabitants.

A devastating midday heat greeted us on Bali, the island of 'Gods and Demons', when leaving the aircraft to stretch our legs during the short stop-over.

After lift-off and while the Dakota gained height, we had, beyond Bali's famous terraced rice fields, a good view of Goenoeng Agoeng, at 3140 metres high in 1946, i.e. before losing some height after the 1963 eruption, and G Batur, where the Balinese believe the Gods reside, which are situated on the wide northern part of this beautiful island with its fascinating Hindu culture.

By the time I turned my gaze away from Sanur on Bali's east coast, we were over the coast of Lombok. Mount Rindjani's peak was partially clothed by clouds while the surface of the island seemed decidedly less lush than on the islands to its west.

Flying over Soembawa I had hoped to be able to look down, from high above, on the flat top of Mount Tambora with its 'new' small cone-shaped volcano in its crater which cannot be observed from the sea, but we were on a flight path too far south to see into Tambora's crater. A fellow passenger, with a similar interest in the history of the volcano Tambora, mentioned that some 10,000 people perished in the flows of pyroplastic mud, stones and other debris from the mighty 1815 eruption. Since the Tambora is now still 2821 metres above sea level, it must once have been one of the highest volcanoes on earth.

The flight across Java had been spectacular and could not but hold one's interest. Now, crossing high in the sky over the Lesser Sunda Islands, having visited them the year before on the Australian Corvette HMAS 'Gladstone', they still held my attention for a while.

After overflying the irregular-shaped Komodo Islands we soon sighted, on starboard, the plain but peaceful island of Soemba which I had left only 10 days earlier. It looked so much drier than fertile Java and Bali and even more so compared with the wildly beautiful, deep green, highlands of New Guinea. I did not for a moment think that I would ever return to Waingapoe, yet, in 1993, my wife and I, during a cruise of the Lesser Sunda Islands on the P & O's 'Explorer', would step ashore at Waingapoe and be met by Mary Elim and Ing, the daughter and son of the late Mea, the chief mechanic and old friend. Ing would tour us around in his four-wheel drive and show us all the old familiar places. The TNT's Commanding Officer now occupied 'our' house on the *aloeng-aloeng*. The airfield can now be reached by a bridge over the *kali* (river), while the Catholic Church must have made more converts since 1946, as their church on the main road in the town looked very well-kept and had a statue of Christ dressed in Soemba-kains on the front lawn."

I can't remember much of the rest of the flight to Brisbane, and the overnight stop, except for landing the next day for a refuelling stop at Cloncurry or Mount Isa, where in the airport WC I spotted a sign I had not earlier come across in Australia: *"Kilroy was here"*. I had forgotten all about Kilroy's notice to advise others of having sat there on the throne before. The previous sighting had been more than a year earlier when visiting the loo at the Humboldt Bay US Base in New Guinea where a joker had put up a "Kilroy was here" sign on a plank nailed on a tree behind the open-air latrines. The Americans claim that they started the lark but the English maintain that they or the Scots had been the first and that it was hi-jacked by the Yanks. Obviously an Australian of Scottish descent, or a stray Yank, must have visited this convenience in Cloncurry.

Funny how unimportant thoughts can somehow be retained in your memory and yet names and some important events cannot be recalled at all.

After an otherwise uneventful trip across and high above the terracotta coloured fifth continent, called New Holland when first sighted by Dutch explorers on the yacht called 'Duyfken' in 1606 and now known as Australia, the Dakota set down on the tarmac of Brisbane's Archerfield Airport in the late cool hours of the 18th of June 1946.

40. The Commitment of a Lifetime

The next morning, the day before her birthday, I phoned a pleasantly surprised Berna and asked her, *"What do you want for your birthday?"* Her simple reply was *"You!"* I could tell her that I had already 'booked' a seat on the ANA plane for the next day, the 20th of June 1946.

To see a young woman and a uniformed young man rush towards each other with outstretched arms, embrace like lovers and obviously overwhelmingly pleased to see each other again, was such a common sight during the war and immediate post-war years, that it did not attract any attention from bystanders. Berna, turning 21 years of age on that very day, could now marry without her parents' consent and throughout the next two weeks we busied ourselves with the wedding's legal and religious requirements to enable us to stand before a priest and be married at an altar of St Patrick's Cathedral in Melbourne. I wrote "an" and not "the" altar, since we could only be married at an altar in the chapel because I was not a Catholic.

As a result of my upbringing I had, and have, only a cultural attachment to Christianity. My parents were not religious and we never attended church and were at no time affiliated with a Protestant denomination but my family adhered to Christian principles. No objections were consequently raised for me to marry a Catholic girl.

I was, however, to receive instruction from a Catholic priest and to agree that any offspring would be raised in the Catholic faith. I became friends with the nice, wise and understanding Franciscan Priest who seemed more interested in my wartime experiences than indoctrinating me in matters of the Catholic faith.

In between all these activities I would call at the Colonial Mutual at closing time and we would sit most evenings facing one another at Molino's on Collins Street or in one of our other, always Italian, restaurants, or in the Dutch Club in Elizabeth Street—unless we went to the Floyd and Binnington families in Bethel Street, Ormond where I had found a second home in 1944-46.

We should perhaps have been beset by misgivings about the future we were facing in a post-war world but, like most young people, we took the consequences of our actions in our stride and faced the future with the confidence of the young.

Australia in 1946 was still a 'wowser' country, with too many restrictions. There were no Sunday papers and any publication, whether book or newspaper, that openly mentioned sex was promptly banned, while the pubs were still not allowed to keep their doors open after 6 o'clock p.m. Consequently, our wedding reception had to be held at 5 o'clock in the afternoon to allow a toast with a glass of champagne (read Australian sparkling white burgundy).

To find a retreat, suitable and affordable for a honeymooning couple in 1946, was not easy. On advice received I had booked us in at the Clifton Springs Hotel, a short train-ride from Melbourne and situated not far from Barwon Heads on the State of Victoria's south coast. I must confess that the hotel having a 9-hole golf course had somewhat influenced my choice of our honeymoon retreat.

We had arrived after dark—July is mid-winter in the Southern Hemisphere—and when my young bride opened the curtains to enjoy the panoramic view, she noted that she was also overlooking a golf course. I would never live down my decision to book us into the Clifton Springs Hotel for our honeymoon.

You may well ask how my beloved could not have noticed my golf bag among our luggage when checking out of the King George Hotel in St Kilda and when moving into our hotel room. However, when I, in my desperate defence, made this observation I did not receive her explanation but was derided for having even thought about playing the ancient game of golf on our honeymoon. I was often reminded of this transgression in later years.

Among the many honeymooners we met was a couple Berna dubbed 'the No-can-dos' (after a popular song of that time). The young woman, to our mutual astonishment, had confessed to Berna that she never had been told the facts of life by her mother and she was afraid to "let him". Consequently, they had (still) not yet done it! Three weeks later when Mr. and Mrs. No-can-do by pure chance moved into one of the apartments in the mansion in which we lived, poor Mr. F. must, by that time, have been climbing walls for Mrs. No-can-do admitted to Berna that they had still not consummated the marriage!

At Clifton Springs we had a table next to a nice young man occasionally suffering from an attack of what was then described as shell-shock and which now is known as post-traumatic stress disorder. A pharmacist had also chosen Clifton Springs to spend his holidays, not only for the lovely countryside and the golf course, but in the knowledge that it was a known honeymooners' retreat. He would at every opportunity advertise his chemist business and in particular the wide range, in quality and price, of condoms carried in his shops, thus combining pleasure with business.

The day after our return to Melbourne we moved into our first home, a rented very large room in a grand old mansion in Clendon Road in the exclusive suburb of Toorak. It had a small kitchen and a bathroom in the hall that we had to share with others. We really could not afford the £4 a week rent on my Lieutenant's pay without dipping into the money saved during my months 'in the islands' and which I had deposited in the Bank of New South Wales. The favourable balance had however been seriously reduced by the cost of the wedding since Berna's father had remained totally opposed to our getting married and, while Berna's mother was present, he would not attend the wedding ceremony nor the incongruously-named wedding breakfast, held in the early evening at Navarettis, a well-known restaurant which catered for weddings. I should mention that Berna's father would eventually come to fully accept me as the husband of his only daughter. It had been her uncle and godfather, Les McCarthy, who had given her away at the wedding, while Berna's best friend, Val Binnington, and Henk Baxmeier had been our bridesmaid and best man. Couples tend to remember their wedding day forever and we the more so for when the Priest asked me whether I, Pieter Rudolph Zeeman, would take Marie Bernadette Mortimer to be my wedded wife, I sprang to attention, saluted and replied *"Yes, Sir!"* This reply was hastily corrected into *"I do"*, when prompted by the good Father.

One of my old friends who was not in Melbourne and therefore not able to attend our wedding was Karel Michielsen, who, as I wrote earlier, had the distinction of being one of the first three *Engelandvaarders* to cross the North Sea in July 1940 and had fought as a Navy Lt. Navigator on Dornier Flying Boats against the Japanese in the NEI. After the fall of Java his Dornier, together with other Dutch Navy flying boats and Air Force planes had escaped to Australia where he continued flying in Catalinas, enduring the interminably long flights from Western Australia to Ceylon. He was also involved in the landing and recovering of the Dutch Intelligence Officer, Oscar Drijber, off the east coast of Borneo by the RNN Catalina under the command of Gerard Reynders. They had been forced to fly within striking distance of the Japanese fleet and air base of Ambon to the east coast of Borneo to pick up Lt. Drijber and his patrol some distance away from the town of Tarakan, where they had gathered vital intelligence for the planned AIF landing.

Lt. Oscar Drijber was one of those idiosyncratic characters that wars tend to throw up and his exploits would make good subjects for war-time movies. After Holland's capitulation he had been locked up in Germany's Colditz Castle and was one of the few who managed to escape from this infamous POW camp. After reaching England he had joined NEFIS (Netherlands East Indies Intelligence) in Australia.

Only two weeks or so before the German attack on the 10th of May 1940, Karel, in the uniform of *Vaandrig* (Sub Lt.), and I had painted Amsterdam town red. The next time we met in Melbourne in 1945 he was in the dark blue uniform of Lieutenant in the RN Navy and I in the deep green American officer's uniform which had been adopted by the KNIL (Netherlands East Indies Army) as their official dress. The Dutch Army and Air Force wore British uniforms.

The *Bebek* (Malay for duck), the 12-foot dinghy belonging to Kees van Eendenburg, had in June been moved from the Kaag Lakes in the province of South Holland to the beach at the seaside town of Noordwijk. In full view of German sentries and German officers, seated on the terrace of the well-known 'Huis ter Duin' Hotel, the threesome over several days had taken the small craft to sea, pottered around a bit beyond the breakers and returned shortly afterwards. The *Wehrmacht* chaps had got used to their activities and soon paid them no attention anymore. On the evening of the 5th of July, earlier than planned because the Germans had just issued a prohibition against keeping any privately-owned boats, even canoes and dinghies, anywhere on the Dutch coast, the three of them carried the small craft down the beach. When challenged by a German sentry they asked him whether he really believed that they were going to attempt a crossing of the North Sea in that ridiculously small boat. The sentry let them go. It was about 7 o'clock in the evening when they pushed the dinghy through the surf and boarded it. Karel, a member of Njord Rowing Club of Leiden University and a powerful rower, immediately started rowing like mad. By the time the boys of the *Wehrmacht* realised what was happening and started shooting, a rain squall came to the rower's aid. Once out of sight of the coast they hoisted a sail and nearly two days later, on the 7th of July, 1940, after an eventful and dangerous voyage, they were hailed by a RN Auxiliary Minesweeper, 20 miles or so off the coast of Yarmouth.

Kees van Eendenburg and Freddie vas Nunes joined the RAF and all three survived the war. The *Bebek* must have been a 'lucky ship' since van Eendenburg survived a crash of his downed Spitfire at St Omer in France in September 1944.

This first escape by sea after the German Occupation of Holland is comprehensively described by Frank Visser in his book *De Schakel,* written and published in the Dutch language in 1976. Erik, who had assisted in the preparations of the attempt, wrote, also in Dutch, an extensive account in his book, *Tegen De Vlagen Van De Oostenwind.* Karel himself would tell me anecdotes of their experiences when we met up again in Australia in 1945, which I would years later read in Frank Visser's book.

In August 1945, when Karel Michielsen was on leave in Melbourne with his Australian artist wife Narelle and their newborn first son, also named Karel, we met again for the first time since a couple of weeks before the German invasion on the 10th of May 1940. He would finally retire from the Shell Company, settle in Canberra and later in Robe, South Australia. Our friendship, started in 1929, lasted until I wrote his obituary for the *Engelandvaarder* Association's quarterly, De Schakel, a few years ago.

After our honeymoon our financial situation soon became precarious. My depleted bank account, and Berna having spent most of her savings on her wedding dress, forced me to dispose of some of my possessions acquired during my time 'up North', to improve the credit balance of our bank account.

I cannot recall every item we sold but a portable Hermes typewriter fetched a good price. By the time we packed our bags to board the MV 'Sibajak' for Holland we had to buy winter clothing and other items not available in war-ravaged Europe and were forced to sell some of our wedding gifts.

Since virtually every man, woman and child in the Low Countries dash around on bicycles I thought it was a logical decision to buy a bicycle for Berna. The pink painted "Malvern Star" ladies bike never turned a wheel in the streets of Amsterdam with Berna on the pedals. Some purchases were also 'removed' from our unaccompanied baggage before it arrived at No 96 de Lairessestraat in Amsterdam.

One of the consequences of married life for Berna would be to endure and learn to cope with my nightmares from which I, as mentioned earlier, suffered during the immediate post-war years and, later in life, an inability to fall asleep and restless sleep. Research by Dutch doctors ascertained that, after turning 60 years of age, 80 percent of the ex-Resistance members suffered from post-traumatic stress disorder.

While my one and only had to put up with my nightmares, I had to face her cooking skills, an important part of a happy married life, and to which I had given no thought at all until then. I should mention that I had been spoiled by the cooking expertise of my mother and grandmother.

On one of the first evenings at our Clendon Road flat, Berna presented me with the first meal she, as I would learn, had ever prepared. It was a total disaster and I had to go into Toorak village to purchase a tin of Heinz spaghetti. Soon thereafter I came home from the KNIL Air Traffic Section, where I worked to earn my Lieutenant's pay, and was welcomed with the exciting news that Berna and Bev Floyd had cooked me meatballs and potatoes. The meatballs were as hard as stones and quite inedible. After a good laugh (what else can a young husband do in such circumstances) I took the two 'cooks' to the Chinese for dinner. My stoicism in facing a life of inedible dinners was, however, years later, and after the culinary delights of the cooks we employed in Indonesia, Hong Kong and Singapore, fully rewarded. Berna (then addressed as 'Missy' by the cooks) had somehow acquired skills worthy of an Escofier by the time we lived in The Hague, when I was transferred to the Head Office of my employers, Internatio, in 1961.

41. Return to the Old Country

Sometime in the first week of August I learned that we were to be repatriated to Holland on the MV 'Sibajak' at the end of August 1946. Berna's mother and some of our friends saw us off and remained on the quay while to our gleeful satisfaction our ship's captain expertly manoeuvred the 12,500-ton liner from the quay and through the harbour into Port Philip Bay without the assistance of tugboats. This was necessary because on the 23rd of September, 1945, the Communist-controlled Seamen and Waterside Workers Union had black-banned Dutch ships in support of their 'brothers' in Indonesia seeking self-determination. They also sought an end to colonial rule.

Humanitarian aid was obviously secondary to aiding their comrades in the NEI. The wharfies had forced the Dutch to fly in food and medicines to the over 100,000 half-starved POWs and the men, women and children of the internment camps, thus seriously hampering the relief effort

The MV 'Sibajak' was no longer the luxurious, by pre-War standards, passenger liner. Early in the war it had been converted into a troopship. All women and children were allotted one of the four to six sleeping berths in the cabins but the men were billeted in the cargo holds. Berna shared a cabin with a woman and her two children as did the ex-internees from the Indies who had been evacuated to Australia to recuperate. I had a canvas-covered bunk in the baggage room, slightly superior to a berth in the cargo hold where in pre-War days passengers' trunks would be stored and from which, during the day, passengers could retrieve, or store, personal items.

Junior officers and other married men shared the baggage room with me. My bunk was situated not far from the bottom of the only access to the baggage room, through a metal staircase. I can still hear the clanking noise of boots coming down or going up those metal steps.

Another great annoyance was being awoken early every morning for 43 days by the playing of the, at that time, popular song which I came to hate called "Que sera sera". I could have strangled the chap who must have loved it and played it every morning on the ship's loudspeakers.

The military officers were enrolled for supervising jobs and as the appointed ship's Fire Officer I would regularly perform my obligations to the stern's inspection tours.

On this overcrowded troop ship with segregation of men and women, quiet nooks on the upper decks and in the lifeboats were much sought after. When strolling along on my inspection rounds, with flashlight in hand, Berna would quite often accompany me to have a giggle at embarrassed lovers inadvertently caught by the light of my flashlight or the slightly swaying lifeboats and, occasionally, sounds, muffled or otherwise, emanating from under the canvas covers.

The 'Sibajak' called at Brisbane before sailing around the north of the Australian Continent and Berna and I went ashore to contribute our last £11 to the economy of the 'Sunshine State' of Queensland. The captain and crew, after sailing up the Brisbane River, moored, loaded and departed again from the wharf without assistance from the wharfies and tugboats.

There was little entertainment aboard the ship apart from playing shuffleboard or deck tennis. Every afternoon, and occasionally in the morning as well, we played Contract Bridge.

The war and the part we individuals had played in it were, unavoidably, topics of discussion. During this long 43-day voyage not one of the *Engelandvaarders* among us, like Bart van Hasselt, or indeed other *Engelandvaarders* I spoke with later, believed in predestination and in implicit ill-fate or mere chance, but all agreed that without luck, with a capital 'L', we would not have succeeded. Providence had nothing to do with it.

The 'Sibajak' did not call at any port during the long uneventful voyage through the Indonesian Archipelago to Sabang. We would often see land or pass sailing vessels and occasionally we would, when close enough to make out human figures on the decks, wave to the passengers and crew of a passing ship, as people at sea always tend to do.

In the Java Sea we did enjoy the tropical sunsets, which no words can ever fully describe. Sailing through the Strait of Malacca I could see a narrow strip of land which I knew to be the tops of the mountains on the slopes of which were the extensive tea-growing area of North Sumatra. My brother would never return and again walk the dirt roads and paths between the row upon row of tea bushes, through which hosts of women in their colourful sarongs and kebajas would move plucking young tea leaves, their heads shielded from the tropical sun by very large, woven, bamboo hats.

My sister-in-law, Hetty, after she and her three-year-old daughter, Patricia, had been rescued from an internment camp in Sumatra and had learnt of Tommy's execution by the Japanese, had passed through the Strait aboard the MV 'Nieuw Holland' when evacuated to Holland from Singapore. I could not but wonder what her thoughts had been when passing this area where she had known happiness, privation and tragedy.

On the opposite side of Sumatra on the Straits of Malacca, way over the horizon, I knew to be the island called Penang where we had lived in the early 1920s. My father had managed the branch of the Netherlands Trading Society (as the NHM was called outside the Indies in the Far East) and was also the Honorary Dutch Consul. My earliest memory in life, as a 4-year-old boy, is of Penang and the two-storied, stucco brick house set in an expanse of lawns opposite a grassy square.

After the bunkering port on the island of Sabang off the northern tip of Sumatra, we did not spy any vessels in the Indian Ocean until days later when, nearing the island of Socotra off the Somali coast, we encountered the first Arab dhows and cargo ships. Socotra and the Horn of Africa looked hot, barren and most uninviting as, in fact, did all the lands bordering the Red Sea. In the Red Sea, we passed a few Dutch troopships bound for the NEI where in the next two years these troops would re-occupy much of the Indies and, after an air assault, men under the command of the Intelligence Officer and *Engelandvaarder,* Jan A. Bakker, would succeed in taking the Republican leaders, Soekarno and Hatta, into custody in Djokjakarta, the then provisional capital of the Repoeblik of Indonesia.

The heat in the Red Sea and when negotiating the Suez Canal was not as stupefying as I remembered from the mid-summer crossing on the MV 'Marnix van St Aldegonde' in 1934 when, already in the early part of the morning, the heat caused the horizon to shimmer above the sands of the desert to the east. However, by the time the coasts of the African and Asian parts of Egypt converged at the town of Suez, it had become uncomfortably hot below deck for it was still in the days before air conditioning and the air funnelled through air scoops placed in the portholes, or blown through the large scoops on the open decks, brought only small relief below decks.

A few days before reaching the Suez Canal, Berna and I could not but overhear a conversation between a young blond Australian woman and a ship's crewman. It appeared that she had married an Arab sailor in Australia and was to leave the ship in Suez to travel on to the Saudi Arabian port of Jeddah to join her husband. The import of her conversation made it clear to us that she was most certainly a, shall I say, free spirit. Berna can also still clearly remember, as if it happened yesterday, when at anchor at Suez, she watched this lady leave the ship down the ship's gangway ladder portside and saw her step into a rowing boat crewed by two Egyptians with the, at that time customary, red Fez on their heads. Ever since, Berna and I have wondered what fate awaited her in the conservative Wahabist Islamic society of Jeddah.

Towards dusk, our ship, sailing in the usual convoy, passed the familiar Suez Canal Authority's cluster of buildings, the palm tree-fringed quay and signal station and the lights of the town twinkling in the fading light in the background. In my lifetime I would travel 12 times by ship through the Suez Canal and Berna did it four times. I cannot recall my first trip at the age of three on an SMN passenger ship from the Far East to Holland, but thereafter we children always looked forward to the voyage and particularly the passage through 'the Suez'.

The 'Gilli-gilli man' in Port Said, with his conjuring tricks with few-days old bright yellow chickens, was always a highlight. It never occurred to us youngsters that the chicks must have suffered during the exhibitions.

Sailing through the canal, built by the French engineer Ferdinand de Lesseps in 1869, much seemed not to have changed since the time of the Pharaohs with mud huts amongst the greenery and palm trees encountered here and there on the West Bank. We would often see the occasional donkey and cart, or a rider in flowing robe astride a donkey, or a man walking in front of a heavily-laden camel. Sometimes these *fellahin* would wave to us but one chap found it funny, or intended to show his disregard for infidels, by turning his back to us, lifting his robe and exposing his bottom. "Oelewappers" was what we used to call these men in their 'nightshirts' because when walking the sound made by their long gowns sounded like *oule-wap, oule-wap, oule-wap.* The stark difference between the lush greenery often seen on the West Bank and the harsh dry land of the Sinai Peninsular to the East leaves a lasting impression on travellers.

In spite of the heat haze so often hanging over the sand and rocks of the Sinai, the desert can somehow look fresh in the very early morning while moonlight and stars at night would induce many a passenger to stay on deck till late. Port Said still had pontoon bridges connecting passenger ships with the quay, and Simon Artz's department store—an institution to all travellers to and from the East—was open for business but offering a poor selection of goods because of the War. We did not wander far from the ship into the side streets of the boulevard along the Canal for we had been warned that it was not safe to do so.

Leaving Port Said, the ships used to pass the statue of Ferdinand de Lesseps. I say "used to" because the Egyptians removed it many years later. The 'Sibajak' then left the shores of Asia and Africa and entered the Mediterranean Sea and headed for Gibraltar and the Atlantic Ocean and not for Marseille, from which in pre-War days passengers could disembark and catch the "boat-train" to Holland.

On our voyage there was not much to distract the passengers except for a glimpse of the coast of Malta and the sighting of Cape Bon on the North African coast. On a glorious day, where the coasts of Africa and Europe nearly converge at the Strait of Gibraltar, we saw the mysterious mountainous coastline of North Africa with the mass of the Zoco el Tzelacza, one of the pillars of Hercules, seemingly rising straight from the sea into the sky. On the north side was the other pillar of Hercules, the Rock of Gibraltar.

By evening we had lost sight of the coasts of Spain and Morocco and the big swell in the Atlantic Ocean made the 'Sibajak' sway enough from portside to starboard, and for the bow to move up and down, to cause the woodwork to squeak. A day or so later, when nearing and passing Cape Finisterre, the notorious Bay of Biscay did not fail its reputation for rough seas and frequent storms. It was actually only somewhat blustery compared to the true Atlantic storm once experienced by me on the 'Marnix van St Aldegonde' in 1934. On that voyage only three passengers attended dinner: my father, another passenger and me. Quite a few aboard the 'Sibajak' nevertheless spent their day lying under a blanket in a deckchair in the fresh air of the promenade deck, some looking slightly yellow with sea-sickness and eyes glazed from misery.

The inclement weather of the Gulf of Biscay did not however interrupt our daily afternoon game of Bridge in the ship's salon. But there was no relief for those affected by *"malade du mal de mer"* until we had sailed well into The Channel. The sea had become quite benign by the time we sighted, between rain squalls and in the gloom of late evening, the white cliffs of Dover.

It was a dismal deep grey morning on the day we rose very early and sighted the low coast of Holland. The sky brightened to a lighter grey by the time we approached the Waterweg at the small town called Hoek van Holland. While the 'Sibajak' had crept towards the entrance of the Waterweg and was still on the North Sea, the harbor pilot had boarded the ship to guide her through this busy shipping canal to Rotterdam. We could soon clearly see the buildings and wharf of the Hoek of Holland to Harwich Ferry, and people walking or bicycling, but very few motor cars.

Here and there we noted war-damaged buildings when proceeding towards the city of Rotterdam and while passing the towns of Vlaardingen, Maassluis, and Schiedam—the town famous for its gin distilleries. While the grey-hulled 'Sibajak' was manoeuvred by tugboats towards the Rotterdam-Lloyd wharf, Berna and I, hanging over the railing of the promenade deck, strained our eyes to spot my parents amongst the small crowd allowed on the quay. I quite soon recognised two familiar figures.

It was two years, ten months and 14 days since I had left Amsterdam when Berna and I walked down the gang plank to step ashore and embrace my mother and father.

Berna would live amongst people whose language she did not speak but she would find a very warm welcome from my family for whom English was their second language. My father would come to call her

'Aussie Doll'. As for my mother, well, don't they say that men tend to marry girls like their mothers? They got along famously.

RMS 'Queen Mary' painted wartime grey.

With Ata Ceurvorst on the balcony at the Grammercy Park Hotel.

Postcard of Times Square, New York City, with Pepsi Cola Centre.

The KNIL-ML contingent which left London on 10 July 1944 aboard the 'Lurline'. Back row: Lt. M Groen on the left and Lt. van Kregten in the centre. Front row (from left): Jongeneel, van Nouhuys, Baxmeier and myself.

The weekend B25 'bus' from Canberra's Fairbairn to Melbourne's Essendon Airport.

Jim Jongeneel,
Henk Baxmeier,
myself and Herman
van Nouhuys
aboard the 'Lurline'.

Christmas 1944: From left to right: myself, Henk Baxmeier, and Dimmie Vermeulen on the beach near RAAF Sommers.

Fountain-pen drawing of the view from my hut over Lake Sentani, New Guinea.

My 'bedroom' on the corvette.

October 1944: Major Baillieu (second from right) and the Commanding Officer of our corvette, the HMAS Gladstone, with the CO of the Japanese Imperial Army (second from left) and his adjutant, on the island of Soemba after the surrender ceremony on the town square of Waingapoe.

Berna Mortimer and I were engaged in September 1945.

4 July 1946: Lt. and Mrs. Rudy Zeeman on our wedding day.

1966: With Karel (Ady) Michielsen (left) at his country home near Canberra, ACT.

September 1977, The Hague: Albert Starink and Robert van Exter at my first meeting with Albert since 21 January 1944.

1982: The Engelandvaarder Reunion. From left: Cees van Brink, Dr Hans Hers, myself, HRH Prince Bernhard of the Netherlands and Hans Fanoy.

1984: The Engelandvaarder Reunion. From left to right: GAM Hazelzet, myself, Cees van Brink, Hans Fanoy, Mrs Fanoy, Prince Bernhard, Henk Brinkman, Pierre van de Veer, H Snelleman and Hugo (Tip) Visser.

1984: Eddy Jonker in London, looking hardly any older than in January 1942.

Pierre (Palo) Treillet and Sam Timmers Verhoeven—two of the survivors of the 6 February 1944 German ambush—standing near the Cabane des Evadees Monument.

June 1994: Standing at the entrance to the Hotel Eychenne in St Girons. From left to right: myself, my wife Berna, Pierre Treillet, Jeanette Treillet and Nancy Gesner van der Voort.

London, 1952: The only time we were all together! Front row: My father, my mother and Mr 'Willy' van de Stadt. Back row: My sister Mary, myself, my sister Anita (Ann), Rory Connor, Richard Saunders and Berna.

1984: The Engelandvaarder Reunion in London, on the steps of the (former) entrance to the Oranjehaven Club. Fred Beukers, in blazer and tie, is in the front row. In the back row are Eddy Jonker (3rd from left), myself and, seated on the balustrade, Sam Timmers Verhoeven.

Epilogue

The Title: Luck Through Adversity

If Hitler's Army had not invaded the Netherlands in 1940, I would not have escaped to England and my life would quite likely not have been so fortunate.

If Robert and I had not met with adversity in Paris, we would not have reached Spain in January of 1944, but have joined the unlucky group of Sam Timmers Verhoeven which was ambushed by the Germans in the Pyrenean Mountains. Even if very lucky, like Sam, and I had eluded the German soldiers, I would not have reached England before D-Day.

If, to my great disappointment, the RAF had not suspended pilot training shortly before my release from RVPS British Intelligence, I would not have joined the KNIL Air Force and been sent to Australia. As a consequence, I would never have met an Australian girl who would become my wife.

If, in 1961, I had not been transferred by my employers from Singapore to the head office in Rotterdam, where we were most unhappy, we would not have emigrated to Australia and would now not live in Tasmania which, all things considered, is for us, and the likes of us, the best place on Earth.

Nostalgic Visit to the Pyrenees in 1994

Like so many *Engelandvaarders* I have made the 'pilgrimage' to and over the Pyrenees and, when on home leave from Hong Kong in 1956, my wife,

Berna, and I toured by motor car from Amsterdam to Belgium, Luxemburg, France, the Iberian Peninsular and Gibraltar.

I remember as if it was yesterday that Berna, who was at the wheel of our Morris Minor in order that I could do the navigating, touched the edge of the pavement at virtually the exact spot where I had stood on the 22nd of January 1944, after leaving the Gare Matabiau in Toulouse, to be collected by Jacques and the *passeurs*.

When, in 1944, we had parted company with our *passeurs* at the French-Spanish Border, 'Palo' had given me his real name, Pierre Treillet, and told me that the chaps at the *Hotel de Ville* at St Girons would always be able to provide me with his or his sister's address. On our trip in 1956 they could tell me at the town hall that Pierre and his wife were somewhere in Morocco They did not have his address but gave me the name and abode of his sister. Early 1957, back in Hong Kong, I wrote 'Palo', care of his sister, but as before with my letter of the 28th of March 1945 from Hollandia in New Guinea to the care of the town hall of St Girons, I did not receive a reply.

In 1994, accompanied by our intimate widow friend, Nancy Gesner van der Voort, we again visited the Pyrenees and booked into the Hotel Eychenne in St Girons with the intention of visiting for the last time the area I had journeyed through 50 years earlier during WWII.

In the dining room we introduced ourselves to the occupants of the table next to ours. This was a charming English couple, the retired Colonel Ronald Arnold and his wife Marjorie. After ordering dinner, I excused myself and went to the reception where I explained to the young lady at the desk that I wanted to find my wartime *passeur,* Monsieur Pierre Treillet whose address I did not know but which could possibly be obtained through his sister. I showed the receptionist the note which the *"Ville de St Girons—Département de L'Ariege"* had given me in 1956. *"Ah, monsieur",* was the immediate and excited reaction of the young woman, *"she is my Godmother!"*

"Life hangs together by coincidences," wrote the *Engelandvaarder* Hugo Pos.

Nancy, Berna and the Arnolds were most intrigued and I had to relate my wartime experiences to the Arnolds. The Colonel was well-informed about the WWII Resistance Movement and particularly the French *Maquis.*

Perhaps 20 minutes later a waiter informed us that the receptionist had obtained the address and telephone number of Monsieur Treillet and, excusing myself again, I went to the reception and phoned 'Palo'; it was well after 9 o'clock. Pierre himself answered the call and, after listening to the reasons for my phoning him, his reaction was decidedly cool and on guard. I would later learn that his friends had many a time made a fool of him by phoning and posing as one of the men he had guided over the Pyrenees.

Noting his constrained demeanour, I asked him whether he had ever received my letters from Hollandia and Hong Kong in which I had mentioned that, having lost one of my sheepskin-lined gloves in the snow at the iced-over rivulet, I had given him the other glove at the border in the hope he would come across it on his return trip. *"Excusez-moi un moment"* was his reaction and, after some minutes during which he seemed to have a discussion with his wife, it was a delighted Pierre who told me without any further ado that Jeannette and he would call at the Hotel Echeynne next morning at 10 o'clock.

On Sunday the 5th of June of 1994, 50 years and nearly four months after the snowbound mountain top parting, Pierre parked his car near the entrance of the Hotel Echeynne.

Colonel Arnold took some excellent photos of our reunion and this unforgettable day cemented a lifelong friendship between Pierre and Jeanette Treillet and us. It would also lead to a friendship between the Arnolds and us and between the Treillets and Sam and Marina Timmers Verhoeven, leading to their presence at the inauguration of the Evadde Monument on the Col de Portet d'Aspet.

Two days later Pierre and Jeannette had Nancy and us for a superb lunch at their home in the old part of the ancient city of Toulouse. Jeanette showed me the letters I had written to Pierre which she had fortunately kept all these years and which had convinced Palo that my phone call was not a hoax. Jeannette also showed me Pierre's Croix de Guerre and foreign decorations as well as personal letters he had received from General Eisenhower and Prince Bernhard. Life is full of memories.

Touring Spain in 1956

When my wife and I visited Vielha, the capital of the Aran Valley, in 1956, the slate-roofed houses, Romanesque Church, bridge over the Rio Negre and Hotel Serrano were still there. However, on our next visit, in 1994, Vielha had changed beyond recognition. Situated at nearly 1000 metres it had become the village centre of a ski-resort with ultra-modern chalets and hotels, as well as ski-lifts, spread out over a spur of the Maladetta chain to the west and south of the Aran Valley and mountains which we crossed on foot on our way from Vielha to Sort. Beech and fir trees had, on some parts of the slopes, made way for the ski-lifts and runs.

I could not recognise the Vielha of old and turning the Renault Laguna around headed back to Bossost, where we and our dearest friend, Nancy Gesner van der Voort, partook of that marvellous dish called *paella*, while seated under a large umbrella on the terrace of a restaurant near the Garonne River.

The Fonda Pessits in Sort had made a quite favourable impression on me at that time but when my wife and I stayed there overnight in September of 1956 we found it to be a run-down village hotel. However, the marvellous reception we received from the owner Don Jose Farrar y Rafel and his wife made our short stay a memorable and worthwhile experience. A bottle of sherry was opened and we were shown old files with the names of all those foreigners who had been registered as guests of the hotel from 1940 to 1944. My name was especially pointed out. We conversed in very simple broken Spanish, French and English sentences aided by facial expressions and our hands until, according to Spanish custom, we sat down for a very good dinner sometime after nine p.m.

The street noise that evening made sleeping difficult, as had been the case 12 years earlier, when we were so desperately tired. Life in a small town, especially in southern Europe, can be noisy at night.

My wife and I stayed at the Fonda d'Agramunt in Lerida in 1956 in the same room and, apart from enjoying the good food and view, received special treatment afforded by Senor & Senora Ribs who, like Don Rafael Farrar in Sort, also brought out the files and photos of the War years. Many *Engelandvaarders* have had the same experiences on return visits to the Fonda d'Agramunt and other hotels they stayed at in Spain before moving on to Allied territory.

In October 1956, walking the beach of Puerta de Sta Maria near Cadiz around sunset, I came across a *Guardia Civil* pounding the deserted beach on guard duty who reminded me of 'our' *Guardia*. I took a photo of him and, armed with only my few words of Spanish, aided by a Berlitz Spanish phrase book, I discovered that he had served in the Pyrenees in the WWII years and had escorted *Americanos* and *Estranjeros* (foreigners) from the frontier areas to Lerida and Madrid. The coincidence that he was 'our' *Guardia* may seem far-fetched but it did intrigue me and has ever since.

The Monument on the Col de Portet d'Aspet

At the very spot where we, in January 1944, crossed the road and on the *cabane*'s side, a Brazilian marble monument was erected and unveiled on the 5th October in 1996 as *'a memorial to those who crossed this mountain pass on their way to freedom and those who, after their arrest on the 6th of February 1944, perished in their endeavours'*. The inscription reads:

LA CABANE DES EVADES

HOMAGE

AUX PASSEURS FRANCAIS QUI ON GUIDE

DE NOMBREUX EVADES DE TOUTE NATIONALITE

PAR LES MONTAGNES VERS LA LIBERTE ULTIME

A CES EVADES DE GUERRE QUI FURENT

ARRETES ET DEPORTES LE 6 FEVRIER 1944

A CEUX QUI NON-SONT JAMAIS REVENUS

A l'initiative de Jean-Louis Beraza 1945-1996

The French *Ministre de l'Environnement* has declared this *cabane* to be a site classé.

The Mayor of Portet d'Aspet, Paul Tancrede, made the inauguration speech and among those attending, apart from the new owners of the *'Cabane des Evades'*, M. and Mme. Beraza, was one of the wartime guides of

the Maquis Patriotique, Pierre ("Palo") Treillet and his wife Jeanette, and
Engelandvaarder Sam Timmers Verhoeven and his wife Marina. Also
present were the brothers Arnold and Piet Hijmans, whose brother Arjan
was arrested on that fateful 6th of February and never heard of again.

Sam, one of the few survivors of that fateful 6th of February of 1944,
was interviewed by French TV and the event was reported, with photo, in
the "La Depeche du Midi" newspaper.

A Camelhair Overcoat and a Soft Felt Hat

In 1943 my companion Robert and I had by great good fortune avoided
a confrontation with Gestapo agents at a safe house in Brussels. Albert
Starink had that unpleasant surprise at another 'safe house' in Brussels in
1944 but managed to elude the waiting Gestapo agents by instinctively
sprinting away before the door was fully opened.

On that fateful day, Albert had worn the overcoat and hat he had
inherited from me on that nearly disastrous 14th of January in 1944 and
believed that these garments brought bad luck. I, however, managed to
convince Albert that since neither of us ended up in a Gestapo
interrogation room that overcoat and hat had brought us luck with a
capital L.

Eddy Jonker and the Tonny Schrader Escape Organisation

After the winter of 1942/1943, I would not meet up with Eddy until 1984
when, on an organised trip of *Engelandvaarders* in London, we would
literally walk towards each other at, of all places, the Mill Hill War
Cemetery. We, to this day, still correspond regularly.

His sea crossing story is worth recounting, also because I can include
one of those extraordinary events that occurred during World War II.

After Eddy and I had completed our Indology Course at the Colonial
Institute, he, with a view to crossing the North Sea by boat, had followed
a one-year course at the Kweekschool Voor de Scheepvaart (Navigational
Training College) in Amsterdam to learn about navigation, tides,
sandbanks, etc. It was at that time he had the good fortune to meet the

intelligent and brave Resistance leader, Tonny Schrader, who through his job and organisational talents at the Rijksbureau Voedselvoorziening (Food Distribution Board) had landed the plum (and important) appointment as supervisor at the Bureau Grondstoffen (Bureau of Raw Materials). His job made it possible to travel around and use for these trips one of the cars of Queen Wilhelmina, complete with her chauffeur Gerard Bruyne, because all the cars of the Royal Family had been confiscated by the Germans. In his key position Schrader was able to organise an escape route over the North Sea.

Schrader and his helpers clandestinely also engaged in the collecting, transport and hiding of downed Allied Aircrew. It was during one of those inspection trips by Schrader that, after collecting a New Zealander (Cyril Mora) at Utrecht-Tuindorp, the car was halted in the town of Woerden by German soldiers. Asked whether they could give a German General a lift to The Hague because the General's car had broken down, Tonny Schrader replied *"selbverstandlich"* (of course). The General took a seat in the back next to him and started an animated conversation. When dropped off in The Hague, the *Herr Generaal* invited Schrader to come and have a drink at his place soon.

All that time the New Zealander had remained fast asleep in the front seat next to the driver. The German General never found out about the unusual company he had been keeping that morning and the New Zealander could, on his return to his base in England, tell the amazing story of having travelled in a car with a German General and a few Dutch Resistance men among whom was the former chauffeur of Queen Wilhelmina!

On the 25th of July the *barkas* (launch) with which Eddy and nine others—A. le Comte, C. T. K. van Dam, D. van Dam, H. Elfrink, H. Herklotz, W. Koole, D. Otten, the RAF Pilot A. Hagens and the Dutch RAF Pilot J. B. Haye—were to make the escape attempt was loaded into the hold of the 40-ton freighter 'Nooit Gedacht' (which was chartered by the Food Distribution Board) near the Ravensteijn Wharf in Leidschendam (near The Hague) on the waterway called de Vliet. The escape boat had been hidden in a large shed where the brothers Piet and Joop Meyer, who worked at the Ravensteijn Wharf, prepared the boat for its crossing over the North Sea and also assisted in the other seven such escapes. After covering the small vessel, and Doffie le Comte (who preferred this mode of travel), with empty potato bags, the skipper Kees Koole took his freighter through one of the locks near Rotterdam and via the New and Old Maas (Meuse) to the Spui River.

The nine men, all dressed as farm labourers and provided with falsified documents complete with German stamps were transported by a truck of the Department of the Food Distribution Board to board the freighter 'Nooit Gedacht' of Kees Koole at a spot between the islands of Voorne Putten and de Hoekschewaard on the Spui waterway. On reaching the broad outlet of the Great Rivers to the North Sea, called Haringvliet, the escape boat was unloaded and boarded just after midnight by the 10 would-be *Engelandvaarders*. After silently, using a rubber hose connected to the exhaust pipe to hang below the water to dampen the noise from the exhaust, and cautiously motoring the 20 kilometres down the Haringvliet in darkness and assisted by a ground mist, they passed unnoticed by the home port of the German E-booten (MTBs) of the Kriegsmarine at Hellevoetsluis. They nearly had heart attacks when they passed by a German patrol boat which was anchored only 40 metres away in the middle of the Haringvliet waterway. For those interested in history, the Dutch William III and his Queen Mary sailed to England from Hellevoetsluis in 1680 to rule England.

Before reaching the sea, they had an anxious moment when momentarily stuck on a sandbank. Then, in the low hanging mist, they sailed past and between three German E-boats returning from a sea patrol. A machine gun fired in their general direction but with the strong tide in their favour they sailed unscathed into the calm North Sea at about 4 a.m. After changing course several times to avoid sandbanks, and not long after they discovered that their boat was not watertight, the engine conked out just after noon. The outboard motor they had taken along for such an emergency proved to be a dud and was jettisoned. Rowing was not possible because of the high sides of the vessel and they therefore paddled with four paddles which they had on board. Twelve hours after their departure, and now well into the North Sea, the wind increased into a SW storm and the sea became very rough. A sea anchor was cast overboard, and those not violently sea-sick bailed with the one bucket while their boat was tossed about and drifted in the North Sea. Eddy remembered that, surprisingly, throughout the frightening ordeal, neither he nor any of the others were actually afraid that night, in spite of the extreme danger of foundering though they realised how helpless and totally at the mercy of the elements they were. It was however a humbling experience which would strongly influence him for the rest of his life.

Luckily the storm blew out as quickly as it had started. Drifting under a fierce August sun, the heat drove them to cool off in the sea and so it happened, that in the middle of the North Sea during the War, 10 naked men spent the time diving into its cool waters. *"It must have been a comical sight"* wrote Jonker, *"but we were all the time aware of the danger and dire consequences of being spotted by a patrol boat of the Kriegsmarine."*

Having expected to complete the approximately 83 sea-mile (150 kilometres) trip to England in two days, they ran out of provisions and water. After spending another hot day paddling as best they could with their blistered hands, followed by an evening and night with rising seas, they saw the English coast on the horizon on the fourth day. A little later a convoy, escorted by warships, passed by some miles away and since it appeared at first that their flares had not been noticed they continued paddling in the direction of the convoy and the English coast. After a long while a destroyer, the HMS 'Garth', left the convoy and headed for their launch, on which they had raised the Dutch Flag.

After being greeted with *"Welcome to England boys"*, a Navy sailor said, *"follow me"*. After they and a bag with documents which they had been asked to take to England, had been hoisted aboard the destroyer, the 10 sunburned, filthy men climbed up a wobbling rope-ladder onto the deck of the destroyer. After a clean-up they were taken to the officers' mess but were so exhausted they could not partake of the food that was put before them and nearly all fell promptly asleep.

Before going ashore they asked the Captain why it had taken so long for them to come to their aid. He answered *"We didn't approach you earlier because I considered it rather unwise to enter the minefield in which you boys were crawling about, but I can assure you that we all followed your journey through the minefield with great interest and the best possible wishes."* The Garth then sailed up the Medway, the same waterway that the Dutch General de Ruyter had sailed up in the 17th century to capture Chatham.

When during World War II the Dutch cruiser 'de Ruyter' announced its arrival with *"de Ruyter entering Medway,"* the laconic reply of the RN Duty Officer ashore was: *"What, again?"*

Tonny Schrader himself, who by then had received the sobriquet "the man of the boats", would join the last and seventh escape-boat voyage he had organised. He had always made sure participants had a cover story if arrested—essential for members of the organisation in order to give them time to disperse and go into hiding. This precaution would save Tonny's own life when his sixth crossing failed during August of 1943. The Kriegsmarine intercepted the boat and the crew was arrested by the Gestapo and, many days later, under torture, one man gave Tonny's name away. By the time the Gestapo came calling for him, Schrader had joined the 7th voyage, which he had himself organized, and had successfully reached England.

In England Schrader would join the American OSS (Office of Strategic Services) for whom, after being parachuted into the Netherlands, he did such sterling work that, at the personal recommendation of General Eisenhower, he was awarded the Silver Star medal for outstanding services rendered.

Tonny Schrader was without doubt one of the most successful secret agents in World War II. Dutch readers can read about his exploits in Paul van Beckum's book, *Oranjehaven*.

Air Raids and Aircrew Escape Lines

The route for bombing raids on Germany ran, for the greater part, over the Low Countries and in particular over the triangle of Rotterdam, The Hague and Amsterdam. We would, increasingly after 1941, be subjected to the grim ululations of the air-raid sirens, quickly followed by the drone of hundreds of airplane engines announcing an imminent bombardment of a target in Germany. The searchlights scanning the sky would promptly light up the night sky soon to be followed by the grump of the *Flakgeschutze*. We would make sure not to be in the open when the anti-aircraft shell fragments rained down; these caused a clattering sound when they hit streets and roofs, and the noise would be particularly sharp when they struck metal objects.

The RAF staged the first 1000-plane bombing raids on Bremen in June of 1942, and by 1943 the RAF carried out these attacks as a matter of routine. In the morning, when the bombers returned to their bases on 'the island in a silver sea' (as the author Arthur Bryant described England), we would be awoken by the sound of AA gunfire.

We would often watch this nocturnal spectacle and when a bomber got caught in the crossbeams of searchlights but managed to disengage we were relieved. However, a groan of anguish from the crowd could be heard at the sight of a bomber being hit and falling out of the sky, occasionally in flames.

The losses of the Allies on these 700 to 1000 four-engined aircraft raids were from 8 to 12 per cent or 50 to 100 aircraft per attack. Over the Netherlands 6,700 were shot down of which 100 disappeared into the IJsselmeer. All in all, 55,000 airmen were killed and 10,000 made prisoners of war.

It has been reported that 2250 German, 2500 British and 1750 American aircraft were shot down or crashed in the Netherlands during WWII, and that 20,000 airmen lost their lives. Many of those killed disappeared, still inside their planes, into the soft mud of the Waddenzee and IJsselmeer or slowly sank into bogs and marshes. Since 1946, the recovery of these planes has been ongoing and in the later 1980s a Short Stirling BK657 Bomber was recovered which had crashed near the village of Portengen on the 27th of April, 1943. The crew had parachuted from the bomber and were all arrested by the Germans except for the radio-operator, a New Zealander named Cyril Mike Mora, who was whisked off by the Resistance and would be back in England ten days later by crossing the North Sea with Tonny Schrader's escape line.

Curiously, Portengen is the village named after the ancestors of my mother Eugenie Maria Portengen. A very distant relative, Jan Portengen, has written a book on the ancestry of the family, the descendants of whom he was able to trace back to four brothers who lived in the 16th Century. The family had, as often happened, adopted the name of their village, the existence of which was already documented in 1217.

Up to June of 1944 a combined total of 4500 Allied Airmen received assistance from the population in Holland, Belgium and France and two thirds of these reached neutral countries through the local resistance and escape lines. Of these, it is estimated that 1500 to 2000 came from Holland alone.

At the Koninginneweg (Queen Street) 151, Amsterdam, the author E de Neve was in contact with the RAF in England, and downed airmen had this street number sown as a laundry tag on their shirt collars and had been told to go to Queen Street when, after having been shot down, they evaded capture (usually with assistance from the Dutch Resistance and ordinary people). After reaching No 151 the helpers of the escape line would escort them along a chain of safe houses stretching from Holland to the foothills of the Pyrenees.

Airmen who had parachuted to earth were often intercepted by the overwhelmingly anti-Nazi population, who would hide them and then hand them on to the *Ondergrondse* (Underground) as the Resistance was known in the Low Countries. Their equivalents were called *Maquis* in France and *Partizans* in the Slavic countries. On their way to, usually, Brussels the airmen were mostly guided across the Dutch-Belgian border by Dutch *Marechaussees* (state police) who, ironically, were authorised by the Germans to patrol along the border area.

Through betrayals or simply bad luck, some aircrew and their helpers would run into the unwelcome arms of the Gestapo (or French *Milice*) and successful escape lines to England (e.g. O'Leary, Dutch-Paris, Comet, and others) were therefore, of necessity, forced to change routes fairly frequently—often at the cost of their operatives perishing in a concentration camp or being executed. According to the Rules of the Geneva Convention, airmen who were arrested on the run should end up in a POW camp, but there were many instances of summary executions.

One of the most tragic cases of a victim of summary justice meted out by the SD to members of the Resistance or merely patriots happened on the 7th of September in 1944. Just days before the southern provinces of Brabant and Limburg were liberated by the advancing Allies, the house of the veterinary surgeon P. Leermakers, a member of an escape line, was surrounded by the *Sicherheitsdienst*. He was promptly executed while his wife and children were forced to watch. The house was thereupon burned to the ground.

It is amusing to note that downed Allied Airmen were described as '*doofstommen*' (deaf mutes), when they were referred to in conversations, because they were always instructed to act like deaf mutes when approached by strangers or authorities in uniform. Those unaware of this ruse must have wondered about the great increase in the number of deaf mutes that they were encountering.

Once, in the woodlands of the area called De Lage Vuursche, seven airmen were hidden for a whole month before being handed on to escape lines through Belgium and France to reach England, mostly via Spain and Gibraltar.

The Engelandvaarders

Historians have estimated that 45,000 Dutch men and women actively took part in resisting the Nazi Occupiers of the Netherlands. Amongst these were about 1700, mostly men but including 48 young women, who managed to escape from German-occupied Netherlands (or the Netherlands East Indies) by sea, land or air and reach England between 15th of May 1940 and September of 1944.

They were called *Engelandvaarders*. *"Vaaren"* in the Dutch language means to sail/travel over water; thus someone who travels over sea is a *vaarder* The first three young Dutchmen who crossed the North Sea after the Germans had occupied the Netherlands were hailed as having 'sailed' to England and, hence, it is believed that the description *Engelandvaarder* was born and used to depict all who managed to reach England.

The first 400 were 240 soldiers and 160 airmen of the Dutch Forces in the southern province of Zeeland, who in the last days of May crossed over to Britain from the area just south of Dunkirk.

Six men once stole two airplanes and reached England within an hour. However, the KNIL-ML pilot Frits Pelder, who took off from a Japanese-occupied airfield on Java, took more than 13 hours (excluding a refuelling stop in Medan on the island of Sumatra) and nearly ran out of fuel upon reaching Ceylon. However, of the 112 attempts (by 465 men) known to have been made to reach England by crossing the North Sea, only 150 men in 25 boats and 4 canoes (or 26 per cent of the craft) reached England. How many more men tried the sea route and perished will never be known; however, it is likely that only 15 out of every hundred reached the shores of Britain, and over one thousand perished at sea, or were executed, or died in concentration camps.

Of those who took the land route to reach England via neutral Sweden, Switzerland and Spain, about 1550 succeeded and amongst these were 50 men who had escaped from German POW camps.

Dutch historians estimate that a quarter of those who tried to reach neutral countries did not reach England but this number is disputed.

Not all *Engelandvaarders* started their adventures from The Low Countries. For example, two brave men crawled through the sewers of Hong Kong and passed through Japanese-occupied Guandong Province to reach Nationalist China and rejoin the Royal Netherlands Navy in Ceylon (now called Sri Lanka), while another three sailed a 7-metre yacht 3200 miles from Japanese-occupied Java to the island of Rodriguez off the east coast of Africa.

It is quite impossible to arrive at accurate figures for those who drowned in the North Sea or Baltic, or who died in the mountains of France and Switzerland, or who may have disappeared without trace in the Balkans and Italy in their effort to reach freedom. Even the numbers of aspiring *Engelandvaarders* known to have died in Nazi concentration camps, or were executed, or who never left the Gestapo torture chambers alive, are incomplete.

While the flyers made the trip in less than an hour, those sailing across the North Sea needed up to a week. The overlanders required a week to a year. I know of at least one individual who decided to go via Italy and was liberated by the advancing Allied Armies. Two brothers who chose to go through Yugoslavia had to make a getaway from suspicious Tito Partizans who intended to liquidate them.

There were also men who travelled from Sweden or Finland via Russia and Siberia to Japan in the years before "Operation Barbarossa" commenced in June of 1941. These Indian Ocean navigators typically needed about a month for their escape.

Quite a number became double *Engelandvaarders* when engaged in covert operations. They were dropped by parachute over the Netherlands or put ashore on the North Sea coast of Holland, and then had to make their way back to England again.

Frans van der Veen, who retired a Lt. General, escaped from a German POW camp in early 1941, and repeated the feat by escaping a year later from Japanese-occupied Java in a sailing boat.

Early in my life, I had understood that there were the Dutch and then there were the other Dutch. The first grew up in the Netherlands. The others were born, occasionally with a native of the Indies among their ancestors, and had spent part of their lives in the Far East. It is noteworthy that the sons of expatriates, from the East Indies in particular, represented a proportionally large number amongst the *Engelandvaarders* and those who were awarded the highest decoration for valour, the *Militaire Willems Orde* (MWO).

Ereveld (Field of Honour) at Loenen

The Memorial Cemetery at Loenen is situated in the centre of the Netherlands in the Province of Gelderland near Woestenhoeve and Loenen. It is the resting place for 3200 victims of WWII and was inaugurated by HRH Princess Wilhelmina, who, in 1948, abdicated in favour of her daughter Queen Juliana.

Military personnel killed in action, resistance fighters, *Engelandvaarders*, secret agents, executed hostages, and victims of forced labour are all interred in its grounds, A simple monument honouring the victims who died in the notorious Natzweiler concentration camp has been erected behind the chapel. An urn filled with earth from the place of execution stands on a boulder taken from the Natzweiler quarry.

A simple chapel with a thatched roof stands in the centre of this field of honour. The centre panel of the triptych inside the chapel stood originally in the Oranjehaven Club in London and commemorated those *Engelandvaarders* who, at that time, were known to have perished. The first panel of honour, inaugurated in London at Oranjehaven by Queen Wilhelmina four days after D-Day on the 10th of May, 1944, was gifted to the Netherlands War Graves Commission by HRH Queen Wilhelmina on her return to the Netherlands and has been placed in the centre of a triptych. It now has five panels to accommodate the names of all *Engelandvaarders* known to have lost their lives in their attempt to reach England. At the time of writing, the last known figures of those who attempted to get to England but failed are: 53 per cent at sea, 28 per cent over the southern route (Switzerland, Spain, Italy and Yugoslavia), 1 per cent for Scandinavia, while the fates of the remaining 18 per cent known to have made the attempt are unknown. There are now 317 names of *Engelandvaarders* who perished during World War II painted on the oak panels; 200 of these lost their lives trying to reach England, and the others were killed in action or through accidents.

Inside the funeral chapel there are 42 memorial volumes with 125,000 names of Dutch war victims whose last resting place is unknown. Urns filled with the ashes of concentration camp victims can also be found inside the chapel.

Stichting Engelandvaarders

Our Escapees to England Association had come into being through the initiative of a number of *Engelandvaarders* who had started meeting on a regular basis in the 1960s.

During a business and holiday visit to Europe in 1977 I learned about its existence and, with Robert van Exter, attended the annual reunion of 1977. I would, up to 1994, attend all of these reunions when visiting the Netherlands.

The reunion of 1982, organised with great expertise by *Engelandvaarder* Paul Kornmehl, was for me the most memorable. Nine *Engelandvaarders* residing in Australia and New Zealand, four of whom were accompanied by their wives, boarded a KLM Boeing 747, bound for Amsterdam's Schiphol Airport, at Sydney's Mascot Airport in early September. The KLM had upgraded us to Business Class, a gesture that was much appreciated.

It was inside the plane and on the top floor of the Business Class section where the introductions took place. I would shake hands with Pierre van der Veer with whom I had shared a bench in the 5th form at the CAS Primary School in Batavia in 1931.

Engelandvaarders came from all walks of life, from primary school leavers to university graduates and, not surprising, a number were professional or reserve officers or military cadets. However, the proportion of young men who had spent part of their lives in the Indies was relatively great. Quite a few had been friends or schoolmates of mine in Batavia. Others I had come across during my high school days in Holland and would meet up with again in Spain, Gibraltar, England, Australia, New Guinea and, later, at reunions in the Netherlands.

Another surprise encounter was with Tip Visser, with whom I had shared an overcrowded train compartment between Madrid and Villa Real de San Antonio in February of 1944, and whom I had not seen since the summer of 1944 at the Oranjehaven Club in London.

Engelandvaarders Snelleman, van Roosendaal and Gaillard I had not met before; neither had I met Hans Fonay who as a Navy Lt. had seen action on the well-known (also in Australia) cruiser 'Tromp'. Henk Brinkman had already left for Holland and joined us after our arrival in Amsterdam.

I had befriended Cees H. van Brink some years earlier. He had been the second Dutch Secret Agent dropped by parachute over the Gaasterland district at the end of November 1940; this was an area in the Netherlands which he knew well, having often hunted there in pre-War days. Cees received admirable assistance from the country constable and a gamekeeper but his identity papers were useless and he was forced to go into hiding, with his radio transmitter, at his parent's home in Wassenaar, near The Hague—no doubt to his parents' pleasant surprise as Cees had been overseas for some years when the War broke out.

Cees managed to transmit a few dozen messages to England. Figuratively speaking, he carried out these transmissions under the noses of the *Sicherheitsdienst*, since Ranter, the Chief of the Gestapo in the Netherlands, lived in a villa opposite that of his parents.

Rauter tried to be on good terms with his neighbours and would send them flowers from his garden which Mrs. van Brink Snr. always refused to accept. For the same reason, he once gave Cees a lift to The Hague. Hollywood movies are apparently not as far-fetched and unbelievable as they sometimes seem, when compared with a Gestapo General offering an enemy secret agent a lift in his own car!

Subsequently, Cees and I would proudly march in the Netherlands Ex-Servicemen's and Women's Association contingent through the streets of Sydney, Australia on ANZAC day (25 April) every year.

The 1982 Reunion was held on the 10th of September at the Air Base Soesterberg where the Air Force had organised everything to perfection. It was the largest gathering ever of *Engelandvaarders*, and they came from a total of nine foreign countries. The reunion was hosted by our Chairman, Frans Th Dijckmeester, who, by the way, had been one of Tip Visser's and my fellow passengers in the Madrid to Portugal train.

Most *Engelandvaarders*, like many members of the Dutch Resistance, were eligible for the Dutch Verzetsherdenkings (Resistance Cross). HRH

Prince Bernhard, our patron, had pinned the Resistance Cross on the chests of a few recipients.

I was given the opportunity to present His Royal Highness with my painting depicting our crossing of the Pyrenean Mountains in January 1944. It is now at the Resistance and War Museum at Overloon in the Province of Brabant in the south of the Netherlands.

Acknowledgements

I would like to first acknowledge Robyn Post who initially exhorted me to write my wartime Memoir before I left for the Valhalla of my very distant ancestors. Had Robyn—the grand-daughter by marriage of my widowed sister-in-law Hetty—and some other friends not encouraged me to do this, I would not have put pen to paper some 60 years later.

Over the many years that it took me to draft my Memoir, I received much helpful advice, maps, diagrams and photographs from various people who are too numerous to list and most of whom, sadly, are now deceased. However, I would especially like to mention the support given to me in later years by Kurt Ganter, former Executive Director of the Weidner Foundation, and Dr. Megan Koreman, author of *The Escape Line*, the substantive scholarly history of the Dutch-Paris Line.

I would like to thank Dr. Ronald Osborn, current Executive Director of the Weidner Foundation, who persuaded me to allow the Foundation to publish my Memoir, and who subsequently edited my text and turned it into this readable form. I also wish to thank my good friend Professor Emeritus Coleman O'Flaherty who (in my 100th year) helped me in the 'behind-the-scene' work which brought this project to fruition.

Last, but not least, I would like to lovingly thank my wife Berna who has put up with me for 74 years and without whose full support *Luck Through Adversity* would never have been completed.

Rudy Zeeman
Launceston, Tasmania, Australia
June 2020

Pieter Rudolph Zeeman, 10 November 2019

About the Author

Pieter Rudolph (Rudy) Zeeman was born in the Dutch East Indies in 1919 and spent his early childhood years there. After finishing high school in Amsterdam, The Netherlands, he entered tertiary education. In 1943, he escaped the Nazi occupation of Holland to England and joined the Free Dutch Forces. He then served in Australia and the former Dutch East Indies.

After World War II, Rudy was awarded both the *Kruis van Verdienste* (Cross of Merit) and the *Verzetsherdenkings* (Resistance Cross) by the Queen of the Netherlands.

After returning to civil life, Rudy joined a large Dutch international import/export and shipping company in Rotterdam (Internationale Crediet en Handels Mij). He worked mainly in the Far East with this company, exporting such products as rubber, sugar, tea, coffee and essential oils, and rose to the position of Export Manager. In 1963, after a stint at the Company's Head Office in Rotterdam, he decided it was time to return to a warmer climate and moved to Sydney, Australia where he represented a nylon extrusion business and then took up a management role in Real Estate. In 1986, he retired to Tasmania for family reasons.

Aged 100 years at the time of this Memoir's publication, Rudy lives with Berna, his one and only wife for 74 years, in Launceston, Tasmania, Australia.